Notes

* Reading & writing seen as accomplishments. p. 88.

* Generally perceived that knowledge for women posed a threat to patriarchy as it allowed women a means of self - assertion. p. 94.

- Experience of prison on Catto. pp. 162-163.

* Many catholic women used gender defined boundaries to their advantage. p. 61.

on reading & writing
as "two unrelated
accomplishments" 88

REDEFINING FEMALE RELIGIOUS LIFE

§ Focuses on two very particular
religious orders, despite the
broad claims of title.

§ Focus on Ursulines is
actually mainly on
Toulousian nuns (e.g. 84)(114

§ Ward & english ladies
no Institute!

To Simon

Redefining Female Religious Life

French Ursulines and English Ladies in Seventeenth-Century Catholicism

LAURENCE LUX–STERRITT
Université de Provence I, France

ASHGATE

Published by
Ashgate Publishing Limited
Gower House
Croft Road
Aldershot
Hants GU11 3HR
England

Ashgate Publishing Company
Suite 420
101 Cherry Street
Burlington, VT 05401-4405
USA

Ashgate website: http://www.ashgate.com

British Library Cataloguing in Publication Data
Lux-Sterritt, Laurence
    Redifining female religious life : French Ursulines and English Ladies in seventeenth-century Catholicism.—(Catholic Christendom, 1300–1700)
    1.Ursulines—History—17th century 2.Institute of the Blessed Virgin Mary—History—17th century 3.Women in the Catholic Church—History—17th century
    I.Title
    271.9'74

Library of Congress Cataloging-in-Publication Data
Lux-Sterritt, Laurence.
  Redefining female religious life : French Ursulines and English Ladies in seventeenth-century Catholicism / Laurence Lux-Sterritt.
      p. cm.—(Catholic Christendom, 1300–1700)
  Includes bibliographical references and index.
  ISBN 0-7546-3716-6 (alk. paper)
  1. Ursulines—France—History—17th century. 2. Women in the Catholic Church—France—History—17th century. 3. Institute of the Blessed Virgin Mary—History—17th century. 4. Women in the Catholic Church—England—History—17th century. I. Title. II. Series.

  BX4543.F8L89 2006
  271'.974044'09032—dc22

                                                                    2005010976

ISBN-10: 0 7546 3716 6

Printed and bound in Great Britain by MPG Books Ltd, Bodmin, Cornwall

Contents

Series Editor's Preface

The still-usual emphasis on medieval (or Catholic) and reformation (or Protestant) religious history has meant neglect of the middle ground, both chronological and ideological. As a result, continuities between the middle ages and early modern Europe have been overlooked in favor of emphasis on radical discontinuities. Further, especially in the later period, the identification of 'reformation' with various kinds of Protestantism means that the vitality and creativity of the established church, whether in its Roman or local manifestations, has been left out of account. In the last few years, an upsurge of interest in the history of traditional (or catholic) religion makes these inadequacies in received scholarship even more glaring and in need of systematic correction. The series will attempt this by covering all varieties of religious behavior, broadly interpreted, not just (or even especially) traditional institutional and doctrinal church history. It will to the maximum degree possible be interdisciplinary, comparative and global, as well as non-confessional. The goal is to understand religion, primarily of the 'Catholic' variety, as a broadly human phenomenon, rather than as a privileged mode of access to superhuman realms, even implicitly.

The period covered, 1300-1700, embraces the moment which saw an almost complete transformation of the place of religion in the life of Europeans, whether considered as a system of beliefs, as an institution, or as a set of social and cultural practices. In 1300, vast numbers of Europeans, from the pope down, fully expected Jesus's return and the beginning of His reign on earth. By 1700, very few Europeans, of whatever level of education, would have subscribed to such chiliastic beliefs. Pierre Bayle's notorious sarcasms about signs and portents are not idiosyncratic. Likewise, in 1300 the vast majority of Europeans probably regarded the pope as their spiritual head; the institution he headed was probably the most tightly integrated and effective bureaucracy in Europe. Most Europeans were at least nominally Christian, and the pope had at least nominal knowledge of that fact. The papacy, as an institution, played a central role in high politics, and the clergy in general formed an integral part of most governments, whether central or local. By 1700, Europe was divided into a myriad of different religious allegiances, and even those areas officially subordinate to the pope were both more nominally Catholic in belief (despite colossal efforts at imposing uniformity) and also in allegiance than they had been four hundred years earlier. The pope had become only one political factor, and not one of the first rank. The clergy, for its part, had virtually disappeared from secular governments as well as losing much of its local authority. The stage was set for the Enlightenment.

Thomas F. Mayer,
Augustana College

Acknowledgements

I am grateful to staff in the Archives Départementales de la Haute-Garonne and the Bibliothèque Municipale of Toulouse; my special thanks and deep gratitude go to Sister M. Gregory Kirkus, the archivist of the Bar Convent in York, for her insightful discussions and invaluable help during my research stays in this most welcoming house. She has clarified my understanding of the Institute and helped me untangle the many strands which weave its rich and complicated history.

I am also indebted to all the people who helped and encouraged this project, and especially to those who guided me during the early stages of the PhD research from which it derives. At Lancaster University, I would like to thank Dr Sarah Barber, Dr Andrew Jotischky and Professor Michael Mullett, and at Manchester University, Professor Joseph Bergin for his continued support. At York University, Professor Claire Cross had the kindness to read the manuscript and offer her comments, for which I am much obliged.

Lastly, I would like to express my appreciation to the Ashgate Publishing team, and more particularly to Tom Mayer, series editor and to Thomas Gray, commissioning editor, for allowing me to see this study into print.

Laurence Lux-Sterritt
August 2005

List of Abbreviations

ADHG - Archives Départementales de la Haute-Garonne
BA - Bibliothèque de l'Arsenal, Paris
BnF - Bibliothèque Nationale de France, Paris
BCA - Bar Convent Archives, York
MDPU - Mère de Pommereu, Ursuline
WDA - Westminster Diocesan Archives, London

Introduction

According to Pius V's *Circa Pastoralis* (1566) and *Lubricum Vitae Genitus* (1568), women who wished to be recognized as religious had no other option but to become enclosed nuns: this was the only forum for them in the Church. Those willing to embrace vocations which differed from this model would not be received to the bosom of the clerical ranks but were to remain secular; enclosure was a condition *sine qua non* to religious status for female communities.[1] Over two hundred years later, contempt for monastic claustration blossomed in the eighteenth century, an age in which religion lost much of its lustre in public opinion and the cloister was represented as a vacuum, a prison condemning its inmates to a life of unfulfilled promises and maddening isolation. In *La Religieuse*, French writer Denis Diderot wrote of the torment of his young heroine for whom entry into religion represented nothing less than a metaphoric death sentence where the body was maintained alive whilst the mind and soul were deprived of the nutrients necessary for life. Bemoaning her fate, she viewed herself as detested by her relatives and condemned to be 'buried alive' in a cloister. She repeatedly asserted that, had she been given a straightforward choice between perpetual enclosure or death, she would gladly have put an end to her days.[2]

Many of Diderot's contemporaries viewed monasteries as burdens on society and often as commodities for families wishing to dispose of their daughters; the women who entered religion freely were increasingly construed as escapists choosing not to face the reality and the duties of life. The author voiced an anticlericalism representative of his time: 'Why does a husband need so many mad virgins? and why does humankind require so many victims? [...] Where do servitude and despotism reside? Where does hatred never relent? Where are schemes hatched in silence? Where do cruelty and curiosity dwell?'[3] Thus, with more denigration than pity for the monks and nuns it had grown to regard with suspicion, the *siècle des lumières* laid the foundations of a perception that endured

---

[1] On the tensions between the cloister and the apostolate for religious women, see Elizabeth Rapley, *The Dévotes: Women and Church in Seventeenth-century France* (Kingston, Ont., 1990), and Ruth Liebowitz, 'Virgins in the Service of Christ: The Dispute over an Active Apostolate for Women during the Counter-Reformation', in Rosemary Radford Ruether (ed.) *Women of Spirit* (New York, 1979), pp. 131-52.

[2] Denis Diderot, *La Religieuse* (Paris, 1951), p. 257 and p. 287.

[3] *Ibid*, p. 311: 'Quel besoin a l'époux de tant de vierges folles? et l'espèce humaine de tant de victimes? [...] Où est le lieu de la servitude et du despotisme? Où sont les haines qui ne s'éteignent point? Où sont les passions couvées dans le silence? Où est le séjour de la cruauté et de la curiosité?'

until recent days: it assumed that the seventeenth-century explosion of apostolic vocations amongst Catholic women was ample proof of their heartfelt rejection of traditional conventual life. These women saw the worthlessness of the cloister and opted for a different choice, one in which they put their lives to better use, one in which, far from fleeing the world, they embraced and served it. In the enlightened consciousness, action became valued as empowering and liberating, whereas a life of religious contemplation was peremptorily reduced to enforced subjection and constraint.

The present work was born out of a desire to evaluate both the reasons for and the extent of the changes which are commonly acknowledged as typifying seventeenth-century female religious life. In the first decade of that century, the very definition of feminine participation within the Catholic Church underwent tremendous transformations which, in turn, came to affect the positions and the roles of religious women. The rise of the devout wave engendered a tide of new postulants for the cloister while lay society, impregnated with the same spirit, witnessed the unprecedented growth in the numbers of sororities and congregations. Yet, if the feminization of the Church is a defining trait of that era of Catholic renewal, the essential nature of the shift which redefined female religious life remains to be explored more precisely. What were the motives which pushed thousands of women to join the ranks of new apostolic congregations? Can the sources available today help historians bring to life a fuller picture of female religious purpose, rationale and beliefs in early modern Europe?

Since the 1970s, numerous studies have focused upon the daily experiences of women within their social, literary, political or economic contexts, bringing to light the female side of a hitherto prevailingly male history.[4] In the field of Counter-Reformation research, edifying studies have already begun to redress this balance; the historiographical debate which first emerged gave rise to a somewhat restrictive dichotomy portraying the Catholic Church either as a champion of feminine spirituality or as a force of oppression. Those who believed that 'Counter-Reformation Europe was a world in need of religious activism, not passivity' were sometimes a little swift in dismissing the conventual life as an inadequate, constricting and ultimately obsolete expression of female spirituality in

---

[4] See for instance Olwen Hufton, *The Prospect Before Her: A History of Women in Western Europe, 1500-1800* (London, 1997); Sherrin Marshall (ed.) *Women in Reformation and Counter-Reformation Europe: Public and Private Worlds* (Bloomington, Ind., 1989); Christine Meek (ed.) *Women in Renaissance and Early Modern Europe* (Dublin, 2000); Susan Mosher Stuart, Merry Wiesner and Renate Bridenthal (eds.) *Becoming Visible: Women in European History* (Boston, Mass., 1998) and Merry Wiesner, *Women and Gender in Early Modern Europe* (Cambridge, 1993).

the seventeenth century.[5] But history is never best represented in contrasting black and white; much work is yet necessary in order to refine these findings.

To understand the rich, complex and multi-layered nature of the seventeenth-century wave of female apostolic calling, early-modern modern conceptions of the dialectic of action and contemplation must be considered. Through the examples of the French Ursulines and the English Institute of Mary Ward, two pioneering movements claiming to exist outside of conventual enclosure, we will see that innovative enterprises implied neither the rejection of centuries of monastic values nor the female desire to become separated from a Church it had grown estranged from. Apostolic women such as the French Ursulines and the English Ladies wished to become a more intrinsic part of their Church, to help it recover from the blows it had suffered at the hands of the Protestant opponent. Could it be that their active calling, which ultimately challenged the Catholic definitions of gendered roles, paradoxically arose from their will to *serve* the Church to the best of their abilities?

The early history of the Ursulines epitomizes a growing female desire to undertake action within the Catholic Reformation. Founded in 1535 in Brescia by Angela Merici (1474-1540), the Company of Saint Ursula was approved by Paul III in 1544. In 1582, the Milan Archbishop Carlo Borromeo organized them into congregations, where the members lived together as laywomen with an apostolic and educational focus on girls.[6] This uncloistered half-way house between lay and religious soon provided the model for an establishment in Avignon (1592), where Françoise de Bermond (1572-1628) procured Clement VIII's authorization to teach the Christian doctrine to girls and to women.[7] The Ursuline movement rapidly spread across France and, by the end of the century, there were an estimated 320 communities across the realm.[8]

Initially, the Ursulines did not obey any monastic rule nor observe enclosure, but rather strove to rebuild the links between local populations and the Catholic Church by undertaking pastoral work and specializing in girls' education and catechism, a mission which could not be carried out by traditional cloistered nuns. In an effort to reach all layers of secular society, the movement distinguished itself by accepting pupils from even the most humble social backgrounds and teaching them for free. Thus, each Ursuline house functioned on

---

[5] Anne York, 'Women and Silence: Expanding the Boundaries of Seventeenth-Century Women's Religious Congregations', *Proceedings of the Annual Meeting of the Western Society for French History* 24 (1997), p. 442.

[6] Teresa Ledochowska, *Angèle Merici et la compagnie de sainte Ursule à la lumière des documents*, 2 vols (Rome, 1967).

[7] Claude Alain Sarre, *Vivre sa soumission: L'exemple des Ursulines provençales et comtadines 1592-1792* (Paris, 1997).

[8] Elizabeth Rapley, *The Dévotes*, p. 48.

a tripartite organization, training its own members, welcoming a number of boarders and giving lessons to day students.

This pattern was adopted throughout the country, a unifying trait common to Ursuline foundations which, on other accounts, remained quite separate from one another. Each of the main establishments such as those in Toulouse, Bordeaux, Lyon, Dijon, Tulle or Paris wrote its own constitutions and created its own filial branches. Thus, Toulouse opened smaller rural establishments in towns such as Brive-la-Gaillarde (1608), Limoges (1620) or Bayonne (1621), while Bordeaux, Lyon and Paris founded others. As these lay congregations multiplied, uncentralized, unregulated, yet rapidly increasing in numbers, statutory concerns arose. These were women in uncharted territory, in legal limbo: they were renouncing their lay personae as daughters, mothers, spouses or widows and yet they were not nuns since they wore no habit, obeyed no monastic rule and observed no enclosure.

The first gestures of legitimization came from secular quarters, when the first royal approbation of Ursulines on French soil was granted to the community of Toulouse in 1611, quickly to be followed with recognition by the local Parlement in 1612. Henceforth, communities of Ursulines across the realm gradually gained the assent of secular authorities in quick succession. The Ursuline profile, however, was more dramatically transformed when in 1612 the Parisian community initiated the general movement of conventualization of Ursulines by closing its doors on the world. In the matter of becoming religious, the *Toulousaines* had been ahead of their compatriots when they requested their elevation into religion in 1609. However, they encountered much delay and were only to become nuns officially in 1616, four years after their sisters in Paris.

Yet even when all houses became convents, the Ursuline family never evolved into a fully unified movement: when they were transformed into nunneries, all major branches received separate papal Bulls at different dates, specifically addressed to them and their satellites. As lay *congrégées* became religious and fluid interaction with secular pupils was replaced with the formality of the conventual school, the spontaneous missionary impulse of the women was curbed and brought under episcopal control. The novelty of its active apostolate, engaging with girls of all social backgrounds, led to the official enclosure of the movement.

Mary Ward (1585-1645) and her English Ladies, on the contrary, were never to be so subdued. Like the original Ursuline project, her English Institute partook in the evangelical drive of the Counter-Reformation, undertaking the secular and religious instruction of girls on a systematic basis. Also like its French counterpart, it strove to strengthen the faith in women and, through the training of young girls, to shape the piety of the wives and mothers of future generations. Inspired by the model of the missionary priests working for the conversion of England, Mary Ward braved the penal laws of her country: she settled her first house in St Omer (then in the Spanish Netherlands) to provide a boarding school and a religious centre for English expatriates, adopting the organization of Jesuit colleges. The Institute was also comparable to the Ursuline movement in its organization, which had three major dimensions: a school for boarders - often the daughters of English recusant families - as well as one for local day pupils, and a religious college training its own members, some of whom returned undercover as missionaries on English soil. In this way, the Institute's activities reached far beyond the accepted sphere of female engagement with the Catholic Church.

Like the initial Ursulines in France, the English Institute was a canonical novelty and did not obey any approved Rule. Its members were emphatically not nuns and yet, congregated with the common purpose of furthering the Catholic faith in England and elsewhere, they viewed themselves as religious. Even more explicitly than the Ursulines, the English Ladies inscribed themselves within the ongoing mission of Catholic recovery in England by imitating its most successful element, the Society of Jesus, the formula of which they adopted as faithfully as was possible for women. Within a few years, houses were opened across the Continent: after St Omer (1609) came Liège (1616), followed by Cologne and Trier (1620-1), Rome (1622), Naples and Perugia (1623), Munich and Vienna (1627) and finally Pressburg and Prague (1628).

The bold novelty of Mary Ward's mission, combined with the canonical infringements it entailed and aggravated by her total dedication to the creation of an independent Society of Jesus for women, were all elements which would coalesce to condemn her work. After years of a bitter controversy in which she faced as much hostility from the clerical ranks of the Church she aimed to serve as she did from Protestants, Mary Ward was condemned by Urban VIII in 1631; the pope, in his Bull *Pastoralis Romani Pontificis,* denounced her as a heretic and ordered the English Ladies to disband, thereby signalling the end of the first English Institute.

However, the demise of the institution did not bring about the total cessation of the activities of the English Ladies. If the Bull suppressed the Institute as a religious establishment, a canonical monstrosity who could not be suffered to live, it did not condemn the more humble work of its schools: what was being eradicated was the institution which claimed to be a female Society of Jesus, but there was no express opposition to the Ladies' teaching, provided they did so as independent lay individuals, not as members of any new Order. Hence, although the English Institute ceased to exist as a religious congregation, the devout Elector of Bavaria, Maximilian I (1573-1651), decided to preserve the establishment in Munich as a simple school for girls.[9] Except for those who stayed behind in Munich, the English Ladies mainly retreated to England and Mary Ward herself travelled back to her homeland in 1639. There, with a few companions, she once

---

[9] Frances Bedingfield (1616-1704) was the Superioress of this house. From its initial 26 members in early 1631, Munich retained only two in 1635. Henriette Peters, *Mary Ward: A World in Contemplation*, trans. by Helen Butterworth (Leominster, 1994), pp. 594-97.

more turned her attention to the English mission not, this time, as a member of the Institute but as a lay individual. From the beginning, the English Ladies had run a recusant centre in Spitalfields. In 1639, it was relocated to Hungerford House, in the Strand and later to Knightsbridge. As the conflicts between the king and parliament intensified in 1642, Ward and her companions left the capital, which had become unsafe, and headed north to Hutton Rudby, in the North Riding of Yorkshire, before settling at Heworth Manor, just outside the city of York, where Ward died on 20 January 1645.

Her death, however, did not seal the fate of her project; her companions, scattered across the country, continued their apostolic work as secular women running unofficial colleges and Catholic centres. After a difficult interval, Frances Bedingfield, the superioress of the only official remnant of the Institute, left Munich to begin a new phase of organization for the English Ladies. Back in London, she lived in St Martin's Lane, with the patronage of Queen Catherine of Braganza. In 1669, she purchased a house in Hammersmith which became a permanent centre for priests and an elementary Catholic school, the government of which she entrusted to the supervision of Cecilia Cornwallis (1656-1723). In 1686, she repeated her experiment in York, where the Bar Convent still operates today.

Munich became the mother house of this second Institute, which was officially distinct from that founded by Mary Ward and suppressed by Urban VIII. At the time, acknowledgement of their direct relationship with Ward's initial foundation would have jeopardized the Ladies' chances of gaining papal approval. Thus, the new Institute severed its links with Mary Ward's enterprise, claimed a totally separate status and finally gained papal approbation in 1702, later confirmed when, in 1749, Benedict XIV pronounced his Bull *Quamvis Justo*. This new order was named the Institute of the Blessed Virgin Mary (IBVM) and bore, on paper, no relation to Ward's Ignatian foundation, which had never officially been allocated a name. In accordance with usage, this study will refer to it simply as the English Institute and to its members as the English Ladies.

Why limit any investigation to the French Ursulines and the English Institute, two seemingly unrelated endeavours? This choice is not entirely arbitrary: it is hoped it will help to unveil the nature of the relationship between the Catholic Church and the women in its midst as well as to evaluate how female innovators related to their Church and how their Church, in turn, related to them. Such relations between individuals and their Church cannot but be conditioned by national religious backgrounds, since these partly determine women's ideas of the norm of acceptability in female endeavours. Therefore, in order to offer a picture which does not represent solely the particulars of one country, it became necessary to explore movements which spanned the various religious climates of seventeenth-century Europe: the Institute in England and the Ursulines in France emerged from and evolved amidst entirely different national religious and political circumstances which could not fail to have an impact upon their histories.

However, circumstantial divergence cannot hide the underlying similarity between these movements' initial intentions. Both shared the same basic desire to integrate women's efforts into the furtherance of the Roman faith, and both represented a degree of innovation within the Church. They dedicated their work to succouring Catholicism in areas which had become heavily Protestant, teaching girls with a view to forming solid Catholic subjects who would in turn become pillars of the faith within their own households. Their main aim was not merely to train prospective nuns, but rather to form young women to become exemplary Catholic wives and mothers. In order to serve such a vocation, they adopted a non-enclosed lifestyle directly inspired from that of the male clerks regular, and more precisely that of the Society of Jesus.

This work aims to highlight some of the more universal motives which underpinned the sharp increase in female apostolic endeavours in the early decades of the seventeenth century, together with the difficulties they faced as a direct consequence of their gender beyond geographical boundaries. Therefore, although this analysis may lose something of the detail that studies of individual religious houses allow, it is hoped there will also be something to be gained from a broader approach exploring a greater variety of cases. In order to put forward possible interpretations of the movements which drove early seventeenth-century women to embrace an evangelical vocation rather than a contemplative one, this book will begin with a short exploration of the humble beginnings of these Catholic female initiatives in their national contexts. The novelties they proposed and the very nature of their missions, as we will see, could hardly remain unquestioned for long. On the one hand, they represented structural aberrations that fitted neither with the secular nor with the religious; on the other hand, and perhaps more importantly, the independent endeavours of women without any male *custos* symbolized, to the clergy, the quintessential female desire to rule rather than be ruled, and must therefore be quickly brought to heel.

Although the English Institute and the French Ursulines were both accused of flouting canonical and gendered tradition, they opted for very contrasted strategies when facing their adversaries: thus, while Mary Ward refused to compromise what she believed to be her divine mission, the Ursulines chose the route of diplomacy and negotiated their acceptance within the Church by accepting enclosure. As a result of such divergent responses to opposition, both communities were to experience very different futures: the English Institute faced suppression while, on the contrary, the Ursulines gained unprecedented success. Yet even after such opposed outcomes, the movements adopted remarkably comparable ways of life in their socially-inclusive teaching vocations, in their evangelizing activities and in the organization they devised within their respective houses.

The final chapters will consider the spirituality of the English Ladies and of the French Ursulines in an effort to clarify the nature of the relationship between their novel calling and the religious heritage they disrupted. Many have been seduced by the seeming modernity of the women's determination to reach beyond the traditional limits of the cloister and undertake work that had hitherto been reserved exclusively for religious men. However, modern congeniality with the female pioneers of the 'mixed' life has led to a tendency to concentrate on the extraordinary nature of their endeavours, to emphasize their departure from the norm.[10] If these women did indeed initiate fundamental changes in the roles of their sisters within the Church, one must nevertheless be cautious not to identify their motives with what we, in the twenty-first century, recognize as militant feminism.

The English Ladies and the French Ursulines vindicated female worth in an attempt to help a Catholic mission which they saw as incomplete, since it did not directly address the daughters, wives and mothers of the community. In this sense, therefore, they were aware of and alerted their contemporaries to issues of inequality between genders. Yet this study will hope to show that these innovators did not set out to destroy the patriarchal system of the Church, nor to bring down social order; they did not breach *Circa Pastoralis* in a bid to free themselves from a monastic model they found abhorrent because it confined them to obedience and prayer. In fact, sources have shown that most apostolic women demonstrated a spiritual affinity for the cloister and that they all respected the religious values it represented.[11] Thus, far from seeing action as a means to tear down conventual tradition, the French Ursulines and the English Ladies undertook their vocations in the spirit of ultimate self-denial and in the service of their Church: to them, teaching and catechizing duties were a cross, a burden each willingly carried in an unprecedented re-interpretation of the medieval notions of asceticism to meet the new circumstances of the Counter-Reformation.

---

[10] Colleen Marie Seguin, ' "Addicted Unto Piety": Catholic Women in England, 1590-1690' (PhD dissertation, Duke University, 1997), pp. 290-91.

[11] See Penelope D. Johnson, *Equal in Monastic Profession: Religious Women in Medieval France* (Chicago, Ill. and London, 1991), p. 229.

Chapter 1

The Birth of the New Phenomenon of the Teaching Nun

> Since women dominated the early years of their children's lives, their influence was crucial. And whereas their sons might be removed from their influence and given a Catholic education, their daughters, as long as they remained at home, were vulnerable to the mothers' heresy. They, in turn, would pass the contagion on to their own children. There seemed no recourse but to develop feminine institutions analogous to masculine colleges.[1]

The seventeenth century was characterized by what has been described as the 'feminization of the Church', a movement which saw a tremendous increase in the numbers of female initiatives, raising the feminine profile within Catholicism.[2] In this wave of renewed devotion, convents were reformed and welcomed increasing numbers of entrants while secular society partook of the same pious revival and witnessed the adoption of the values of the cloister by mothers, housewives and young women. In England, the recusant household defined its religious identity by integrating intense spiritual elements into its daily life; in France, polite society revived the pursuit of physical and moral purity and the practice of charity. In this *siècle des saints*, conditions were ideal to produce the genesis of a new phenomenon combining elements of secular and religious life and aiming to take the piety of the cloister into the world: this was the advent of the apostolic nun or, to be more exact, of the teaching nun.

The magnitude of female involvement is indisputable, yet the question remains: why were women so prevalent in the offensive of the Counter-Reformation? Through the experiences of Mary Ward's English Institute and those of the French Ursulines, this chapter will attempt to shed some light upon the motives which compelled secular women to work towards the foundation of a new form of female religious life, a 'third way' offering an option for pious souls to enter the great family of the Church without altogether renouncing their interaction with the world. Why did the French Ursulines and the English Ladies feel

---

[1] Elizabeth Rapley, *The Dévotes*, p.43.
[2] *Ibid.*, p. 193.

compelled to inaugurate semi-religious congregations with a specific teaching brief, which had no female antecedent in the Church?

Why found female congregations with a teaching brief?

Over the last three decades, studies have highlighted the prominence of women in early modern English Catholicism. Indeed, the situation was such that by 1610, the English Parliament was forced to acknowledge that women represented a great proportion of the recusant population and was compelled to act accordingly. In an unprecedented move, 'An act for administering the Oath of Allegiance, and reformation of Married Women Recusants' targeted women as the recalcitrant element of recusancy and a recusant woman who remained impenitent once convicted would be committed to prison without bail until she conformed.[3] Should she persist in her ways, her husband could procure liberty only upon payment of a fine of £10 a month or upon the forfeiture of a third of all his lands and tenements.

Many have pondered about the reasons for such high female visibility in recusant England. Historians sometimes hypothesize that women felt linked to the Roman Church because of their very gender. Thus, Godfrey Anstruther has postulated that the womanhood of the 'weaker sex' predisposed it (on some unexplained, genetic or organic level) to be uphold Catholicism, the mysticism and rituals of which appealed to feminine sensitivities. Others, like John Bossy, preferred to highlight the fact that the penal system forced Catholic piety to retreat into the privacy of the household, where women traditionally held greater influence than in the wider public sphere. Such centring upon the private realm considerably increased the importance of female roles in the recusant community. The influence of the penal system was also analyzed by historians such as Alexandra Walsham, who believes that a legal arsenal which concentrated mostly on fines and attacks against property, though most efficacious against men, would have been quite ineffectual against women. Wives were in fact virtually immune from prosecution since, under common law, their possessions were vested in their husbands; according to this arrangement, patriarchal scorn for women as property-owners in fact enabled gentlewomen to enjoy a level of religious freedom which their spouses were denied. Thus it is revealed that, somewhat paradoxically, anti-popery laws offered women an unexpected advantage in recusancy.[4]

---

[3] (7 & 8 Jac. I, c.6), in J. R. Tanner (ed.) *Constitutional Documents of the Reign of James I* (Cambridge, 1930), pp. 105-09.

[4] Godfrey Anstruther, *Vaux of Harrowden, a Recusant Family* (Newport, 1953); John Bossy, *The English Catholic Community, 1570-1850* (London, 1976); Roland Connelly, *Women of the Catholic Resistance: In England 1540-1680* (Durham, 1997); Alexandra Walsham, *Church Papists: Catholicism, Conformity and Confessional Polemic in Early Modern England* (Woodbridge, 1993) and Marie Rowlands, 'Recusant Women 1560-1640', in Mary Prior (ed.) *Women in English Society 1500-1800* (London, 1985), pp. 149-80.

Whatever the reasons for this prominence in militant Catholicism, documents demonstrate that Englishwomen took their role much further than the purely domestic expression of their personal faith: as priests worked for the preservation of Catholicism on English soil, female evangelists distinguished themselves by applying their skills pragmatically where they were most needed, with such success that they provided much of the secular infrastructure without which the English mission could hardly have survived. They were, effectively, considered agents of the mission. As expediency replaced customary gendered specialization, some recusant laywomen were, for the first time, allowed to play roles which would, in ordinary circumstances, incur the censure of the clergy. However, the constant state of danger and emergency which suffused recusant life in seventeenth-century England actually rendered the services of these women too valuable to be foregone by the missionaries.

Today, the histories of many such recusants have been unearthed, counting amongst the most renowned those of Margaret Clitherow (d. 1586), Dorothy Lawson (1580-1632), Anne Line (1567-1601), Magdalen Montague (1538-1608) and the sisters Anne (1562-1637?) and Eleanor Vaux (1560-1626) and their sister-in-law, Elizabeth Vaux, born Roper (d. 1637?).[5] These key characters were all actively involved in the Catholic mission in England; they taught children, succoured the poor, visited the sick and those in prison, and acted as intermediaries between the people and the few missionary priests at work in their neighbourhoods. These women and many others like them were one of the Catholic Church's most powerful allies in its attempt to re-conquer England, and their biographies indicate that the principal female agents in the English mission conceived their role as essential to the success of the whole movement. Yet, if women occupied such a crucial place in the English mission, why did Mary Ward and her supporters feel the urge to create an organized religious Institute? Was there a need for a concerted effort to promote female religious participation in the mission even further?

Born in 1585 at Mulwith near Ripon, Mary Ward was educated in various Yorkshire recusant households, while her father Marmaduke Ward was forced to move to Northumberland to avoid the penalty of *praemunire* and escape the Justices of the Peace. Between 1600 and 1606, whilst living with the Babthorpe family at Osgodby (in the East Riding of Yorkshire), she became convinced of her religious call and, eventually, she left England for the Flemish town of St Omer to become a Poor Clare.[6] After hesitant beginnings, her Ignatian vocation slowly

---

[5] See Godfrey Anstruther, *Vaux of Harrowden*; John Mush, *The Life and Death of Margaret Clitherow, the Martyr of York*, ed. William Nicholson (London, 1849); William Palmes, *The Life of Mrs Dorothy Lawson of St Anthony's near Newcastle-on-Tyne* (London, 1646/1855); Richard Smith, *An Elizabethan Recusant House: Comprising the Life of The Lady Magdalen Viscountess Montague*, ed. A.C. Southern (London, 1609/1954).

[6] M.C.E. Chambers, *The Life of Mary Ward, 1585-1645*, 2 vols (London, 1882-1885); Margaret Littlehales, *Mary Ward (1585-1645). A woman for all seasons: Foundress of the*

revealed itself more fully between 1607 and 1611, in a succession of mystical visions which will be analyzed in further detail later in this study. The first was a revelation received on St Gregory's day in 1607, indicating that she was not meant to be a member of the Flemish Poor Clares of St Omer, but rather to open a separate branch of the Order specifically for English women. Accordingly, she left the town in order to found such a community in Gravelines, but she barely had time to settle there before, on St Athanasius's day in 1609, another vision indicated to her that she should leave that new community altogether and wait for further enlightenment. Bereft, she left for England, there to work for the relief of recusants.[7] It was whilst she engaged with the active apostolate in her native country that Ward experienced a third revelation, known as the 'Glory vision', after which she understood that she was not intended to be a member of any enclosed order at all. Finally, after years of indecision between the contemplative or the active life, she took a decisive turn towards an active apostolate when, in 1611, she received the divine command to 'Take the Same of the Society', an epiphany which prompted her to found a Society of Jesus for women.

Thus, it was within the particular setting of the English mission of Catholic recovery that Mary Ward's Institute found its *raison d'être*; it sought to provide a way of life which would allow women to transcend their secular status of simple helpers in the mission; members of the Institute would be part of the Church, truly religious, yet not condemned to a lifetime of exile in continental cloisters. They would be active in the Catholic mission of recovery, as a female counterpart to the on-going efforts undertaken by priests to re-Catholicize the people. The English Ladies' proposition was of a pragmatic nature: in a quasi-organic response to English circumstances, they aimed to address Englishwomen's spiritual needs, working alongside priestly missionaries in Protestant England. Mary Ward's Yorkshire recusant background certainly influenced her perception of the roles which women could play in the Catholic Church; indeed, when she spent part of her childhood with the Babthorpes at Osgodby, she had experienced both the critical situation of covert Catholicism and the essential part played by housewives in the organization of a recusant network. Yet these women were acting only as secular individuals moved by their own intentions.

Despite the privileged position held by female recusants in the specific circumstances of Catholic England, there remained gender-specific limitations to their roles. Mary Ward highlighted three main reasons why Englishwomen, if they wished to become involved in the Church, did not enjoy the same opportunities as their male counterparts. First, she noted, Englishwomen seeking to become religious had no other alternative but to leave for one of the many convents on the

Institute of the Blessed Virgin Mary (London, 1974) and Mary Ward, *Pilgrim and Mystic (London, 1998); Margarita O'Connor, That Incomparable Woman* (Montreal, Quebec, 1962); Emmanuel Orchard (ed.) *Till God Will*; M.P. Parker, *The Spirit of Mary Ward* (London, 1963) and Henriette Peters, *Mary Ward*.
[7] Henriette Peters, *Mary Ward*, p. 106 and M.C.E. Chambers, *Life*, vol. 1, p. 227.

Continent, since there were, of course, no nunneries in their own country. Thus, entering the Church was irrevocably synonymous with perpetual exile. Second, an increasing number of devout young women preferred to remain at home in order to work alongside missionary priests but found that this alternative option was more limited for women than for men, who could be ordained and trained on the Continent, to return to England as missionaries. Although they enjoyed a degree of participation within the mission, recusants of the 'weaker sex' remained constricted within a niche of secular activism which left many longing for a form of participation which could be recognized as truly religious. Lastly, Ward realized that, since priests were traditionally discouraged from inter-gender mingling, they focused their catechizing and pastoral efforts on men and boys; there was, therefore, an obvious need for a parallel movement which would imitate these endeavours and undertake the salvation and education of girls, a brief which could be more practically allocated to female than male evangelizers.

Under the circumstances of penal England, Mary Ward understood that it would benefit the Church to allow female religious life to flourish outside the cloister. In her view, the women whose vocations were neither solely contemplative nor of a purely secular nature should be allowed to enter the 'mixed life', on the same model as the new orders of clerks regular characteristic of the Catholic Reformation. Ward interpreted the commandment to 'Take the Same of the Society' as an exhortation to start a society of women formed on the institutional model of the Society of Jesus and pursuing the same goals. Thus, by 1611, back in St Omer and helped by a handful of followers, she set out to cast the foundations of a religious movement whose missionary spirit and Ignatian inspiration would revolutionize the seventeenth-century conception of religious women.

In subsequent years, the foundress endeavoured to provide appropriate definitions both of its nature and of its goals. This task would occupy her throughout her life, in documents addressed to clergymen or to the Curia, and particularly in three main Plans she drafted as the constitutions of her Institute. The first of these, the *Schola Beatae Mariae* written in 1612 in collaboration with her spiritual director, the Jesuit Roger Lee, was followed by the *Ratio Instituti* in 1616 and by the *Institutum* in 1621. Although these three Plans expound slightly different versions of the structure of the Institute, they are united in their clear definition of its nature and aims. Thus, the opening lines of the *Schola Beatae Mariae* present Ward's project as one born out of the urgency of the English Catholic crisis:

> Since the very distressed condition of England, our native land, is greatly in need of spiritual workers, just as the priests both religious and secular, exercise an increasing apostolate in this harvest, so it seems right that [...] women also should and can provide something more than ordinary in the face of this common spiritual need.[8]

Crucially, the *Schola* anchored its proposal in the context of the English Catholic crisis; the tone was one of pressing necessity, the word 'need' being repeated twice at short intervals. Without being alarmist, Mary Ward did not shrink from stating what she believed was fact: the mission needed to enrol female workers if Catholicism was to survive in England. The first item on the agenda was, therefore, to form a corps of religious women who would work alongside the secular and regular clergy. These female apostles, she envisaged, would contribute towards 'something more than ordinary'; indeed, they would transcend the informal lay support provided by recusant women and place the apostolate of recognized female religious within the mission, on a par with that of the missionary priests.

Moreover, Ward highlighted the limitations of the then current religious options open to women; while she remained grateful for the prayers offered by her enclosed religious compatriots on the Continent, she remarked that, in view of the nature of the English predicament, a more active form of religious life might allow women to become more directly implicated in the mission of Catholic recovery in their homeland:

> Since many women outside of England serve God most devoutly in monastic communities and day and night by their prayers to God and good works contribute very much towards the conversion of the Kingdom; so we also feel that God (as we trust) is inspiring us with the pious desire that we also should embrace the religious life and yet that we should strive according to our littleness to render to the neighbour the services of Christian charity which cannot be discharged in monastic life.[9]

In this passage, Ward underlined that nuns could not help their fellow Catholics other than through the intercession of prayer. Consequently, she suggested, a new congregation inaugurating an apostolic brief would be better suited to national circumstances. For the first time, an English foundress proposed a religious institution of women which did not observe the traditional enclosed life of the contemplative nun, but rather pursued an active, evangelical vocation for the service of others.

---

[8] BCA, B18, *Schola Beatae Mariae*, item 1.
[9] *Ibid.*, item 2.

The opening statement of the *Schola Beatae Mariae* expressed Ward's desire for an Institute which would offer an evangelical alternative to the cloister and thereby enable women to join the English mission officially. Although not criticizing the established monastic model, the *Schola* showed that the medieval form of female religious life prescribed by the Council of Trent failed to address the difficulties of the situation in England. Pragmatically, English women could and should do more than become either enclosed nuns on the Continent or ancillary lay helpers of priests at home. Therefore, the 'mixed life' should become an option available to women.

The predicament of Catholicism in her native country remained a primary concern in Mary Ward's later plans; the opening paragraphs of the subsequent 1616 *Ratio Instituti*, for instance, are reminiscent of the *Schola*:

> As the sadly afflicted state of England [...] stands greatly in need of spiritual labourers, and as priests [...] work assiduously as Apostles in this harvest, it seems that *the female sex also in its own measure, should and can in like manner undertake something more than ordinary in this same common spiritual necessity.*[10]

The next passage carried on in the same vein, underlining both the value and the limitations of a cloistered kind of life on the Continent. The foundress seemed keen to clarify that her Institute's novelties and the elements of irregularity it presented were adequate responses to the pressing need to find an efficient answer to the English crisis and were therefore fully justified. This was a trope which would recur in many documents written by the foundress throughout her life. After penning the 1621 *Institutum*, the third Plan she sent to Rome in an attempt to secure papal approval, Mary Ward addressed a brief letter to the pontiff to clarify her most substantial points. This 'covering letter', known as the *Brevis Declaratio*, was very similar to the three Plans which preceded it in that it dwelt upon the extreme circumstances faced by Catholicism in the North of Europe, a quandary Ward suspected the Holy See might not entirely comprehend from the remoteness of its seat in Rome:

> We cannot see without great grief and bitterness of soul the northern parts of Europe; and how by the scattered poison of heretical depravity which is daily spreading itself more widely, many souls redeemed by the precious blood of Christ rush headlong to destruction.[11]

Ward's letter to the pope called to his attention the clandestine and temporary nature of any Catholic endeavours in recusant England; she reminded her reader that such precarious conditions did not allow her followers to follow any structure

---

[10] BCA, B18, *Ratio Instituti,* f. 1 (emphasis mine).
[11] BCA, B 18, *Brevis Declaratio.*

which resembled the traditional Catholic life as prescribed for women by the 1563 Decrees of Trent, since living a conventual type of life would not only have aroused public suspicion, but would also have defeated the object of the missionary work they undertook in England. Since the cloister did not address the particulars of the English situation adequately, Ward believed there must be a way to supplement the limitations of traditional female religious life and provide other avenues for women who wished to serve the Church in England. Her solution to the problem was as clear to her as it appeared radical to others: she proposed nothing less than a female religious congregation based on the model of the Society of Jesus.

Such an innovative vocation implied that religious women, recognized by the pope, would be allowed to leave the enclosure and have daily business with the world, catechizing and educating girls and women. Throughout her life, the foundress had witnessed the disparities between male and female Catholic education and these provided her with the essential vocation of her Institute. She commented on the matter in the *Brevis Declaratio*:

> Since all these things which are approved in the education of boys by the holy Society of Jesus, we see and lament, are wanting for girls, it results that the other part of the human race [...] appears, if not indeed left altogether without help, not to receive much assistance.[12]

In this passage, the foundress did not merely point to the neglect of girls' education: she also remarked that, by such an oversight, the Church failed to address half of humankind, leaving countless souls in perils and, as importantly, depriving the Church of as many faithful servants. Hence, she saw it as the particular brief of her Institute to take care of female instruction, thereby providing a counterpart to the educational drive for boys which spearheaded the mission of Catholic recovery.

Therefore, the early history of Mary Ward's novel Institute (transcending the limitations both of the cloistered isolation prescribed by the Council of Trent and of the lay apostolate of simple recusants) seems to indicate that her apostolic movement was born out of necessity, justified by a situation of emergency in which a female form of the 'mixed life' was indeed a last resort to save the Roman faith from utter extermination. However, Ward's English Ladies were not the only women to articulate a desire to embrace the religious life without committing themselves to the perpetual claustration of traditional convents. Others, particularly in France, were also at that time transgressing the gendered differentiation which allowed the mixed life for men but proscribed it for women. Yet, unlike its English counterpart, French Catholicism was not a religion under

---

[12] *Ibid.*

siege: what were the reasons behind the surge of female vocations which sought a new form of religious, apostolic life?

In the first decade of the seventeenth century, the momentous rise of female involvement in the apostolate was symptomatic of a change in French spirituality, a reaction to circumstances which seemed to call for a reappraisal of women's place in the religious life. First, there was a perceived need to defend the faith against the palpable advances of Calvinism, the widespread progress of which had threatened extensive regions of the country during the Wars of Religion (1562-1598). Second, while Protestantism gained toleration with the 1598 Edict of Nantes, Catholicism itself offered a picture of neglect, riddled with the abuses which must ensue when, for many clergy, religion represented a career rather than a vocation.[13] Sexual misconduct, drunkenness and the assiduous frequenting of fashionable circles figured high on the list of grievances, along with the more specifically clerical failings of non-residence, lack of training and ignorance of religious duties.

The decadence of the French Church had been a strong, if unwitting ally to the popular rise of Protestantism. However, when in dioceses such as Paris, Toulouse or Bordeaux, bishops effected a thorough and speedy reformation, their energy seeped out into the secular world and the laity (particularly women) became eagerly involved in religious endeavours. A spiritual revival was gathering momentum, as more and more women dedicated their lives to devotion and forsook the frivolities of the world to enter the cloister. This decidedly feminine leadership in the resurgence of conventual devotion can be illustrated by the famous example of the Cistercian sisters of Port Royal who, in 1609, after years of non-observance, reinstated the strictest enclosure and ceased all contact with the world. By the middle of the seventeenth century, there were in France more nuns than monks and friars and, in parallel, the proportions of women in mixed lay confraternities increased sometimes to more than 80 per cent.[14]

The rekindling of female devotion also manifested itself in the new *engouement* of the *dévotes* who rediscovered the practice of charity and dedicated their time to good works, following the example of renowned *Parisiennes* such as Madame Acarie (1566-1618) or Madame de Sainte Beuve (1562-1630).[15] One

---

[13] Henri Brémond, *Histoire littéraire du sentiment religieux en France depuis la fin des guerres de religion jusqu'à nos jours*, 11 vols (Paris, 1967-8); Louis Cognet, *Post-Reformation Spirituality* (trans. by P. J. Hepburne-Scot, New York, 1959); Pierre Janelle, *The Catholic Reformation* (Milwaukee, Wis., 1963); François Le Brun (ed.) *Histoire des catholiques en France du XV° siècle à nos jours* (Toulouse, 1980); René Taveneaux, *Catholicisme postridentin, la réforme catholique* (Paris, 1972) and Jean de Viguerie, *Le Catholicisme des Français dans l'ancienne France* (Paris, 1988).

[14] Jean Viguerie, *Le Catholicisme des Français*, p. 166.

[15] Hélène de Leymont, *Madame de Sainte Beuve et les Ursulines de Paris, 1562-1630* (Lyon, 1890) and F. Ellen Weaver, 'Cloister and Salon in Seventeenth-Century Paris:

could say that in French salons, the seriousness of unworldly pursuits had come to replace the usual levity of fashionable distractions. Characteristically, female lay involvement in the French Catholic Reformation was even more ardent than its male counterpart and, in the first decades of the century, women's opportunities reached far beyond their traditional roles both within the Church and in society at large.[16] This stirring new breath of devotion, rekindling the fire of popular piety from its barely glowing embers, owed much to the influence of François de Sales (1567-1622), the bishop of Geneva. Faced directly with Calvinism, Sales proposed to relax the formalism which had vitiated Catholic piety; he advocated a more personal, inner religion, allied to a moral life free of formal limitations. In 1608, his *Introduction à la Vie Dévote* involved the whole life of the believers into their religious experiences:

> Almost all the writers who have discussed devotion have considered the instruction of people far removed from the bustle of the world or, at least, they have taught a kind of devotion which leads to this type of complete retreat. My intention is to instruct those who live in towns, in households, at court, and who are obliged by their condition to share the lives of others in the world.[17]

The novelty in François de Sales's message was an exhortation for the mystically minded not to shrink from the concrete world but, on the contrary, to anchor their existence (including secular concerns) in religion. Salesian writings encapsulated the spirit of the age, an era in which public *engouement* for a devout life was manifest in the multiplication of new religious congregations which, in their turn, began the delicate and demanding task of rebuilding a trusting relationship between the people and their Church, working daily in the world to strengthen the links between secular and religious.

In France, male companies such as César de Bus's Fathers of the Christian Doctrine (1598), Pierre de Bérulle's Oratory (1611) or Vincent de Paul's Fathers of the Mission (1625) became extraordinarily successful. On the other hand, new female endeavours such as the Congrégation de Notre-Dame (1597), François de Sales's Visitation (1610-1616) or the Filles de la Charité (1634)

Introduction to a Study in Women's History', in Rita M. Gross, *Beyond Androcentrism. New Essays on Women and Religion* (Missoula, Mt., 1977).

[16] Louis Châtelier, *L'Europe des dévots*; H. O. Evennett, *The Spirit of the Counter-Reformation* (Cambridge, 1968) and Elizabeth Rapley, *The Dévotes*. Also M. C. Gueudré, 'La Femme et la vie spirituelle' and Caritas McCarthy, 'Ignatian Charism in Women's Congregation', *The Way*, supplement 20 (1973) 10-18.

[17] François de Sales, *Introduction à la vie dévote* (Paris, 1969), p. 37: 'Ceux qui ont traité de la dévotion ont presque tous regardé l'instruction des personnes fort retirées du commerce du monde, ou au moins ont enseigné une sorte de dévotion qui conduit à cette entière retraite. Mon intention est d'instruire ceux qui vivent dans les villes, en ménages, en la cour, et qui par leur condition sont obligés de faire une vie commune quant à l'extérieur.'

flourished alongside their male counterparts and shared the same apostolic essence. Their main vocation was not the observance of a monastic way of life but rather an evangelical brief which implied constant interaction with others. They taught, visited hospitals and prisons, helped the poor and generally aimed to restore the damaged links between the people and the Catholic Church.

Since in the first decade of the century France had yet officially to receive the Decrees of the Council of Trent and the restricting laws they imposed on female religious life, these were times when an efflorescence of individual initiatives was allowed to bloom. Therefore, the seventeenth century began during an era of relative liberty in which the Catholic revival was free to express itself in many ways which would come under questioning when, in 1615, the assembly of the clergy of France finally endorsed the Tridentine canons. It was during that time that France experienced some of its most significant changes in female Catholic involvement.

C. A. Sarre argues that just before the enforcement of the Tridentine Decrees, and more particularly during the years between 1592 and *c.* 1610, Catholic France presented opportunities for capable catechizers regardless of gender.[18] His view is shared by Lierheimer, who referred to these years as 'a unique moment' during which female endeavours were not only tolerated but welcomed by the French Church.[19] This opinion is confirmed by contemporaneous documents and, to name but one, the Augustinian Parayre justified the multiplication of Ursuline houses all over France by reminding his readers that the country was, at that particular juncture, in pressing need for spiritual renewal. He argued that the new communities were a timely response to a necessity:

> This congregation [began] at a time when [the Church] needed it the most; indeed, heresy was multiplying its efforts to corrupt, pervert all young women and steep them in error, and to corrupt their understanding from their earliest childhood [...] In order to prevent this, God inspired diverse people, particularly in France, to establish the Company of St Ursula, whose principal end is to teach girls in their homes in order to give them safeguards against heresy; they could not have undertaken this role if they had been cloistered from the beginning.[20]

---

[18] Claude Alain Sarre, *Vivre sa soumission*, p. 5.

[19] Linda Lierheimer, 'Female Eloquence and Maternal Ministry: The Apostolate of Ursuline Nuns in Seventeenth-Century France', unpublished PhD dissertation, Princeton University, 1994, p. 15.

[20] R. P. Parayre, *Chronique*, part 1, pp. 26-27: 'Cette congrégation [commença] en un temps, où [l'Église] en avait plus de besoin; car l'hérésie faisait tous ses efforts pour corrompre, pervertir, et imbiber toutes les jeunes filles de l'erreur, et corrompre leur créance dès ce premier âge de l'enfance [...]. Pour empêcher cela, Dieu inspira diverses personnes en France particulièrement, d'établir la Compagnie de sainte Ursule, dont la principale fin est d'aller par les maisons instruire les jeunes filles, et leur donner par là des préservatifs contre les hérésies, ce qui n'eût pas pu se faire, si d'abord elles se fussent cloîtrées.'

In the chronicler's opinion, therefore, the Ursuline *via media* was particularly adapted to French circumstances. Indeed, not unlike Mary Ward's English Ladies, they proposed a new religious institution which would allow women to work alongside the clerks regular, educating and catechizing the female half of the population which was, thus far, all but bypassed by the efforts of male Orders such as the Society of Jesus.

The vocations of the first French Ursulines sprung from this new trend. The reputed *siècle des saints* saw an increasing need for a formula which would allow women to undertake apostolic work and yet be considered religious. Guided by this innovative spirit, the French Ursulines, like the English Ladies, founded establishments in which women were more than mere ancillary lay helpers of the Catholic movement of recovery but were not required to become cloistered nuns, born into religion only by dying to the world. Their educational vocations, like those of Mary Ward's followers, proposed to combine the spirit of devotion of the convent with the pragmatic duties of the apostolate in an evangelical life which adapted the idea of the mixed life to congregations of women. When looking back on the early history of the Ursulines, Parayre described their mission as follows:

> To remove souls from vice and instruct girls in virtue, to teach them Christian doctrine and piety, to engrave in their hearts both the love and fear of God, and to form them to the exercises befitting their sex. [...] In order to teach the mysteries of our religion and the practice of good virtue to young women [the Ursulines] combine contemplation and the instruction of souls, which is their principal aim. [21]

This definition could easily be applied to all French Ursuline houses; in fact, Mère de Pommereu began her general chronicle of the French Order in a similar manner and individual establishments kept, in their own archives, declarations much to the same effect. Since women had not been specifically included in the educational drive led by male religious communities such as the Society of Jesus and the Fathers of the Christian Doctrine, the Ursulines developed their educational mission in an attempt to redress this imbalance: the new female institution was, first and foremost, a teaching and catechizing congregation, its essential core resting with its apostolic brief. The first Ursulines were therefore more than a simple lay sorority, since they lived in a community with its own hierarchy and regulations; nonetheless, they were emphatically not nuns, since they took no

---

[21] R. P. Parayre, *Chronique*, part 1, pp. 20-21. The French text reads: 'retirer les âmes du vice et instruire à la vertu les jeunes filles, leur apprendre la doctrine chrétienne, la piété, graver dans les cœurs l'amour avec la crainte de Dieu, et les former aux exercices convenables à leur sexe. [...] Elles rapportent la contemplation à l'instruction des âmes, comme à leur fin principale, pour apprendre aux jeunes filles les mystères de la religion Chrétienne et la pratique des vertus.'

solemn vows and did not observe strict enclosure. In their original and, practically speaking, highly successful form, they were *congrégées* working assiduously for the Church, and yet in breach of Church decrees.

The first French Ursuline settlements were unregulated affairs, spontaneous gatherings which often operated without so much as a letter of recognition from either municipality or king nor local ordinaries or pope. Typically, they established their houses in urban centres of wealth and power such as Avignon, Toulouse, Bordeaux and Paris. Founded in 1604 by Marguerite de Vigier (1575-1639) and Françoise de Blanchet (no dates), two *congrégées* who had been delegated from Avignon, the Toulouse house was the first foundation to emerge from Provence and the Comtat Venaissin. This community was also the first to secure temporal recognition by gaining approval from Louis XIII in 1611 and from the Parlement in 1612, thereby leading the way towards the global legitimization of the Ursuline movement in the country. Surprisingly, the *congrégées* had remained entirely unapproved until then; yet, the monarch appeared undisturbed by the fact that the *congrégées* had previously been working without licence; nor did he appear perturbed by their lack of religious status, since he not only praised them as an establishment of 'great profit and edification' but trusted them 'to promote by all necessary means the service of God and the salvation of souls'.[22] It seems that the king, perhaps influenced by royal and Gallican habits of less than absolute deference to the prescriptions of Rome, did not consider the community's lack of papal approval as an essential weakness. The Ursuline initiative was responding to a profound need for female catechizers, and they had found an efficient mode of operating: this in itself was enough to gain the royal *lettres patentes*. Therefore, the Toulouse establishment was the first in France to see its educational efforts recognized and encouraged by the crown, a distinction which immediately improved its position within the city itself.

Although this first royal approval covered only Toulouse and the small branch it had founded in 1608 in the town of Brive-la-Gaillarde, a precedent had been created and over the next few years many letters would be issued in approval of the Ursulines of Bordeaux, Paris, Lyon, Orléans or Troyes for instance, and all their sub-foundations.[23] Soon after the Toulouse establishment was founded, others sprang up in all the major cities of the realm. Although independent from one another, they were aware of the global need for their concerted efforts and they consciously pursued a common goal in the re-Catholicization of women. Thus, when one considers the early phases of the French Ursuline movement, documents found in the archives of the community of Toulouse show some degree of national, rather than purely regional, awareness. The manuscript book entitled *Mémoires du*

---

[22] ADHG, 221H-4, *Lettre Patente*: '[le] grand profit et édification qu'apportent à ses sujets les congrégations établies depuis peu d'années en ce royaume sous le nom de Ste Ursule pour vaquer à l'instruction des petites filles, à la piété et aux bonnes mœurs' and 'promouvoir par tous les moyens le service de Dieu et le salut des âmes.'
[23] R. P. Parayre, *Chronique*, part 1, p. 124.

commencement et progrés de l'ordre de sainte Ursule declared that their unusual profile sprang from the particular circumstances which affected France in the first decade of the seventeenth century, 'for them, in particular, in their days'; firmly anchored in this context, the Ursulines worked and prayed for the furtherance of the faith. This 'new way' they extolled would be similar to that of the English Ladies in its binary nature, allying the prayers of the traditional convent with the apostolate thus far restricted to secular women only.[24]

Like Ward's Institute, the Ursulines recognized the good work undertaken by the *dévotes*, but aimed to transcend this status of informal, secular helpers to provide women with a truly religious station which incorporated them within the mission of Catholic recovery. Like Mary Ward's English Ladies, they were responding to local circumstances on a pragmatic level: aware that women could take a more active part in the movement of Catholic revival, they found a niche for their vocation in catechizing local girls. In Toulouse and in St Omer, the members of both congregations were transgressing the established order and laying the foundations of a new, apostolic way of life for women within the Catholic Church. Born out of a real sense of urgency and necessity, how did these evangelical communities construct their own definitions of themselves? As they responded to a need in a religiously buoyant era, these women were attempting nothing less than to inscribe women within the mission of the Counter-Reformation; this was entirely new and required the implementation of an adapted framework to suit the new model of the teaching religious. How did the French Ursulines and the English Ladies conceptualize their vocations?

Inscribing women into the Catholic movement of recovery

Both French Ursulines' and English Ladies' vocations can be described as initially sharing a common catechizing goal which necessitated the abandonment of the traditional monastic model in favour of the adoption of a 'mixed' way of life. Although they would, in time, develop more contrasting definitions of their vocations and organizations, the fledgling communities shared an understanding of the religious instruction of girls as a universal and conceptual ideal, one which would complete the educational mission headed by male missionary movements such as the Society of Jesus. To them, female religious welfare was a global objective. Since such an evangelical type of vocation privileged interaction between the congregations' members and the girls they aimed to teach, both communities defined their dual essence as an alternative to the contemplative and enclosed religious life which was, thus far, the only recognized place for women within the institution of the Church.

---

[24] ADHG, 221h-37, *Mémoires du commencement et progrés de l'ordre de sainte Ursule, 1604-1621*, f. 3: 'pour elles en particulier en leurs jours'.

Women had been highly receptive to the Protestant movement in France and they remained beyond the reach of the male colleges which were attempting, from the 1590s, to re-Catholicize French society.   Female institutions with a specific educational purpose were, therefore, considered a priority in order to match the movement of the male colleges which worked for the re-conversion and Catholicization of boys.[25] Thus, the Ursulines found justification for their teaching efforts in the sense of emergency which pervaded their local circumstances. Indeed, southern France gave particular emphasis to the educational impulse of the Catholic mission; thus, in heavily Protestantized areas such as the Midi, for instance, Ursuline establishments provided a harmonious response to their regional contexts. Since Protestant schools addressing both female and male audiences had secured deep roots in Dauphiné, Guyenne or Languedoc, the Catholic response was to confront them by founding colleges to catechize people. Thus, the Ursulines played their part in the overall movement of the French Catholic renaissance. Even more essentially, they completed it by providing their own particular note: their educational and catechizing vocation for local girls.[26]

The parallel between French Ursulines and English Ladies is particularly evident in the communities' educational vocation. Despite widely varying national circumstances, both movements began with an ideal which targeted a simple, common goal: the consolidation and the expansion of Catholicism through the medium of the education of girls. Like the Ursulines, Mary Ward's followers did not wish to recruit girls who felt called to the religious life only. On the contrary, they hoped to train pupils who would later become exemplary Catholic wives and mothers in England, thereby influencing everyone in their direct domestic spheres. Both congregations strove, from the beginning, to strengthen the faith in young women in order to allow it to be passed on naturally through the main channel of female influence in seventeenth-century England and France, the household.

The 1612 *Schola Beatae Mariae* presented the Institute's vocation in terms which were strikingly similar to those used by the French Ursulines; its *raison d'être* was:

> [to] educate maidens and girls of tender years in piety, in the
> Christian virtues and liberal arts so that they may be able

---

[25] R. B. Escoupérié-Merle, 'Marthe de Flottes, directrice des Filles de la Providence de Toulouse ou l'enseignement féminin sous l'Ancien Régime' *Auta* 632 (1998) 8-13 and 633 (1998) 57-63; M. C. Gueudré, *'La Femme et la vie spirituelle'*.

[26] An indicative review of literature treating of the Ursulines as a teaching order should include titles such as Hélène Leymont, *Madame de Sainte Beuve et les Ursulines de Paris, 1562-1630* (Lyon, 1890); Marie Martin, *L'Éducation des Ursulines* (Rome, 1947); M. C. Gueudré, *Histoire de l'ordre des Ursulines* and Georges Snyders, *La Pédagogie en France aux XVII° et XVIII° siècles* (Paris, 1965) . Articles such as Yves Poutet, 'L'Enseignement des pauvres dans la France du XVII° siècle', *Dix-Septième Siècle*, 90 (1971) 87-110 and Elfreida Dubois, 'The Education of Women in Seventeenth-century France', *French Studies* 32.1 (1978) 1-19 are also extremely valuable.

> thereafter to undertake more fruitfully the secular and
> domestic life or the religious and monastic life, according to
> the vocation of each.[27]

The text required prospective English Ladies to be entirely 'resigned to teaching for life', thereby placing the educational apostolate unquestionably at the forefront of the proposal. Ward's second Plan, the 1616 *Ratio Instituti*, placed the English Ladies' teaching duties even more explicitly to the forefront of the proposal, where it was henceforth to remain as the chief purpose of their mission. The *Ratio* declared:

> [The English Ladies] are not called to a life in which they
> can devote themselves only to themselves; [...] they are to
> prepare themselves to undertake any labour whatsoever in
> the education or instruction of virgins and young girls; in the
> first place, by instructing them generally in their duties
> towards God.[28]

Between 1612 and 1616, the Institute's vocation had become more clearly defined as one focused on teaching; any prospective member was reminded that her life would not be one of quiet contemplation but one primarily defined by its educational mission.

However, it was in the third Plan, the 1621 *Institutum,* that the exact and mature expression of what Mary Ward wanted for her congregation finally found its voice. As with the Ursulines, secular knowledge was considered ancillary to Catholic doctrine and the absolute priority was to catechize:

> The members of this Institute [...] shall instruct young girls
> in spiritual practices and simple people in Christian doctrine,
> by teaching the catechism and the reverend use of sacred
> objects, educating girls in day and boarding schools, an
> apostolate which will be particularly efficacious for the
> universal good of the Church and the personal good of
> individuals, whether their vocation is to a life in the world or
> in religion.[29]

Primarily, the English Ladies aimed to further the Catholic cause by instructing simple people, preparing them for Mass and the sacraments and reconciling those whose apostasy put their salvation in peril.[30] In this respect, their core vocation

---

[27] BCA, B18, *Schola Beatae Mariae*, item 3.

[28] BCA, B18, *Ratio Instituti*, f. 5.

[29] BCA, B18, *Institutum*, f. 19.

[30] *Ibid.*: ' [The English Ladies] shall assemble the people and prepare them to attend public sermons and lectures, and shall also undertake any other ministry of the word of God'.

remained comparable with that of the Ursulines, since their major goal was indeed to evangelize the female half of the population.

However, the *Institutum* presented elements which were altogether more radical, especially in its bold transference of the styles of the male priestly congregations of clerks regular to a new religious association of women. Ward went further than her French *consœurs* when she described her Institute's mission as similar to that of the clerks regular, customized for specific purposes:

> to strive for the defence and propagation of the faith and for the progress of souls in Christian life and doctrine, leading them back from heresy and evil ways to the faith, to a Christian manner of life, and to special obedience to the Holy See.[31]

The functions envisaged were, in short, those of ordained men, proposing a female congregation which would act as a counterpart to this so far essentially male mission: the Institute would run a seminary for women on the Continent and send some of its members to England to relieve recusants there, in the same way as seminary priests did.

Therefore, French Ursulines and English Ladies aspired, to varying degrees, to emulate the Society of Jesus, whose ideal offered a compromise between contemplation and action, in order to consolidate the popular basis of Catholicism by means of catechesis.[32] However, the Catholic Reformation was experiencing difficulties in applying its line of action across the boundaries of gender. The crisis thus generated had reached a peak in 1563 when, by endorsing Boniface VIII's Bull *Periculoso* (1298), the Council of Trent defined female religious life as strictly enclosed and denied women the chance of an apostolic mission outside the cloister. Both congregations' claims to work in the world, alongside all manners of people, were remarkably bold endeavours in their time. Militant apostolic work, religious education and the salvation of souls were considered best suited for men whose spiritual constancy had been proved. It was not a common belief that women could endure the difficulties awaiting them when faced with such a duty.[33]

One of the main obstacles hindering women's participation in the active work of the Catholic offensive resided in the belief that women were, by nature,

---

[31] BCA, B18, *Institutum*, f. 19.

[32] For literature on the Jesuits, see William V. Bangert, *A History of the Society of Jesus* (Saint Louis, Mo, 1986) and Martin A. Lynn, *The Jesuit Mind: The Mentality of an Elite in Early Modern France*, (Ithaca NY, 1988).

[33] Rapley, *The Dévotes*, pp. 5-6. Also Ruth Liebowitz, 'Virgins in the Service of Christ', pp. 31-52 and Elizabeth Rapley, 'Women and the Religious Vocation in Seventeenth-Century France', *French Historical Studies* 18.3 (1994) 613-31.

flawed and therefore unsuitable for such missionary ventures.[34] This combination of religious tradition and vivid suspicion of female constancy made the idea of women missionaries unacceptable to Church authorities. However, congregations such as the French Ursulines and the English Institute tried to abolish these gender-defined distinctions. Their calling implied innovations for which the Counter-Reformation Church was not as yet prepared: though their vocations were, theoretically, suited to the catechizing mission advocated by the Council of Trent, they brought profound changes to traditional female religious life and the adoption of both structures and roles which, thus far, remained a male preserve. Such undertakings could not fail to arouse opposition from ecclesiastical ranks and, at least, a degree of suspicion from the laity.

When both the Ursulines and the English Ladies undertook the re-Catholicization of the women in their neighbourhoods, their endeavours put them on a similar level with that of the clerks regular. Although the Church accepted schooling as an appropriate occupation for women's congregations, the English Ladies' and the French Ursulines' ambitions overstepped the habitual limits ascribed by gender-definitions. In England and in France, the women in this study adopted a lifestyle geared towards the apostolate and took it upon themselves to become active agents of the Catholic mission. Beyond geographical and national differences, their common aim transcended their contextual differences. Thus, the members of the Institute of Mary Ward and the Ursuline *congrégées* of Toulouse (and of France) were laying the foundations of religious movements which exploded the rigid confines of traditional female involvement in Catholicism.

Therefore, neither of the two congregations could be content with the traditional formula of female religious life, which the Council of Trent had re-defined in 1563 as enclosed, contemplative and utterly separated from the activities of the secular world. Both establishments needed to create a space to initiate a new level of female involvement in the early modern Catholic revival which used proselytizing and catechizing as its main tools. In this way, two female movements which sprang from their pragmatic response to Catholicism's chronic need for female workers in a mission of recovery which, thus far, catered mostly for men, found that their initial common goal involved too many innovations to be wholeheartedly accepted by either the Church or indeed society at large. French Ursulines and English Ladies were compelled to compromise with their initial designs in order to save their enterprises from utter destruction; in the end, it was only by embracing enclosure or by returning to the secular sphere that they were allowed to thrive and catechize the young, an area which remained within the sphere which the Catholic Church believed was suitable for feminine activity.

---

[34] Barbara Newman, *From Virile Woman to WomanChrist: Studies in Medieval Religion and Literature* (Philadelphia, Penn., 1995) and Julian O'Faolain and Lauro Martines, *Not in God's Image* (London, 1979).

These two institutions are of such momentous importance in the history of female religious congregations because, despite working from within the patriarchal confines imposed upon them and remaining within gender-allocated role distributions, they managed to lay the foundations of a new system of education for women; indeed their activities enlarged the pre-existing feminine roles within the Church. Their vocations not only participated in the re-Catholicization of Europe but also brought about a new understanding of female education in a world where nobody had, thus far, attempted to give the teaching of girls any formal expression.

Chapter 2

The Improper Institutions of Troublesome Women

> Une religieuse hors de sa clôture est [. . .] comme un arbre
> hors de terre; [...] comme un poisson hors de l'eau [...];
> comme une brebis hors de sa bergerie et en danger d'être
> dévorée des loups [...] et par conséquent dans un état tout à
> fait opposé à la vie Régulière qu'elle a embrassée.[1]

We have seen that the French Ursulines and the English Ladies perceived their vocations as an integral part of the on-going movement of the Catholic Reformation. Hence, they defined themselves in religious rather than lay terms and their educational calling paralleled the extensive effort undertaken in boys' schooling by male communities such as the Society of Jesus or the Fathers of the Christian Doctrine. However, whilst the communities spent their first few years focusing primarily on the work at hand, their institutional status remained too loosely defined to allow clear-cut definition. Since Pius V's *Circa Pastoralis* (1566), simple vows were no longer recognized as defining a religious state; therefore, though they pursued goals which were essentially in tune with the spirit of the Catholic revival, their lack of statutory clarity was to be one of the main sources of difficulties for both the Ursulines and the English Ladies. Without the official approval of the Roman Curia, their endeavours lacked the stable formality and the propriety of prestigious convents, a situation which undoubtedly deterred wealthy and influential patrons from supporting their cause. Since the differentiation between religious and lay was one of the main axes of Tridentine Reform, such loosely-defined female movements could not go unquestioned.

Nevertheless, at least during the first years of their project, the English Institute and the French Ursulines shared the opinion that lack of formal recognition did not undermine the intrinsic value of their work. Though their communities did not correspond to any existing form of female religious life, they were convinced of the worth of their enterprises. This was eloquently expressed by Anne de Xainctonge (1567-1621), foundress of the Ursulines in Burgundy who, in a document clarifying the essence of her establishment in Dole, in the region of Franche-Comté, declared: 'You will give this body [of congregated women] any name you wish; it matters little to me. Names do not glorify God, and they do not

---

[1] Jean Bâptiste Thiers, *Traité de la clôture des religieuses* (Paris, 1681), p. 243.

increase or diminish the perfection of the sacrifices one makes [for God].'[2] She went on to proclaim that women responding to this new type of vocation should not feel any shame or regret about not enjoying as high a reputation as some more prestigious convents; she exhorted her followers to take comfort in the fact that their simple vows and their adoption of the mixed life were more faithful to the example set by Christ himself. Such views proved that the Ursulines, like the English Ladies, considered their vocation to have precedence over official ecclesiastical recognition.

However, early modern Catholicism usually considered any innovative undertakings with a degree of suspicion and this chapter will illustrate that although they proposed to serve the Church in its movement of recovery, the first members both of the English Institute and of the French Ursulines came under close scrutiny and often found opposition where they could have expected support. Statutory objections were raised against new enterprises which flouted Tridentine Decrees; moreover, documents will also show that organizational objections were underpinned by the deep-seated misogyny which was typical of early modern society. The women would have to win two battles: one on institutional grounds, the other on the related issues of gender.

The unthinkable: a Society of Jesus for women

In order to counteract the novelties introduced by the Protestant doctrine, the Catholic Reformation across Europe generally advocated a return to the traditional positions of the Church. It provided a clear image of society, one in which each person or group played a specific role, according to their stations in life. Tridentine emphasis upon the divide between lay and religious was a vivid illustration of the Catholic world picture, which functioned in a compartmentalized manner. Conformity to the established order was a prerequisite for any movement which endeavoured to take part in the Catholic Reformation. This was particularly acute in the Church's relationship to women. Since the Council of Trent had endorsed Boniface VIII's Bull *Periculoso* in 1563, one of these norms was the restriction of female religious life within the convent and the decree uncompromisingly equated female religious life with the strictest enclosure:

---

[2] In Gaétan Bernoville, *Le Cloître dans le monde: Anne de Xainctonge, fondatrice de la compagnie de Sainte Ursule 1576-1621* (Paris, 1956), p. 130. In French: 'On donnera à ce corps le nom qu'on voudra; il ne m'importe. Ce ne sont pas les noms qui glorifient Dieu, comme ce ne sont point eux qui augmentent ou diminuent la perfection des sacrifices.'

After religious profession no nun may go out of her monastery on any pretext even for a short time, except for a legitimate reason approved by the bishop [...]. And no one of kind or condition or sex or age may enter within the confines of a monastery without the permission of the bishop or superior given in writing, under pain of excommunication.[3]

However, bishops consistently met with difficulties in enforcing these measures and, at the close of the sixteenth century, convents across the Continent were questioning the Tridentine rulings and even denouncing the limitations of enclosure. Indeed, the evangelizing drive of the Catholic Reformation implied that educational provisions had to be made by women's institutions in order to rally the female population to the faith. This presented the Holy See with a dilemma: if women were to remain enclosed, how could they undertake a catechizing mission? More importantly, should the Church implement changes which would irremediably alter the definition of female religious life? Should congregations such as the French Ursulines or the English Institute be allowed to inaugurate movements which, in harmony with the Counter-Reformation effort, reconciled an educational vocation with traditional religious life even if, in so doing, they distorted established conventual patterns?[4]

The case of Mary Ward's Institute provides the most eloquent illustration of Counter-Reformation issues concerning matters of structure. Although the Institute's aim to evangelize women in England and on the Continent was in tune with the spirit of the Catholic Reformation, its vocation did not fit comfortably within the Tridentine framework of female religious life. With this in mind, and despite ecclesiastical support in towns such as St Omer, Liège and Cologne (where bishop Blaes, vicar general Jean de Chokier and Nuncio Pietro Francesco Montorio wrote to the pope in defence of the Institute), Urban VIII's decision to suppress Mary Ward's foundations in 1631 came as no surprise. Yet although both the Institute and its foundress herself have generated much research in recent years, very few works have attempted to unravel the complicated history behind this cruel fate. The abolition of the Institute seems to contradict the missionary spirit of the Counter-Reformation Church and the factors leading to the promulgation of the Bull still remain somewhat unclear.

---

[3] Session 25, 3-4 December 1563, in Norman Tanner, *Decrees of the Ecumenical Councils*, vol. 2, p. 778.

[4] On the tensions between the cloister and the apostolate for religious women, see Ruth Liebowitz, 'Virgins in the Service of Christ', pp. 131-52; Linda Lierheimer, 'Redefining Convent Space', and James Cain, 'The Influence of the Cloister on the Apostolate of Congregations of Religious Women', unpublished PhD thesis, Pontifical Lateran University, Rome, 1965.

Some of the reasons for the violent controversy which led Pope Urban VIII to pronounce the suppression of Mary Ward's work may be gleaned from one of the Order's most essential documents, the *Institutum,* which the foundress addressed to the Curia in 1621 exposing, without any dissimulation, the Institute's faithful emulation of the Society of Jesus and its desire to be recognized as its independent female counterpart. Even with its opening words, the Plan offered an unmistakable vindication of its Jesuit-like nature, borrowing the military taxonomy of the Jesuits and deriving an estimated 85 per cent of its text from the *Formula Instituti*:

> Whoever wishes to serve beneath the banner of the cross as a soldier of God in our Society, which we desire to be designated by the name of Jesus [...] is a member of a Society founded primarily for this purpose: to strive for the defence and propagation of the faith.[5]

In an unprecedented move, Ward claimed the title of 'Society of Jesus' for her own Institute and proceeded to show how she adopted the Jesuit model in matters vocational but also institutional. In addition to an educational and missionary vocation which did not allow claustration, she departed drastically from the norm of women's religious Orders by creating the first female generalate. At the head of the Institute, the Mother Superior General acted as a central figure of authority, governing and co-ordinating all the branches across Europe. According to the *Institutum*, the superiors of each establishment would look to their Superior General for direction and advice. Therefore, Mary Ward, as foundress and Superior General, eluded the usual channels of authority embodied in local bishops and ordinaries and declined to submit to any episcopal control; like the Society of Jesus, the Institute was to be self-governed.

The principle of a female generalate was but one aspect of the proposed structure which not only flouted centuries of Church establishment but flew in the face of Tridentine Decrees and implied the rejection of the traditional hierarchy of male authority. To the clergy in general, it represented little less than an open criticism of their ancestral definition of female religious life, a conviction which was reinforced by a further passage of the text in which the foundress requested to be dispensed from all forms of episcopal control, writing: 'We therefore most humbly beg that the entire hierarchical structure of this work should depend entirely on the Holy See and not on any other authority.'[6] Predictably, the clergy were incensed by what they perceived as the Yorkshire woman's presumption not only to organize her female Institute as a generalate but to dispense with male jurisdiction altogether. Mary Ward's wish to be answerable to the sovereign

---

[5] BCA, B 18, *Institutum,* f. 19, my italics.
[6] *Ibid.*, f. 22.

pontiff only was a daring innovation, which she reiterated in a letter addressed to Pope Gregory XV in January 1622; she explained:

> That kind of government [religious life under episcopal control], though holy in itself and helpful to other religious communities [is] not only contrary to the Institute allotted unto us, but would moreover [...] much molest and hinder us [in] the service we are to perform towards our neighbours.[7]

Therefore, like their Jesuit exemplars, the English Ladies requested self-government and wished to vow direct obedience to the pope as their only authority outside the Institute's Mother Superior General.

Such a principle of autonomous generalate took Ward's imitation of the Society of Jesus to its apex. It enabled her Institute to work hand in hand with, yet independently from, the Society of Jesus, unfettered by the supervision of episcopal authority. Since the Jesuit constitutions offered the ideal balance between the traditional female religious *modus operandi* and the flexibility the English Institute required in order to operate in such varied circumstances as they would find on the Continent or in England, the *Institutum* mirrored, almost word for word, the Ignatian *Formula,* embracing not only the Society's goals but also its manner of life.

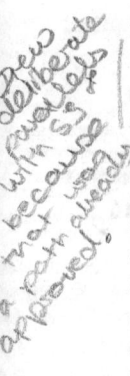

Mary Ward thus introduced her request to the pope with a reminder that the way of life she and her followers had adopted was already approved, and therefore could contain no objectionable elements. In the text, she carefully headed off predictable criticism by recognizing some gender-defined limitations in her project: though her followers walked in the Jesuits' footsteps, they would not meddle with exclusively male functions, which she enumerated as 'ministering sacraments, public preaching, teaching and public disputing of matters of divinity, and all such things as are lawful only for priests to exercize'.[8] Nonetheless, she continued, at a time when the Church needed every advantage it could summon, a congregation of women working to catechize the female half of the population would represent a formidable asset.

For the Institute, she insisted, adaptability should prevail over the observance of traditional usage: these circumstances, therefore, accounted for her request for the relaxation of choral Office (as traditionally practised in monastic houses) in favour of private and unsung prayer, in order to devote more time to the practical purposes of an educational vocation. It also explained why, when working under cover, the English Ladies were not required by their Rules to wear a religious habit but rather to dress according to the fashion suited to 'virtuous ladies'. The members of the community working in various countries across the Continent wore a practical but sober dress in lieu of religious habit and, if on a

---

[7] BCA, B18, *Memorial to Gregory XV.*
[8] *Ibid.*

mission in hostile parts, they would avoid detection by reverting to garments in line with those sported by local women of equivalent social standing.[9] Thus, in their attire, their flexibility and their organization, Ward and her followers were faithful to the Jesuit model. Therefore, if the Institute was to be so similar to the Society of Jesus, what were the reasons for the antagonism which it encountered in Rome?

In fact, its Ignatian vocation, far from facilitating its progress, threw countless difficulties in its path. By the 1620s, the Society of Jesus was at the centre of a deep-seated dispute with the secular clergy. In the English mission particularly, the tension had started during Queen Elizabeth's reign, as soon as secular priests and Jesuit missionaries came into conflict for the control of the mission and the spiritual direction of leading recusant families. This quarrel reached a climax in the 1600s, as a pamphlet published in 1601 testified in its eloquent title: *A true relation of a faction begun at Wisbich by Fa. Edmonds, alias Weston, a Jesuite, 1595 and continued since by Fa. Walley, alias Garnet, the Provinciall of the Jesuits in England, and by Fa Parsons in Rome, with their adherents: Against us the Secular Priests their brethren and fellow Prisoners, that disliked of novelties, and thought it dishonourable to the ancient Ecclesiastical Discipline of the Catholicke Church, that Secular Priests should be governed by Jesuits.*[10] In such an unstable context, Mary Ward was far from increasing her chances of speedy approval when she committed herself to adopting the Society of Jesus as her model. On the contrary, when she undertook dealings with Urban VIII (1623-44), a reputedly choleric and anti-Jesuit pope, she became unwittingly caught in the long-drawn acrimonious disputes between Jesuits and seculars. Was Mary Ward unaware of the increasing drift in the post-Reformation Catholic Church which pitched the secular clergy against the regulars, and more particularly the Jesuits?

It was predictable that the enemies of the Society of Jesus would also oppose a female Order which claimed to imitate it; it is therefore not surprising that, in response to the 1621 *Institutum*, the English secular clergy presented to the Holy See a Memorial against the English Ladies.[11] They expressed concerns which derived from the Tridentine Church's compulsion to categorize religious life according to established denominations; their main objections seemed to address the Institute's status rather than the nature of its vocation. Such vituperation was expressed by the coinage of the label of 'Jesuitesses', a term which showed a somewhat contemptuous separation between the seculars and the Ladies whose organization they mocked. This term also showed that the secular clergy misconstrued the Institute's imitation of the Society of Jesus for some sort of

---

[9] BCA, B18, *Ratio Instituti*, f. 4.
[10] The text of this publication is reproduced in Thomas Law Graves, *A Historical Sketch of the Conflicts between Jesuits and Seculars in the Reign of Queen Elizabeth* (London, 1889).
[11] Westminster Diocesan Archives, vol. 16, ff. 201-207, in conjunction with a translation into English kept in the BCA, C1, J3, 'Translation of documents re. Jesuitesses'.

assimilation into the Ignatian fraternity. Deliberate or not, this was a considerable mistake indeed.[12]

Although they were correct in their claim that Mary Ward's followers lived 'according to the rule and institute of the Jesuit Fathers', it was a mistake to assume, as they did, that the Ladies were directly 'under their government and discipline' since they were, on the contrary, determined to be entirely independent.[13] This is an important clarification, since it shows that Ward not only knew the Jesuit *Formula* forbade any female branch of its Order but also that she did not wish to be ruled by the Society at all. Her foundation, she insisted, was to be entirely parallel to its Ignatian model, but it would submit to no other male jurisdiction than that of the pope, whom she begged 'to receive this our whole company into [his] especial care and protection, not suffering bishops in their particular dioceses or others whomsoever, to have any ordinary authority or jurisdiction over us.'[14]   The clergy's statement, therefore, was a patent misrepresentation of the community's intentions, arising from a point-blank assumption that the self-rule of autonomous female congregations was inconceivable; furthermore, it was intended to expose and ridicule the Jesuits for directing an illicit female phalanx, thereby tarring both congregations with the same brush.

As if opposition from the enemies of the Jesuits was not enough to contend with, Mary Ward also faced antipathy from within the Society, some members of which proved sensitive to accusations and calumny concerning their alleged approval of the Institute.[15] The prevailing fear was that the Society might be compromised by women following its code of life. Despite the foundress's clarity on this point, the poisonous epithet of 'Jesuitesses' used by the English secular clergy had blurred the boundaries between Jesuits and English Ladies in the public eye. A contemporaneous report publicized this crisis in edifying words:

> [The Jesuits] are grown to a faction about the Jesuitrices or
> Wandering Nuns, some allowing them, some disliking them
> utterly. [The English Ladies] observe the Ignatian habit, and
> go clad very like to the Jesuits, in this only differing from
> other nuns: they walk abroad in the world, and preach the
> Gospel to their sex in England and elsewhere.[16]

It is true that the Ladies' chosen attire on the Continent, which closely resembled that of the Jesuits, added further to the confusion. Though they did not wear a religious habit as such, they all wore (whenever possible) the same simple black dresses which visually expressed their closeness to the Society and made a number

---

[12] Margaret Littlehales, *Mary Ward, Pilgrim and Mystic*, pp. 110-3.

[13] Westminster Diocesan Archives (henceforth WDA) vol. 16, f. 202 and BCA, C1, J3, f. 2.

[14] *Ibid.*

[15] Henriette Peters, *Mary Ward*, p. 123.

[16] James Wadsworth, *English Spanish Pilgrim* (London, 1629), p. 30.

of Jesuits uneasy. Indeed, as a consequence of this popular misconception linking the Society of Jesus and the Institute, many priests decided to detach themselves officially and firmly from the female congregation. The few who supported the Ladies, such as Roger Lee (1568-1615), John Gerard (1564-1637) or Edward Burton (d. 1624), incurred reprimands from their superiors and the official line was conveyed in 1623 by the Jesuit General's order 'not [to] meddle with any thing belonging to the temporals of Mrs Mary Ward, or any of her company'.[17] Above all, the Fathers should make it quite clear that their Order, in keeping with the rulings of St Ignatius, did not harbour any female branch, that it had no more particular link with these women than they did with any other penitents. Slander had thus left a deep scar in the relationship between English Ladies and the Society they so admired. The Jesuits were anxious to dissociate themselves from the so-called 'galloping girls' or 'wandering nuns'.[18]

But association with the Society of Jesus was not the only difficulty: the Institute's most public and perhaps most damning departure from the norm of established female religious life was its non-enclosure, which the foundress claimed was essential to its missionary purpose. Beyond the disputes which opposed the secular clergy to the Jesuits and those they spitefully called their 'Jesuitesses', the broad spectrum of the English Catholic clergy agreed on one account: if the English Institute was a religious Order, then its early form was in breach of the Decrees of the Council of Trent and its members should submit to claustration. This was exemplified in Liège in 1619, when Ward's new establishment prompted local Jesuits to compile a short questionnaire in order to determine its nature and function. Revealingly, their very first question referred to enclosure:

> When the English Ladies found houses and accommodate them according to their needs, do they observe the same kind of enclosure as is customary in the Society? First, are men prohibited from entering their houses, just as women do not enter ours?[19]

Mary Ward's answer showed both her determination to emulate the Society and her refusal to compromise her Institute's freedom of movement. She replied:

---

[17] Mutius Vitelleschi's letter, dated 19 July 1623: directions for the colleges of Louvain and St Omer. A copy is preserved in BCA, C1, J3.

[18] WDA, vol. 16, f. 207 and BCA, C1, J3, f. 5. Ward's followers were mockingly called 'wandering nuns' because of their refusal to accept traditional enclosure. In her article ' "Wandering Nuns": The Return of the Institute of the Blessed Virgin Mary to the South of England, 1862-1945', *Recusant History* 24.3 (1999) 384-96, Sr. M. Gregory Kirkus, IBVM, explores what she calls 'the purposeful mobility' of the members of the Institute in more recent years.

[19] BCA, B9, *various papers*.

> It was always intended after our houses were built
> commodious, to observe the same enclosure that the Society
> does from women, and hitherto we have practised as much
> as the incommodity of our houses would permit.[20]

Such an answer could not be deemed satisfactory by most clerics, especially with
the addition of this last proviso, 'as much as the incommodity of our houses would
permit'. This was probably intended to refer to houses in England, where her
missionaries did not have the necessary building arrangements to observe any form
of enclosure at all, even if they had wished to do so. But enclosure was never on
the agenda for the English Ladies; on the contrary, they were proud of their ideal of
the mixed life, which emulated Christ's way of life whilst being perfectly tailored
to their particular vocation. Even in 1612, the reputedly timorous *Schola Beatae
Mariae* had already insisted upon the importance of the 'mixed life' when the
foundress candidly declared: 'We have in mind the mixed life, such a life as we
learn Christ Our Lord and Master taught his chosen ones [...] so that in this way
we may more easily educate maidens and girls.'[21]

When, in 1615, the Jesuit canonist Francisco Suarez (1548-1617) engaged
in the debate concerning the English Institute, his appreciation of Mary Ward's
foundation led him to draft a list of four main inconveniences which worked
against the general approbation of the foundress's work by most clerics.
Unsurprisingly, the first of these concerned the Ladies' lack of enclosure. He
wrote: 'they go up and down the land with little of the decorum of the feminine
sex, and to the ignominy of the Catholic religion, practising great liberty with
young people.'[22]

Suarez's disapproval of the Institute's way of life was later endorsed
wholeheartedly by many and came to represent a complete consensus between the
Society and the secular clergy. As we have seen, the seculars objected to the
structure of the Institute which, in their 1621 Memorial, they accused of being
'directly contrary to the decrees of the Sacred Council of Trent'.[23]   Later, in
October 1622, the English secular priest John Colleton (1548-1635), made this
point one of his main preoccupations.[24]   After a description of the Institute's
activities and of its way of life, he wrote:

---

[20] *Ibid.*

[21] BCA, B18, *Schola Beatae Mariae*, item 3.

[22] BCA, C1, *Letters against the Jesuitesses*, f. 297.

[23] WDA, vol. 16, f. 206, and in translation from the Latin in BCA, C1, J3, f. 4.

[24] John Colleton formed the Association of the Clergy of England, an independent body in
charge of regulating the affairs of the secular clergy. He was later suspended for
aggravating the schism between the seculars and the Society of Jesus. See Ethelred Taunton,
The History of the Jesuits in England, pp. 256-57.

> If [the Institute] abode within its cells and walls, after the example of other religious communities, [it] would perhaps deserve much praise, but when it claims the duties of the apostolic office, wanders unrestrainedly about hither and thither [...] undertakes the management of families, in fact does all sorts of things under pretence of practising charity to its neighbours, and in spite of this insists on being numbered amongst the religious communities, [it] is certainly exposed to the censures and reproaches of many pious people.[25]

These were women without a *custos*, who brazenly refused male supervision and the propriety of the cloister. This point was reiterated in the Memorial of the English clergy, the authors of which recognized the Ladies' teaching work as worthy of praise (since religious instruction and girls' education were fully in keeping with the spirit of the Catholic Reformation) while nevertheless insisting that these teachers could not be considered religious if they would continue travelling at will and dressing in secular fashion.

Many other members of the clergy supported this view and felt equally angered by Mary Ward's refusal of traditional enclosure. In the same year as Colleton expressed his suspicions, Fr. John Bennet (d. 1623), the agent for the English secular clergy in Rome, wrote: 'Briefly closure they must embrace, and some Order already approved, or else dissolve. But of closure they will not hear.'[26] Some years later, in 1630, Francesco Ingoli, secretary of *Propaganda Fide,* wrote along the same lines.[27] In his *Compendium of the process made by the Nuncio of Cologne against the Jesuitesses in the year 1630 and month September* he described the Institute as 'a new form of religious life without the license of the Apostolic See, [...] without enclosure, against the pontifical bulls'.[28] He added: 'In this Institute, there are many inconveniences, such as intercourse with men [and] wandering about the world.'[29] The objections to such unchecked geographical mobility were many, and Ingoli alleged that the English Ladies were publicly called whores in England and that one of them had an illegitimate child. Their impudence knew no bounds since they preached publicly, taught theology and dared to think themselves equal to priests.

Mary Ward's wish to develop an international Society of Jesus for women took the ideal of female ministry further than the more localized endeavours of the French Ursulines. Yet, there remained some similarities with the endeavours of the first Ursulines *congrégées* of France: they too proposed to adapt the 'mixed' life of the clerks regular, to a female community. Although they did not claim to imitate

[handwritten marginal note: Although Ward went further than the Ursulines / still some parallels]

---

[25] BCA, C1, J3, *translation of documents re. Jesuitesses.*

[26] WDA, B 25, 54.

[27] Henriette Peters, *Mary Ward*, p. 356.

[28] BCA, C1, *Letters against the Jesuitesses*, f. 311.

[29] *Ibid.*, f. 312.

any male congregation as openly as Ward emulated the Jesuits, they nevertheless worked closely with the Society and presented a profile which did not comply with the established definitions of female religious life. We will see that initially, the *congrégées* particularly puzzled the local elites, since they followed no recognized Rule and lived an evangelical life.

The Ursuline mixed life under suspicion

The French Ursulines, like the English Ladies, considered that their vocation called for the kind of 'mixed' life which Tridentine decrees had prohibited for religious women; they felt that the traditional monastic model did not correspond to their particular vocation, which was of a more evangelical nature. Thus, the *congrégées* gave priority to concrete and urgent matters: they focused on opening schools and started teaching and living in simple congregations as a practical and efficient way to kick-start their catechizing enterprise. They appeared little preoccupied with the adoption of a recognized way of life, thereby implicitly treating Tridentine categorizations and ecclesiastical recognition as matters of lesser importance to them than the pursuit of their essential goal.

The Ursulines were very aware of their canonical irregularity; yet, at that juncture, budding establishments were often more preoccupied with carving a niche for their educational vocation amongst local women than with ecclesiastical recognition. Toulouse exemplifies this situation eloquently since ten years elapsed between its settlement in the city in 1604 and its papal approbation as a religious community in 1614. Moreover, these early congregations seemed to regard their hybrid status with more than simple indifference: they were truly committed to living a 'mixed' kind of life bringing both the spirituality of the cloister and the activity of the world into play. The Toulouse community, like all others throughout France, underlined the excellence of its chosen style of life:

> The life of the Ursulines is none other than that which the Son of God Himself led in this world; it is the same as his Holy mother and his apostles lived when He went to Heaven. Here are the models and the exemplars of their status and their profession: it is the mixed life, combining both contemplation and action.[30]

Such ambiguities would need to be resolved if the Ursulines were to secure official acceptance for the work they insisted on carrying out; indeed, although the French Church generally welcomed the Ursulines, this was not always

---

[30] ADHG, 221H-37, f. 2, *Mémoires*: 'La vie des Ursulines n'est autre que celle que le fils de Dieu a menée en ce monde, et sa Sainte mère avec les apôtres après sa montée au ciel. Voilà les modèles et les exemplaires de leur état et profession: c'est la vie mixte mêlée de la contemplation et de l'action.'

the case, and some early *congrégées* suffered directly from their perceived lawlessness. Thus, when in 1606, Geneviève de Valembert and Christine Peiron set up an Ursuline congregation in Grenoble, they fell prey to public opprobrium; although their group had been licensed locally by the diocese of Avignon, a preacher took it upon himself to speak against them in a crowded church and, 'pointing them out and naming their names, he said quantities of things that were most damaging to them.'[31] In this instance, the attacks came from a member of the clergy, but it was even more usual for difficulties to arise from lay, public opinion.

For Françoise de Xainctonge, for instance, starting a congregation in Dijon proved to be an ordeal, upsetting family and acquaintances who could not comprehend such a choice. She and her companions were exposed to local suspicion: why would young ladies of high social status decide to bring shame on their families and deny themselves the chance of good repute by casting off respectable society and abasing themselves by being school teachers for poor children?[32] Such was public puzzlement that the women came to be entirely alienated; they represented rogue elements which had willingly opted out of a system which was deemed reputable. As a result, children acted out the spite which adults dared only speak, jeering, spitting or flinging mud at these eccentric deviants. Antoinette Micolon suffered a string of similar humiliations during her lifetime and faced the same popular antipathy in each of the six congregations she founded in Ambert, Clermont, Tulle, Beaulieu, Espalion and Arlanc. In her memoirs, she recalled founding the house in Ambert whilst the whole town united in opposing her: local boys penned a lewd song about her, children pointed and whistled at her when she went out, and women afflicted her with verbal and physical attacks.[33]

Popular and lay opposition was therefore the most overt form of antagonism met by the new venture. It was not unusual to find hostility even against congregations which were publicly endorsed by local ecclesiasts. We have seen that for Mary Ward, the active support of certain bishops and vicars did not suffice to quell the quarrel regarding the Institute. This was also the case in France where cardinals, bishops and parish priests usually defended their Ursulines against the criticism they occasionally encountered. In other respects, however, the Frenchwomen fared a little better than their English counterparts; they benefited from wider clerical support, and active Orders such as the Fathers of the Christian Doctrine or Society of Jesus welcomed their work as a complement to their own.[34]

---

[31] MDPU, *Les Chroniques de l'ordre des Ursulines*, part 1, p. 84: 'Un fameux prédicateur déclama contre elles en pleine chaire dans l'église de sainte Claire, et les montrant du doigt et les nommant par leur nom, dit quantité de choses qui leur étaient très désavantageuses.'

[32] *Ibid.*, part 4, pp. 3-9.

[33] Henri Pourrat (ed.), *Mémoires de la mère Micolon (1592-1659)* (Clermont-Ferrand, 1981); p. 81.

[34] M. C. Gueudré, *Histoire de l'ordre des Ursulines,* vol. 1, pp. 151-54.

One Jesuit was reported to have spoken these encouraging words to the Ursuline congregation of Paris:

> Our blessed Father Ignatius worked towards this end, directing our Company to the sound education of young boys. It would be a praiseworthy and useful work to establish a congregation into which one could transplant young girls, as though into a fertile soil; the girls, after being well instructed, could leave the congregations to bring virtue into their families.[35]

Such positive endorsement may owe much to the fact the Ursulines, unlike Mary Ward's followers, were never suspected *as a group* of unsavoury relationships with Ignatians. The *congrégées* did complete the educational work undertaken by the priests, yet did not claim any particular closeness with them; they therefore represented much less of a threat for the Society's reputation. Thus, despite some examples of hostility, the overall dissemination of the Ursuline movement across France was allowed to follow its course with little organized opposition, provided that its establishments complied with the traditional requirements for female religious endeavours and did not upset the stability of the local social order. In Toulouse, for instance, the presence of the *congrégées* seems to have been generally well accepted and their school won outspoken praise from among laity and ecclesiastics. However, even in the pious atmosphere of the *ville rose*, renowned as the cradle of provincial Catholic revival, women's freedom to teach or innovate with the established mode of religious life came under the vigilant scrutiny of local authorities, both lay and religious.

Thus, although in a different way from Mary Ward's Institute, the Toulousain house provides another eloquent example of early modern preoccupations with status classification and order. Aware of the spirit of her time, Marguerite de Vigier soon decided to take drastic measures in order to secure the future of her life-long commitment to the Ursuline project. She knew from experience that women carrying out religious works outside enclosure and beyond episcopal authority were at odds with accepted seventeenth-century preconceptions.

We must remember that, in their very first years, Ursuline congregations functioned without any official authorization and it was not uncommon for local authorities (*Parliaments* and *municipalités*) and their Ursuline settlers to develop rather tense relationships. Even an essentially Catholic body such as the *Parlement* of Toulouse had shown strong reluctance to recognize its local community before the royal approval of 1611. In her authoritative study of the Ursuline Order in France, M. C. Gueudré stated that this predicament was in fact replicated

---

[35] Père Marin, SJ, to Madame de Sainte Beuve, foundress of the Ursulines of the Faubourg Saint Jacques in Paris, in Elizabeth Rapley, *The Dévotes*, p. 53.

throughout France.[36] Generally, she found that most municipalities showed no inclination to regularize the administrative situation of new Ursuline houses; on the contrary, the *congrégées* often experienced difficulties in gaining approbation from their local authorities. How can such a seemingly paradoxical situation be explained?

Several factors compounded to create unexpected hostility from localities whose Catholic commitment should have otherwise guaranteed their support of the Ursuline cause. Many municipalities, like that of Toulouse, were actively involved in the movement of the Catholic renaissance and would, from a religious point of view, have welcomed the women's contribution to that process. Yet it is arguable that their Gallican values prevented them from officially receiving a new community of foreign origin until it was approved by the crown. When congregations were eventually accepted by the king, then the cities' officials usually showed no hesitation in receiving them wholeheartedly, even when, as was the case for the earliest settlements, they were not as yet approved by the pope. Thus it was that the community of Toulouse, who had remained in official limbo since its arrival in 1604, became registered by the city of Toulouse in April 1612, barely four months after the 1611 publication of the royal *lettres patentes* approving its existence and praising its work.

Entrenched Gallicanism apart, there were additional factors to delay the official reception of Ursuline congregations in French cities. At the root of local concern was the unprecedented increase in the sheer numbers of religious establishments, and the pressures this put upon urban centres. In Toulouse, as elsewhere in France, the seventeenth century witnessed a proliferation of monasteries which even affluent conurbations could barely sustain. Between 1590 and 1709, an estimated twenty-one new religious Orders came to settle in the *ville rose*, fourteen of which were female congregations.[37] Since monasteries were exempt from taxation, it is easy to see the economic strain they represented in the eyes of the municipality; moreover, such multiplication of establishments led to increasing competition for space, leaving the *Parlement* with no choice other than to prohibit the building of new religious houses in 1623, 1665 and 1667; thus, new communities often struggled for years before securing a property inside the city walls.

The last, but not the least of local preoccupations concerned the welfare of the daughters of well-to-do society. Indeed, the Ursulines hoped to recruit from amongst the ranks of influential and wealthy families, to secure their patronage and to benefit from their connections in spheres of power; they therefore targeted the upper classes and particularly the *Parlementaires* in cities which (like Toulouse) had a Parlement. However, the prospect of seeing one or several daughters join an

---

[36] M. C. Gueudré, *Histoire de l'ordre des Ursulines,* vol. 1, p. 132. 'Les fondations ne furent que rarement l'œuvre des municipalités et, pour prendre racine, elles eurent parfois des résistances à vaincre et des concessions à faire.'

[37] Philippe Wolff (ed.), *Histoire de Toulouse* (Toulouse, 1974), p. 316.

indigent congregation of no approved status was certainly far from pleasing to their intended catchment area. Therefore, it is plausible that municipal representatives' reluctance to recognize the initial Ursulines was caused by a combination of suspicion towards this ill-defined group and of fear for their own family interests. Securing a good alliance for their daughters or allowing them to enter a prestigious religious establishment would be immensely more beneficial than letting them join a poor community as yet unrecognized by either king or pope.[38]

Consequently, in the early years of their residence as lay congregations in French towns, the Ursulines needed to exercise extreme caution in their daily dealings with their neighbourhood. First, their houses and schools had to gain public confidence by proving their value and, above all, by demonstrating qualities that would inspire trust. Yet, though educational excellence was a primary condition in order to win the support of noble and gentle patrons, it alone would not suffice without the correlatives of stability, status and all the virtues commendable in religious women.

Across France, these new congregations were highly aware both of the public mistrust of novelty and of the fragility of the reputation of female enterprises: Marguerite de Vigier, the foundress of the Toulouse establishment, had experienced it first hand when, during her initial journey from Avignon in 1604, she and her companions had been arrested on suspicion that they were *'gens de mauvaise vie'*. As she and her companion, Françoise de Blanchet, travelled towards Toulouse under the tutelage of two Fathers of the Christian Doctrine (her own brother, Antoine de Vigier, and his acolyte Pierre Sisoine), the four missionaries were seized and imprisoned in the town of Pezenas, an episode which not only bears witness to early modern fears of vagrants but also indicates that women, travelling freely in the company of men, were immediately construed as being prostitutes.[39] This anecdote illustrates vividly how seventeenth-century perceptions frowned upon geographical mobility in general and upon that of unmarried women in particular. Indeed, it is strongly reminiscent of the criticisms ridiculing Mary Ward's followers with such sobriquets as 'wandering nuns' or 'galloping girls'. In a climate which understood women as confined either within the sphere of their household or that of a convent, early Ursuline settlements in France (and indeed most non-enclosed communities of women across Europe) were viewed with the same kind of suspicion as the English Institute.

Parayre's *Chronique* illustrated polite society's misgivings regarding the fledgling community of Toulouse, with which some young women found sanctuary when absconding from marriage arrangements they could not bring themselves to honour. One incident concerned Magdelaine Despanez (1594-1677), in religion *sœur* de Jésus, whose father, a *trésorier général de France*, had arranged an

---

[38] See Elizabeth Rapley, *The Dévotes*, pp. 57-60, for her interpretation of the relationships between influential families and their local Ursuline communities.
[39] ADHG, 221H-37, *Mémoires*, f. 2.

advantageous marriage for her in 1606. However, the young girl, who was not yet twelve years old, flouted her family's project and broke all the arrangements when she escaped and found refuge with the Ursulines.[40] One can understand her family's discontent at the loss of potential income and status, which was in this case further aggravated by the blatant disobedience of their child. Yet, the girl's parents, and especially her mother, were of a devout disposition: eventually, they complied with their daughter's choice, without attacking the community as virulently as might have been expected. In this case, a well-to-do family relinquished personal interest and social alliances to oblige their daughter's desire to stay with the Ursulines and become a *congrégée*.

Things did not go so well, however, for the young Marie de Liberos (born in 1574), in religion *sœur* de la Trinité. Like Magdelaine Despanez, she also fled a pre-arranged union to find refuge with the Ursulines.[41] In her case, however, parental consent was not easily gained. Originally from the smaller town of Agen, where her family lived, she had been sent to Toulouse under her uncle's tutelage, in order to meet her future husband and finalize the settlement. When she ran away to the Ursuline establishment, both uncle and suitor attempted to break down the house's doors and kidnap her. A raging and embarrassingly public battle of wills followed; when the use of force was finally abandoned, it was substituted with court action on the part of the enraged uncle, who sued the Ursulines for holding his niece illegally. The community eventually won after a long-drawn-out legal battle and Marie de Liberos was soon sent to a new branch, in the nearby town of Brive-la-Gaillarde.

Things were even bleaker for Françoise Rabonite, in religion *sœur* de Sainte Claire, who came from a similar *Parlementaire* milieu and was destined to follow in the footsteps of her sisters, who were nuns in the city's prestigious convent of St Claire. After completing her education in its boarding school, she refused to enter the novitiate.[42] Instead, she preferred the poverty of the fledgling Ursuline house, whose reputation had already won her heart and which she secretly joined in 1607. On discovering her initiative, her mother was deeply upset, but her ultimatum reinforced her daughter's determination to stay with the *congrégées*; the community's manuscript memoirs recalled:

> Françoise Rabonite [...] presented herself to the community with such fervour and such generosity that she resolved, for the love of God, never to see her mother again, the later having opposed and resisted [her daughter's] decision as much as she could, and declared that she would never see her again in her life.[43]

---

[40] R. P. Parayre, *Chronique*, part 2, pp. 240-264.

[41] *Ibid.*, pp. 338-375.

[42] *Ibid.*, pp. 87-116.

[43] ADHG, 221H-37, *Mémoires*.

One of her uncles, a *procureur au Parlement*, even tried to get her out by force. Significantly, respectable neighbouring families united to support Madame Rabonite in her plight and stood at the Ursulines' doors demanding Françoise's release and shouting abuse at the community. Indeed, although most Catholic families approved of the *congrégées'* religious cause, their lack of institutional status implied that the Ursulines' financial stability remained uncertain. Thus, most fathers of influential households preferred placing their daughters in convents whose prestige was proven and long-established. Françoise Rabonite's choice ran against early modern preconceptions when she refused the grandeur and *kudos* of the St Claire convent in favour of the small, fragile and unrecognized Ursuline community, much to her parents' distress. One feels tempted to postulate that it was as a tribute to the Order she turned down, and perhaps as an homage to her family's wishes, that she chose the name of Sainte Claire when she later took the habit.

Such vicissitudes affected many other Ursuline communities across France and it would be impossible to give more than a very cursory glimpse of such difficult times in this chapter. Similar opposition to that encountered in Toulouse was recorded, for instance, in Bordeaux where Françoise de Cazères (in religion *sœur* de la Croix) founded a small congregation.[44] Initial opposition did not rise from ecclesiastical quarters but rather from the local people who mocked the *congrégées* and derided their practice of covering their heads with veils when on their way to church. Cruel tortures were designed to victimize them in church, such as pricking their shoulders with long needles during the sermon. The Ursulines were a laughing stock and the butt of regular booing and hissing.

Unsurprisingly therefore, when Françoise de Cazères received into her congregation and promptly cut the hair of two of the daughters of an influential local family, the girls' parents took immediate action, libelling the congregation throughout the town and spreading 'a thousand insulting and hurtful rumours' against the local foundress before resorting to violence and raiding the house by breaking down its doors. Upon discovering that their daughters had been removed to a safe haven, they began legal proceedings against the congregation. Predictably, the Parlement sided with the family and decreed that the two girls should be handed back to their family for the duration of the trial; the final verdict was that they should enter an approved Order of their own choice. Clearly, the issue here was not that the daughters wished to become religious, since the family agreed to the verdict without difficulty. The source of their outrage was evidently the ambiguous and unrecognized nature of the Ursuline congregation and on this occasion, slander and scandal reached beyond the small establishment of Ursulines.

---

[44] Charles Sainte-Foi, *Vies des premières Ursulines de France tirées des chroniques de l'Ordre* (Paris, 1856), 198-205 : 'Le monde, d'un côté, le poursuivait de sa haine, de son mépris et de ses calomnies' alors que 'les hommes les plus pieux, soit parmi les laïques, soit parmi le clergé, regardaient comme impossible cette œuvre, et n'en voulaient point entendre parler.'

The girls' family took it upon itself to tarnish the reputation of the *congrégées'* most fervent patron, the Cardinal-Archbishop François de Sourdis, whose episcopal letter had supported the Ursulines' case during the trial. Because of his association with these women, Sourdis's reputation suffered grievously; accused of improper relations with Françoise de Cazères, he faced public opprobrium when 'the people hunt[ed] him down with hatred, spite and calumny'. It was reported that 'even the most pious of men, either secular or amongst the clergy, regarded [the Ursuline] enterprise as impossible and did not want to hear anything about it.'

These examples illustrate how the initial years of the Ursuline settlements in France were episodically blighted by conflict, and this despite the intensity of the Catholic revival effort in many cities. The opposition and difficulties which faced the French sisters were not entirely of the same nature as those encountered by Mary Ward's English Institute; since the community evolved in an atmosphere which was favourable to Catholic initiatives, they, at least, did not have to contend with persecution from a Protestant government. However, like the English Ladies, they did find that at popular level and within the Catholic Church itself, their congregational form and the novelty of their unapproved structure constituted a considerable obstacle to their success with the city's Catholic elite whose support was so essential to the attainment of their goal.

Thus, these endeavours met with opposition, sometimes from the most unlikely quarters. Since these movements were entirely devoted to the Church, one would logically have expected whole-hearted support from Catholic clerics, counter-balanced by fierce opposition from Protestant opponents. However, when dealing with female initiatives (whether these were social, economic, political or religious), gender issues cannot be ignored. In a century of unprecedented religious changes, medieval gender definitions were strong enough to taint the Church's relations with some of its most zealous proselytizers, simply because they were women.

Beyond structural objections: gender as the essential limitation

Elizabeth Rapley has emphasized the importance of what she called 'a growing male-female dichotomy, an aggressive antifeminism, an irresistible trend towards patriarchy'.[45] Both Mary Ward's Institute and French Ursuline communities aroused opposition which was articulated on two overlapping levels, the one canonical and the other anthropological. Whilst the clergy opposed the women's innovations on institutional grounds, their arguments inexorably pointed to the same question: could women be the soldiers of God? Even in the objections they

---

[45] Elizabeth Rapley, *The Dévotes*, p. 3.

presented as entirely preoccupied with the uncanonical nature of these unorthodox missions, they repeatedly expressed the underlying misogyny which bolstered the double standards of the Counter-Reformation. The English Ladies and the French Ursulines were not only in breach of canon law, they were also women daring to adopt the roles and the structures devised for men.

The French Ursulines usually appear to have been aware of the fragility of their project; with some notable exceptions such as Antoinette Micolon (who, we will see, went so far as to preach publicly) the early *congrégées* usually pushed the boundaries of female acceptability with extreme care, ensuring that they did not overtly step out of the sphere which befitted women. Hence, they appear to have faced relatively few objections based *purely* on the grounds of gender and their archives yield fewer examples of the crudely-stated misogyny which punctuated the history of Mary Ward's Institute: opposition to the Ursulines' undertakings was more frequently articulated along the lines of social and religious acceptability and propriety. When they found themselves the object of mockery or diatribe, it was usually because they flaunted social protocol, by inciting the daughters of respectable families to lower themselves to teaching, for instance. They were also perceived to be damaging social networks: when marriageable daughters fled their engagements to enter Ursuline congregations, families bore the shame of their children's rebelliousness but also lost profitable alliances, both financially and socially. On examination of the documents, these seem to have been the concerns at the forefront of lay and indeed clerical disapproval whenever it was expressed.

Thus, for the Ursulines, gender in itself was rarely avowed as the principal reason for opposition: its omnipresence remained more subconscious, and somewhat more understated than in the proceedings against Mary Ward. Presumably, since the Ursulines did not propose to become the exact female counterparts to any male Order, nor openly to challenge the sphere of accepted feminine activity in seventeenth-century France, the animosity they generated was less intensely focused upon gender. Yet it would be naïve to infer that misogyny was not as pervading in France as it was in England at the time, and if the Ursulines were not exposed to the same concentration of gendered hatred generated against Mary Ward's Institute, their sex did indeed determine their fate, albeit in a more diffuse manner.

Even in the more favourable context of *dévot* France, the general acceptance of women undertaking religious work outside of enclosure was a lengthy process: it was only during Louis XIV's reign (1661-1715) that uncloistered female teaching institutes were allowed to flourish on French soil thanks to the charitable *filles séculières,* unmarried women who practised all the virtues of religion without however withdrawing from the world, taking any vows or submitting to any monastic rule.[46] The slow recognition of such groups was

---

[46] René Taveneaux, *Le Catholicisme dans la France classique*, vol. 2, pp. 401-409.

greatly aided by their adoption of a particular profile which suited contemporaneous conceptions of feminine virtue. Since the *filles séculières* mostly belonged to the lower classes and limited themselves to duties suited the image of womanly care, they were not considered as a threat by either the Church or the upper echelons of society. They merely helped the poor, cared for children and visited prisons and hospitals, thereby fulfilling a function which was consistent with the expected station of a pious woman, humble and circumscribed within gender-assigned limits. Female innovations were not to be allowed to threaten either the order of the Catholic Church or the traditional patterns of society. In many ways, the age-old tradition of subjection to masculine will was reinforced during the seventeenth century.

The case of Mary Ward's Institute provides a striking counterpoint to the Ursuline venture and uncovers the root of the early modern Catholic Church's difficulties in providing for the women in its midst in the same way as it did for men. Ward's determination to imitate the Society of Jesus 'both in matter and manner' constituted one of the main stumbling blocks on her way to recognition.[47] However, her adoption of the Jesuit structure and way of life constituted only one of the factors which brought about the suppression of the Institute in 1631. If the idea of a female Society of Jesus caused division amongst clerical ranks, there was one factor which united all of Ward's adversaries, secular and regular: the English Ladies were women who behaved in unwomanly ways.

Undoubtedly, one of the most acute aspects of the controversy about Mary Ward's project was centred on the relationship between religious life and gender and more precisely on gendered role-definitions within the Catholic Church. Clerical divisions were momentarily abandoned to champion the established order against innovations which religious men deemed essentially unsuitable for women. With hindsight, it is possible to untangle the elements of the controversy and uncover the clergy's main argument as twofold. On the one hand, the Institute's detractors dismissed it as insignificant and ridiculed what they saw as the feeble attempts of weak women. On the other hand, some of their objections were not so light-hearted. They denounced the Institute's vocation as unfeminine and condemned the lack of propriety of its members, who defied pre-defined female categories. The English Ladies, they claimed, were usurping roles which were rightfully male.

First, there were the contemptuous judgements which dismissed the Ladies' Institute as a laughable aberration. In their 1621 Memorial, the English secular clergy decried what they caricatured as nothing more than the 'senseless notions of a few insignificant women'. They predicted that the Englishwoman's project was inexorably doomed to ruin, since women's lesser capability could lead

---

[47]BCA, B5, letter 4 to Mgr Albergati, 1620.

them only to failure.[48] This frame of mind was also reflected in the very wording of the Memorial: the authors remarked that the Institute was 'incongruous' and 'ridiculous' and treated it with 'contempt' and 'mockery'.[49] According to them, most of the innovations suggested in the *Institutum*, such as the government of the whole congregation by a Mother Superior General, would necessarily occasion further ridicule: the secular clergy believed, quite simply, that a woman was not capable of governing in such posts.

In 1617, at a meeting in Rome, a Jesuit had expressed a point of view that was shared across the clerical board. He doubted the English Ladies' positive input in the Catholic mission, pithily declaring: '[the English Ladies'] fervour will decay, and when all is done, they are but women'.[50] Women, it was universally admitted, did have a place in the Church, but their communities should submit to male jurisdiction and focus upon activities within their limited scope. Their intellects, as well as their bodies, were deemed less fit than those of men trained for missionary or evangelizing purposes. Thus, many of the Institute's detractors, secular or regular, decried it as worthless and ludicrous because it was composed of women.

Nevertheless, it would be simplistic to dismiss the Institute merely as a laughing stock for the sport of clerics. Had that been the case, they would not have felt moved to press so hard for its suppression. There were deeper concerns about the Institute, and the clergy's scorn revealed their growing unease at the very nature of what Ward's Ladies were proposing to undertake. Far from being amused by the Englishwomen's endeavours, the secular clergy - and, arguably, some, at least, of the Jesuits themselves - were profoundly disturbed by the fact that they proposed a new form of female religious life which threatened male supremacy.

The unease of ecclesiastics is apparent in a series of documents written at the time of the controversy, when the Institute's fate was being decided in Rome. In 1630, the secretary of *Propaganda Fide*, Francesco Ingoli, was in charge of the investigation dealing with the accusations against Mary Ward. The interrogation of seven members of the Institute enabled him to compile the *Compendium of the Process made by the Nuncio of Cologne against the Jesuitesses*.[51] Significantly, Ingoli's conclusion highlighted his dismay at the foundress's transgressing of gender boundaries; to him, she was a woman who not only cast down all her feminine virtues but also usurped the essential traits of masculinity. She was, he wrote, 'a virgin of virile spirit'.[52] Similar language, referring to the foundress in

---

[48] *Ibid.*, f. 201, and in translation *Ibid.*, f. 1.

[49] *Ibid.* f. 202, and in translation *Ibid.*, f. 2.

[50] M.C.E. Chambers, *Life*, vol. 1, p. 408.

[51] BCA, C1, *Letters against the Jesuitesses*, ff. 309-312. The seven members who were questioned were Maria Clopey, Leizabeth Hall, Anna Morgan, Catherine Smith, Brigida Heyd, Winefrid Campion and Anna Micel.

[52] *Ibid.*, f. 312.

terms of manly qualities, can be found in a prior report against the Institute, which described her as 'a young woman with a masculine mind'.[53] Indeed, in the eyes of the clergy, Ward and her followers lacked proper feminine humility and reserve and showed no sense of their intrinsic limitations. Thus, both members of the secular clergy and of the regular Orders expressed their indignation that a woman would choose to behave in ways which were traditionally construed as virile.

The Institute's involvement with the English mission was one of its most controversial aspects and had aroused clerical concern as early as September 1612. A document, entitled *On certain English Virgins residing at St Omer*, explained that Mary Ward's followers enticed young English girls into their boarding schools on the Continent while, at the same time, some of the Ladies themselves were dispatched into England.[54] The author estimated that, at the time of writing, six of these female missionaries were working covertly in their native land. This, he explained, was doubly inappropriate: on the one hand, there was no need for a seminary for English girls, since recognized religious communities such as the convents of St Benedict in Brussels, St Augustine in Louvain or St Clare in Gravelines already welcomed them, and that within the safety and propriety of enclosure. On the other hand, the author complained that the Lady-missionary in England simply usurped male roles and connived to obtain control over respectable and influential recusant families. Once they gained the trust of a household, he explained, they would then divert its occupants from the ministry of the secular priests and direct them to the care of Jesuits.

In short, even as the clergy scorned the Ladies for their pre-supposed intrinsic female weaknesses, they felt undermined by their ambitious work. Their Memorial opened with a sentence reclaiming the male missionary prerogative: 'the Catholic faith has been hitherto propagated in the world only by apostolic men of approved virtue and constancy'.[55] The text reads like a list of grievances: the Ladies had undertaken their work without securing the approval of the Holy See, and they most inappropriately worked for the conversion of England, a mission which the religious men saw as a male preserve. The priests' indignation was mixed with deep concern regarding those 'women who [did] not fear to mix themselves up in the conversion of England, to approach and attempt that most difficult of all undertakings'.[56] This manner of life, it was concluded, was 'not only a scorn but a great scandal to many pious people' and 'unbecoming to their sex'.[57]

---

[53] BCA, C18, f. 101, Francesco Ingoli, 1627. See Jeanne Cover, *: Mary Ward's Spirituality and its Significance for Moral Theology* (Milwaukee, Wis., 1997), p. 17.

[54] BCA, C18, ff. 10-12; the author, a Jesuit, is not named. See also Henriette Peters, *Mary Ward*, pp. 164-66.

[55] WDA, vol. 16, f. 201, and in translation from the Latin in BCA, C1, J3, f. 1.

[56] WDA, vol. 16, f. 202, and in translation from the Latin in BCA, C1, J3, f. 2.

[57] WDA, vol. 16, f. 206, and in translation from the Latin in BCA, C1, J3, f. 4.

Thus, when the 1631 Bull *Pastoralis Romani Pontificis* called the women 'Jesuitesses' and described their Institute as a sect, it was clear that Urban VIII had endorsed all the arguments expounded by both secular and regular priests against Mary Ward's enterprise.[58] The women had transgressed the boundaries of gender-defined roles and the pontiff condemned what he termed their 'arrogant contumacy' and 'great temerity'. He also chastised the nature of their work, which, he complained, was 'by no means suiting the weakness of their sex, intellect, womanly modesty and above all virginal purity'. Therefore, he declared the Institute 'null, invalid and of no value or importance', likening its houses to 'dangerous branches', 'plants hurtful to the Church' and to be 'pulled up by the roots and extirpated'. He concluded: 'we entirely and utterly suppress and extinguish them and condemn them to perpetual abolition'.[59] The decree was pronounced as final and was, of course, disastrous for the English Ladies.

Pastoralis Romani Pontificis expressed the Church's perception of independent women's congregations with an active goal. These were indeed the improper institutions of troublesome women. In their time, the French Ursulines and the English Ladies were incongruous, pursuing goals and adopting means which moved away from centuries of tradition and undermined the very definition of female religious life; although they were valuable supporters to the effort of re-Catholicization, they were also a thorn in the side of the Church they sought to succour. Regardless of their institutional eccentricities, one simple fact remained: these women, whose innovations transcended the usual feminine contribution to the Church, acted very much like men. To a degree, they negated their intrinsic femininity in order to take on roles and attributes believed to be better suited to male clerics. It is not surprising, therefore, that the leaders of both movements should have been construed as troublesome women by their contemporaries.

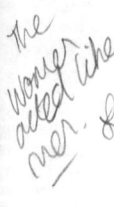

Although both communities defied the patterns of gender norms within the Catholic Church, it appears that Mary Ward's Institute was defined - and condemned - by its belonging to the 'weaker sex' much more than the Ursuline effort ever was. It seems likely that this crucial difference was the result of the profound disparity between the religious and political circumstances which affected the Catholic Church in England and in France. As a response to the acute jeopardy in which her recusant community found itself, Mary Ward distanced herself from the traditional paragon of female perfection to be found in meekness and subjection: her mission was decidedly militant, some would even say aggressive. Conversely, since France had emerged from the Wars of Religion still a Catholic kingdom, the Ursuline schools were perceived to be working within areas suited to female endeavours: their educational concern was unthreatening, partly because it did not offer the image of an explicitly missionary project.

---

[58] BCA, C1, Bull of Suppression of the Institute by Urban VIII, 1631.
[59] BCA, C1, Bull, ff. 1-4.

As they fitted more easily into the established patterns of female roles, the *congrégées* did not threaten male prerogatives in the same overt way as Ward's Institute and consequently did not become the object of the same brand of vitriolic criticism. In fact, the Toulousain Ursuline community soon became expertly adroit at manipulating gender stereotypes: with tact and diplomacy, Marguerite de Vigier and her followers deliberately endorsed many of the gender prejudices of the age in order to placate patriarchal Church authorities and avoid confrontation. Could the destinies of the English Institute and the French Ursulines have been shaped, not only by the national circumstances from which they emerged, but also by the dexterity of their main protagonists to speak the language of the Curia and to manoeuvre in the minefield of its gender politics?

Chapter 3

Religious Change and the Politics of Gender

The advent of the Protestant Reformation led ecclesiastical figures to rally to the defence of their institutions, deflected the attention of many members of religious orders from promoting the cult of the 'living saint' to the doctrinal controversy, and increased caution in preaching and in publicizing visions and spiritual doctrines that would soon come to seem suspect.[1]

Mary Ward is compelling to the modern mind because of her perceived resolve to break free from the prison of the cloister in order to work in the world, catechizing and converting populations alongside male missionaries.[2] Indeed, Retha Warnicke wrote that the Yorkshire woman was 'the first known English feminist' and her opinion seems shared by such renowned historians as Patrick Collinson, who wrote of Mary Ward as an 'unattached, roving, adventurous feminist'.[3] Yet, although apostolic women were often construed by their own contemporaries as dissenters fighting gender unfairness, this chapter will propose a deeper investigation of the rationale behind their female active vocations. It will argue that although the vocations of the English Ladies and of the French Ursulines are undoubtedly more akin to twenty-first-century understanding than those of their cloistered counterparts, their spirituality was too rich and multi-layered to be satisfactorily summarized in this way. In order better to fathom the extent of their gender awareness, it is necessary to re-assess their documents and clarify the ways in which they related with early modern anthropology.

---

[1] Gabiella Zarri, 'Living Saints: A Typology of Female Sanctity in the Early Sixteenth Century', in Daniel Bornstein and Roberto Rusconi (eds.), *Women and Religion in Medieval and Renaissance Italy* (Chicago and London, 1996), p. 248.

[2] Colleen Marie Seguin, ' "Addicted Unto Piety": Catholic Women in England, 1590-1690' (PhD dissertation, Duke University, 1997), pp. 290-91.

[3] Retha Warnicke, *Women of the English Renaissance and Reformation* (Westport, Conn., 1983), p. 179 and Patrick Collinson, ' "Not Sexual in the Ordinary Sense" ', *Elizabethan Essays* (London, 1994), p. 127.

French Ursulines and English Ladies shared the same essential defining feature: they were societies which proposed innovations in the traditional domain of female religious observance in times when femininity was synonymous with inferiority and women were commonly considered less worthy than men. In such a deeply patriarchal society, women did have their place in the life of the Catholic Church, but male hierarchy had the ultimate authority to define patterns of female religious acceptability, at the heart of which were found those most intrinsic of female virtues, humility and obedience. However, though these pre-determined standards of female behaviour were meant to maintain women in a subjugated position, they paradoxically made it possible for some remarkable individuals such as Teresa of Àvila to achieve their goals.[4] Were the English Ladies and the French Ursulines able to use their society's gender stereotypes in order to secure their aims, or were they entirely ignorant of the bargaining power offered by such 'pragmatic stylistics'?

Mary Ward's perceived vindictiveness: a proto-feminist?

As the 1631 Bull of suppression proved, the English Institute's adopted lifestyle (missionary, unenclosed and autonomous) was simply unacceptable to the Church of the seventeenth century. Mary Ward's unwillingness to compromise on the terms of her mission certainly exacerbated the problem facing her project. Her visions had called for a female counterpart to the Society of Jesus and she had no intention of departing from this in any way.[5] Perhaps a leader with more subtle negotiating skills would have managed, in time, to achieve this grand design; but the foundress could bear no delay, firmly believing she had been personally chosen by divine providence as the vehicle of God's will.[6]

As time passed, Ward became increasingly assertive: she moved away from the meekness and humility which her Jesuit director Roger Lee had imparted to the 1612 *Schola Beatae Mariae*. From 1616 onwards, her vindication of female worth and her claims for the Institute's autonomy not only came as blows to the Church hierarchy but began to present a challenge to the received traditional order. We have seen that, in 1617, a Jesuit priest had spoken slightingly of the English Ladies, doubting the constancy of the religious fervour of those he called 'but women'. Later that year, Mary Ward addressed her congregation of St Omer in a series of three speeches, in which she responded to those misogynistic taunts. These sound extraordinarily assertive even to the modern reader and it is easy to

---

[4] Alison Weber, *Teresa of Àvila and the Rhetoric of Femininity* (Princeton, NJ, 1990) and 'Little Women: Counter-Reformation Misogyny', in David Luebke (ed.), *The Counter-Reformation. The Essential Readings* (Oxford, 1999), pp. 143-62.

[5] BCA, B5, letter 4 to Mgr Albergati, 1620.

[6] Margaret Littlehales, *Mary Ward, Pilgrim and Mystic*, p. 108.

understand how ill they fitted within the gender-defined patterns of their society. The foundress wrote:

> There is no such difference between men and women, that women may not do great matters, as we have seen by the example of many Saints who have done great things, and I hope in God it will be seen that women in time to come will do much.[7]

Her defence of women as worthy beings thus showed that she did not share the patriarchal view generally endorsed by the early modern Church. The next passage demonstrates this even further:

> What think you of this word, 'but women'? If we were in all things inferior to some other creature, which I suppose to be men, which I care be bold to say is a lie then, with respect to the good Father, I may say: it is an error. [...] I would to God that all men would understand this verity: that women, if they will, may be perfect, and if they would not make us believe we can do nothing, and that we are but women, we might do great matters.[8]

These words speak for themselves: Ward did not share her contemporaries' conceptions of women. She believed that, when they were inspired by God and dedicated to him entirely, women were as capable and as worthy as men. All beings, regardless of gender, were equal before their creator.

This message sounded somewhat like an attack on men's long-held supremacy over women. This was, perhaps, the most insurmountable obstacle of all and it certainly played a crucial role in the suppression of 1631. Admittedly, these speeches were intended for Ward's fellow sisters only but, although there is no evidence that the Roman Curia ever heard or read them directly, there can be little doubt that, in their dealings with the foundress, they became familiar at least with their spirit. Her strength of conviction, combined with her shortcomings in the art of diplomacy, made it plain in her business with the authorities that she refused to comply with traditional female role-definitions.

In her responses to her antagonists, Mary Ward sometimes lacked tact, defending her vocation with a virulent assertiveness which, in turn, lent weight to clerical complaints about her failings in the timidity and the modesty befitting a religious woman. The 1621 *Institutum*, for instance, displayed none of the diffidence or reserve which was perceived as an essential virtue in early modern

---

[7] BCA, B17, f. 2, *Three speeches of our Reverend Mother Chief Superior made at St Omer having been long absent.*
[8] BCA, B17, f. 3.

women: the plan was clear and to the point, revealing its missionary ambitions and its pioneering organization as a generalate with unusual directness:

> The entire Society and the individual members who make their profession in it are battling for God under faithful obedience to His Holiness Pope Paul V and his successors in the Roman Pontificate. [...] For we are convinced that God speaks through His holy one, and that through the pope, He will guide the Institute for His greater honour and glory. This is what He has already been doing for many years, without the Institute being under the express jurisdiction or care of the Bishops.[9]

Either the foundress expected no difficulties in seeing the Institute being approved, or she was not prepared to compromise what she saw clearly as her divine mission.

It appears that Mary Ward did not clearly comprehend the nature of the opposition she was fighting: she did not recognize that a demonstration of her good faith and sincerity would not be enough to sway the ecclesiastical authorities as they decided her fate.[10] Her papers indicate that, unaware that her loyalty towards the Society could be, in itself, a damning characteristic, she believed the precedent embodied by her Ignatian model would make the approbation of her own Institute a simple matter of course. In the knowledge of the canonical prohibition against the founding of new religious Orders, she believed that her adaptation of the Jesuit rules and customs provided a rational element in support of her Institute. In her 1621 *Brevis Declaratio,* which she presented to the papal authorities to accompany the *Institutum*, she answered those who denounced her foundation as a canonical aberration:

> In custom, perhaps, this way of governing may seem new to some persons, but let those remember how many new things [were implemented] in the case of the one Society of Jesus [...]; all of which things however have been daily examined and approved by the Church. [...] The same rule, altogether the same form of regimen suits us also, since the same means should suit to the same end.[11]

With her unmistakable brand of logic, she assumed that what was recognized as useful and successful in one Society could not fail to be granted for another.

A few months later, in her 1622 Memorial to Gregory XV drawn up in order to clarify her position and to address some of the points raised by the 1621 Memorial of the English clergy, she reminded the pontiff of the non-innovative nature of her project, citing the Society of Jesus as the Institute's model. Because

---

[9] BCA, B18, *Institutum*, ff. 22-3.

[10] Jeanne Cover, *Love, the Driving Force*, pp. 14-15.

[11] BCA, B 18, *Brevis Declaratio.*

the Society of Jesus had created a favourable precedent following its recognition by Paul III in 1540, the foundress seemed to foresee little difficulty in securing approval for an Institute which presented such a similar profile.[12] Her confidence appeared in the 1622 Memorial to Gregory XV, in which she wrote:

> By divine appointment we are to take upon us the same holy Institute and order of life already approved by divers popes of happy memory [...] we humbly beseech that by the authority of the See Apostolic, the aforesaid Institute (holily observed by the said Fathers of the Society of Jesus, with so great fruit to the universal Church) together with their constitutions, manner of life, and approved practice (altogether independent, nevertheless, of the said Fathers) may likewise be approved and confirmed in [...] us.[13]

She saw no reason why her venture should be deemed presumptuous, when it merely followed rules which had been approved for the Jesuits. In another document, revealingly entitled *Reasons why we may not alter*, she gave a list of justifications for her Ignatian project. As naïvely as ever, she argued: 'First, because what we have chosen is already confirmed by the Church and commended in several Bulls and in the Council of Trent as a most fit Institute to help souls.'[14] As she focused on the benefits which her Institute could bring the Catholic Church, Ward failed to recognize that gender definitions in seventeenth-century Catholicism made a mission which was praiseworthy for men quite unacceptable for women - regardless of how beneficial it could be for the Church.

According to Cover, the difficulties Mary Ward experienced in the 1620s sprang from a degree of miscommunication with the Curia which might have been a result of her familiarity with devotional literature such as that of Teresa of Àvila, emphasizing the importance of obedience to divine commandments, whilst praising a lifestyle traced on the sufferings of Christ.[15] Be that as it may, this miscommunication between a woman from the militant recusancy of the English North and Roman Church authorities was one of the most impassable hurdles in the path of the Institute. As Jean Delumeau as noted, the ecumenical intentions of the Council of Trent did not translate into factual reality: the decrees represented mainly southern Europe and failed to recognize the essential difference between an overwhelmingly Catholic South and a Protestantized North.[16] Thus, in the seventeenth-century Church, female spiritual perfection was still held as synonymous with contemplation rather than action. A woman's holiness, it was

---

[12] Anthony Clarkes (ed.), *The Heart and Mind of Mary Ward* (Wheathampstead, 1985), p. 7.

[13] BCA, B18, *Memorial to Gregory XV* .

[14] BCA, B18, *Reasons why we may not alter*.

[15] Jeanne Cover, *Love, the Driving Force*, p. 55.

[16] Jean Delumeau, *Catholicism between Luther and Voltaire*, trans. by Jeremy Moiser (London, 1977), p.7.

tacitly understood, could be achieved only through the channel of monastic life, in complete mental detachment and physical separation from the world. This pervading and essentially medieval concept of perfection was reinforced by early modern anthropology and its rigid definition of woman's worth and capacity.[17]

The Church's androcentrism and misogyny could not envisage female spirituality outside the confines of conventual enclosure. This was to constitute the essential stumbling block for Ward's Institute and its apostolic vocation.[18] Indeed, Rome refused to jeopardize the established order (of which gender norms formed an essential component) by hurriedly approving solutions which, though they addressed the crisis of the English mission, would create precedents endangering the entire framework of the Catholic Church. When female leaders such as Mary Ward failed to think inside the feminine frame of mind shaped by the early modern Church, communication became impossible, as if both parties spoke different languages.

It is of course impossible to assess the degree of sincerity of Mary Ward's declarations; we shall never know whether she genuinely did not understand how her endeavours could be construed as presumptuous or whether she was aware of this dimension but chose to challenge the very idea of acceptable female ambitions in early-modern Europe. What is plain, however, is that she did not believe there was anything intrinsically wrong with what her Institute proposed. After John Bennet accused the English Ladies of pride and immodesty, declaring: 'they presume of their own power that it is omnipotent [and] flatter themselves',[19] Ward, in her 1622 Memorial to Gregory XV, denied that her endeavours were the result of what her adversaries had termed her 'vice of pride'[20] and argued that, on the contrary, they were ordered 'by divine appointment'.[21] This, implicitly, made her position non-negotiable since her vocation, as she understood it, lay in the hands of the Lord and she had no power of influence to change or modify it in any way. Just as she misdiagnosed the seriousness of clerical opposition against a new Institute which emulated of the Society of Jesus, Ward also misread the objections which were based on the gender-defined limitations of any female religious congregation. Indeed, the obdurate manner in which she defended her Institute seemed distinctly arrogant to those ecclesiastical authorities who, in Rome, were deliberating upon the fate of the Institute, and for whom woman's prime virtues were humility, meekness and obedience.

---

[17] Ian Maclean, *The Renaissance Notion of Woman* (Cambridge, 1980); Julia O'Faolain and Lauro Martines, *Not in God's Image* (London, 1979); Katharine Rogers, *The Troublesome Helpmate: A History of Misogyny in Literature* (London, 1966); and Linda Woodbridge, *Women and the English Renaissance: Literature and the Nature of Womankind, 1540-1620* (Urbana, Ill., 1984).

[18] Jeanne Cover, *Love, the Driving Force*, pp. 58-63.

[19] WDA, B 25, f. 56. John Bennet was the agent for the secular clergy in Rome.

[20] BCA, C18, f. 101, *Report on the Institute of the Jesuitesses*.

[21] BCA, B 18. *Memorial to Gregory XV*.

Thus, it is most revealing that, episodically, the members of the Institute were advised to consider embracing the Ursuline way of life.[22] In 1621, for instance, the prelate Juan Bautista Vivès, acting as ambassador for the Spanish Netherlands in Rome, recommended that the English Ladies should become Ursulines; since, by that date, the Ursulines had begun their process of conventualization, this step would resolve the Institute's problems. Moreover, Vivès argued, since the Ursuline vocation was akin to that of the English Ladies, their *modus vivendi* should be easily transferred to them.[23] He reiterated his advice in February 1622, highlighting the advantages the English Ladies would find if they chose to retire to a closed house under an approved rule and educate boarders according to Ursuline usage. However, Vivès's suggestion was dismissed out of hand by Ward's followers, who objected that their Ignatian calling and their undercover work in the English mission would not allow them to become enclosed. Thus, Mary Ward's refusal to accept any form of enclosure, even the *via media* adopted by the teaching nuns, undoubtedly constituted one of the factors which led to the 1631 suppression.

Vivès's was not an isolated argument: such suggestions, aiming to merge Mary Ward's project with that of Continental Ursulines, recurred until the Institute's suppression. Even after 1631, it was considered as a solution to the predicament of the disbanded members. When the English Ladies who worked in Austria were cast out of their establishments, they benefited from the kind hospitality of the neighbouring Ursulines of Hall, but eventually refused to be absorbed into that community. For Ward, and despite their dedication to the schooling of externs, the Ursulines' abandonment of their non-enclosure had corrupted their initial evangelical spirit. This was a risk she was not prepared to take, and she expressed both her determination to pursue her Ignatian vocation and her rejection of any compromise in no uncertain terms, writing: 'If God give health, we shall find another way to serve him than of becoming Ursulines.'[24]

These few words are all the more relevant in that they were written immediately after the Institute's dissolution, when the adoption of the Ursuline way of life was offered as a last resort to salvage some aspects of her work. Ward recognized the contribution which women could make towards the advancement of Catholicism, both in the English mission and on a world-wide level. To her, female engagement, performed in the world outside the limitations of the traditional convent, was not only complementary to the duties undertaken in enclosed religious houses, but was qualitatively as valuable in the eyes of God. She envisaged the mixed type of life, combining action and contemplation, as closer to that actually experienced by Christ himself, and consequently she esteemed it truer to the spirit of God.

---

[22] See M.C.E. Chambers, *Life,* vol. 1, p. 293 and Emmanuel Orchard, *Till God Will*, p. 108.

[23] Henriette Peters, *Mary Ward*, p. 320.

[24] BCA, B5, f. 90. *Letter to her congregation*, 17 February 1631, when in prison in Angers.

It seems highly likely that her understanding of female potency emerged, in the first instance, from her familiarity with English recusancy, in which women were so prominent in the daily running of the endangered Catholic faith.[25] Yet, the interaction between clerics and their female aides was not always a partnership made in heaven. Generally speaking, Catholic clergymen, whether they were secular or regular, struggled to resolve a lingering ambivalence in their attitude towards female helpers who, for centuries, had been pictured as less constant and intrinsically weaker than their male counterparts, a belief which was reinforced by the reforming Decrees of the Council of Trent. Moreover, many zealous recusants also felt it was not a woman's place to become involved in a religious mission. For instance, Lord William Vaux of Harrowden, in Northamptonshire, a staunch recusant himself, wrote to the notorious Lady Montague (1538-1608) in 1581, protesting she was too zealous in matters of religion and that her conduct was not fit for a gentlewoman. He complained:

> I think good to unfold to you some unkindness which I conceived of you at my last being in your company, which was your somewhat too zealous [...] urging me in matters tending to religion [...] since St Paul admonishes that women should learn in silence and in subjection [and] does not permit them to teach in their [husbands'] presence, but to be in silence. For silence extols womanly shamefastness and such comely shamefastness adorns their age.[26]

It is well known that the Vaux family was to produce some of the most remarkable female figures in the English mission and that two of its members, Margaret and Joyce, would later enter Mary Ward's Institute. Yet, although his two daughters and his daughter-in-law were to become pillars of the recusant network, Lord Vaux expounded the patriarchal view, ordering women to remain silent.

The example of the Vaux family demonstrates that traditional gender frontiers still applied even in the English mission, although the permanent danger in which recusant women evolved sometimes allowed them enough leeway to manipulate gender prejudices very shrewdly, transgressing their female roles whilst outwardly appearing to comply with them. The eldest daughter, Eleanor Vaux, used her house at Shoby in Leicestershire as the headquarters where the Jesuit Superior Henry Garnet (1555-1606) held yearly meetings with his missionaries. Since she and her younger sister Anne Vaux hosted these meetings, the future of the entire mission relied solely on the cool-headedness of the young women in the

---

[25] J.C.H Aveling, *Northern Catholics: the Catholic Recusants of the North Riding of Yorkshire, 1558-1790* (London, 1966); J. A. Hilton, *Catholic Lancashire, From Reformation to Renewal, 1559-1991* (Chichester, 1994) and J.S. Leatherbarrow, 'Lancashire Elizabethan Recusants', *Chetham Society* 110 (1947).

[26] Godfrey Anstruther, *Vaux*, p. 118.

face of peril.[27] This was put to the test several times and Henry Garnet recorded one incident when, in October 1591, government searchers raided the manor and jeopardized the secret meeting held there.

Eleanor, the mistress of the house, was timorous in her encounters with pursuivants; when recounting the event, Garnet construed her fear of danger as characteristic of a feminine composure, combining humility, shyness and a lack of bravery in the fragile frame of a weak-bodied woman.[28] He was surprised, however, when Anne boldly stepped in and faced the searchers with aplomb, assuming her older sister's identity. Edified, he reported how she calmly ordered the servants to play for time while all evidence of the Jesuit meeting was hidden away. She cunningly used to her advantage the standards of womanly modesty: since the searchers had arrived in the early hours of the morning, she pretended she had not yet risen and needed to make herself presentable before letting them in. This stratagem gained the household some considerable time to conceal both the priests and the tools of their trade. When she eventually allowed the search party in, she displayed respectful hospitality and offered the men breakfast as a ploy to give her servants an opportunity to go back to the rooms and secrete what was left in them. Thus, she used her role as hostess to throw the pursuivants off the scent: by offering food and drink, she appeared cordial and unthreatening, therefore showing she had nothing to hide.

However, although Anne Vaux's bravery and resourcefulness won Henry Garnet's admiration and respect, it was to be at the price of her femininity. To him, she had become an honorary man, a woman so far above her own kind that she lost the attributes of ordinary womanhood. He later commented:

> The virgin [Anne Vaux] always conducts these arguments
> with such skill and discretion that she certainly counteracts
> their persistence [...]. For though she has all a maiden's
> modesty and even shyness, yet in God's cause and in
> protection of His servants, virgo becomes virago.[29]

This example shows that patriarchal notions defining the nature of woman still pervaded the missionaries' appreciation of their female colleagues. The words used here - *virgo* and *virago* - indicated that Garnet granted his companion the qualities of extraordinary women. She combined manly courage and rationality with virginal purity; moreover, Anne Vaux was indeed a true virgin in the physical sense, which granted her a degree of purity unparalleled by other women, especially since she worked alongside two widows.

---

[27] *Ibid.*, pp. 186-91.
[28] *Ibid.*, p. 185.
[29] Garnet to Jesuit General Aquaviva, 1593, as translated in Godfrey Anstruther, *Vaux*, p. 189.

Such a lexicon (opposing *virgo* and *virago*) also reveals that gender definitions applied even at the core of a mission which allowed Catholic women a degree of involvement they rarely enjoyed elsewhere in Europe, perhaps with the exception of the Netherlands. Far from recognizing the virtues he praised in Anne Vaux as characteristic of an individual's dedication to a cause, Garnet represented them as the extraordinary traits of an incomparable heroine. Anne Vaux did not stand as a representative of womankind, but rather as an exemplary exception. She combined in her person the bodily weakness of the archetypal female, sublimated with the unfailing courage of a true soldier of God. Indeed, there is abundant evidence to show that, in the history of female recusancy, those who won distinction by their services to the Church were generally depicted as women of exceptional virtues; stripped of their supposed intrinsic feminine failings, they served to put ordinary females to shame.

Although not on equal footing with the priests, women such as the Vaux sisters were an integral part of the missionary fabric; they were animated by a strong missionary impulse and conceived their role, *qua* women, as essential to the success of the whole movement. As the aides of priests, they seemed aware that contemporaneous conceptions of women as frail, simple beings actually allowed them an advantageous degree of latitude and immunity. Thus, they knowingly and consciously used gender-definitions to their advantage in order to serve the English mission in ways that were inaccessible to men. Whereas established religious communities functioned in a neatly compartmentalized manner where each individual held a clearly-defined function, English recusants turned their hand to whatever circumstances dictated.

Such examples as those of Anne and Elizabeth Vaux show that early modern conceptions of gender-defined roles were not strictly applicable in the special conditions of the English mission. On Protestant soil and in the face of permanent peril, both male and female Catholics co-operated, contributing to the mission to the best of their abilities. Mutual assistance, resourcefulness, adaptability and delegation of some functions from priests to their female partners in religion, all meant that the English recusant community did not show the same compartmentalization as the more established body of the Catholic Church on the Continent. This was a community in constant movement, which would have only been impaired by the specialization of its members, who needed to be flexible and adaptable to survive.

As a Yorkshire recusant, therefore, Mary Ward may have been predisposed to assume that female religious initiative and leadership were part of the accepted order. Indeed, the urgency and permanent danger which suffused life for the English Catholic community meant that the barriers of traditionally defined behaviour did not apply so closely in recusant networks. From her own childhood experience, Ward knew that women were capable of acting as pillars in the missionary movement; thus, in her view of her Institute, she did not accept the patriarchal beliefs which marked them as unsuited to an active vocation in the mission. However, as the Vaux sisters demonstrated, playing prominent roles in the mission did not necessarily prevent women from keeping a finely tuned sense of their place in the male fabric of the Church and of society at large. Consequently, Mary Ward might have been expected to demonstrate a greater degree of subtlety in her handling of gender politics.

Although, with the passing of time, Ward's requests acquired an increasingly diligent tone, her dealings with Rome had first displayed all the humility and subjection believed to be essential to female virtue. For instance, the 1612 *Schola Beatae Mariae* stressed aspects in which its proposed School of the Blessed Virgin remained in conformity with approved convents, taking care to present its novel vocation in a humble form:

> We also feel that God (as we trust) is inspiring us with the pious desire that we also should embrace the religious life and yet that we should strive according to our littleness to render the neighbour the services of Christian charity which cannot be discharged in monastic life.[30]

In this passage, the emphasis lay strongly on the 'littleness' of the women, who begged to be allowed to 'render services' and insisted on their 'pious desire' and 'strife', in an almost apologetic fashion. Such deferential submissiveness was strewn throughout the entire request; its opening paragraph set the tone when it suggested, almost tentatively, that the English crisis called for a reassessment of female involvement in the meekest of terms, advancing that 'it seem[ed] right that, *according to their condition*, women also should and c[ould] provide something more than ordinary in the face of this common spiritual need'. In its description of the fundamental values expected from the members of the Institute, the Plan became a little more assertive, expecting its members to possess praiseworthy virtues such as a 'spirit of devotion' or 'zeal for perfection', coupled with others which were not specifically feminine, such as 'fortitude of soul' and even 'strength of soul'. However, such declarations were quickly toned-down again and the paragraph ended on a stereotypically gendered note, concluding: 'But let them specially strive to be outstanding in humility and meekness.'[31]

Indeed, the *Schola Beatae Mariae* is a masterpiece of placatory semiotics, displaying astute manipulation of the politics of gender, ensuring its positive reception by presenting even its most novel idea with the vocabulary of modesty and deference. Even the educational vocation at the core of its mission was deliberately described so as not to cause concern for male teaching congregations, since the Ladies aimed to operate only 'in accordance with the

---

[30] BCA, B18, *Schola Beatae Mariae*.
[31] *Ibid.*, item 46.

capacity of our own sex'.[32]   However, in the midst of these two entirely conventional declarations of female humility and subjection, the 1612 *Schola* also offered a glimpse of the innovative nature of Mary Ward's ambitions for female schooling.   Towards the end of the Plan, the foundress exposed her desire to work in conjunction with the Society of Jesus and follow a similar curriculum.   Hence, item 53 contained elements which were atypical in female religious teaching, since it planned to teach girls in such topics as the 'liberal arts, singing, playing musical instruments' and even 'playing the organ'.

However, such unusual subjects were immediately made to sound less threatening by the next paragraph which carefully concentrated on essential female learning; there, the pupils would be taught to 'conduct themselves peacefully in everything, curb passions, restrict inordinate desires, obey parents, turn away from the levity of girls, observe virginal maturity'.[33]   Considering that the *Schola Beatae Mariae* was the first plan the Institute ever submitted for approval in Rome, it is most unlikely that the wording of its requests was ever entrusted to chance.   On the contrary, every sentence was carefully written in order to obtain the desired effect. As the example of paragraph 53 illustrates, the more novel aspects of the education dispensed by the Institute were inserted between more traditional elements.   This was far from accidental: in fact, the author meant to encase the demands which were likely to upset the authorities between, as it were, brackets of conformable female behaviour, in the hope of rendering those radical aspects less obvious or offensive.

Thus far, the *Schola Beatae Mariae* has often been dismissed as unfaithful to Mary Ward's vocation, as a Plan which presented none of the spirit of the foundress.[34]   Yet, it deserves to be reviewed in a more positive light.   Ward's collaboration with her Jesuit director Roger Lee has generally been held responsible for the diluting, even the corrupting of the Englishwoman's ideal as expressed in the document.   Indeed, the *Schola* does not brazenly demand to 'take the same of the Society'; however, Roger Lee's influence may have helped the foundress to speak the language of Roman authorities.   Because of his active part in its drafting, the Plan was, in effect, more likely to have been accepted by the Curia than any of the subsequent Plans, since it acknowledged female humility, timidity and obedience in a manner which neither the 1616 *Ratio Instituti* or the 1621 *Institutum* would do.   Indeed, this alliance of subtlety and diplomacy was very much Roger Lee's contribution to the project and would be fairly absent from the further documents which Mary Ward wrote after his death.   She did not develop a skill for tactical rhetoric or strategies but preferred to speak her mind in a straightforward manner which many found blunt, and others deemed altogether alienating.

---

[32] *Ibid.*, item 5.
[33] *Ibid.*, item 54
[34] Henriette Peters, *Mary Ward*, pp. 129-31.

This close collaboration with a Jesuit who constantly reminded her of the gender-limitations she faced may have prompted Mary Ward to use what Alison Weber has termed 'pragmatic stylistics'.[35] For instance, in defence of her vocation and her Institute, she explained to Lee that women, though spiritually and intellectually weaker than men, were nevertheless capable of a fruitful relationship with the divine. To do this, she appropriated the gender prejudices which pervaded the Church and all but turned them upside down. She argued that women's frailty was in fact a blessing in their relationship with God, since, because of it, they needed His direct guidance more than religious men did. She wrote:

> The Fathers of the Society, being men, wise and learned, they might by their natural parts, perform the function of this Institute without so special occurrence of God's grace [...]. We, wanting that learning, judgement and other parts that men have, [...] should gain at God's hands true wisdom, and ability to perform all such other things as the perfection of this Institute exacts of us.[36]

Here, Mary Ward used female subordination to her advantage and turned women's perceived spiritual weakness into an asset which justified their need for the direct guidance of God. This was also, to an extent, a rationalization used to defend claims to direct divine revelation. Although it emphasized her personal fragility, her understanding of herself as an 'empty vessel' actually rendered her position much stronger. This corresponds closely to the 'pragmatic stylistics' which Alison Weber highlighted in Teresa of Àvila. There was a subtle inversion in which the weakness of the fair sex was transformed into a strength: it was precisely because a woman's judgement was feeble that she needed to let God guide her. Men were not wrong in mistrusting her personal decisions. Yet when she was obeying His commands, all opposition was bound to be futile or misdirected.

However, as opposition to her project became stronger and time brought no papal recognition to her Institute, Mary Ward became increasingly assertive. Her answer in the face of adversity was entirely in keeping with her character. For as long as she lived, and even after the suppression of her life's work, she continued to champion the Institute in the form which she had set out in the 1621 *Institutum* (and in subsequent documents addressed to the Holy See, such as the *Reasons why we may not alter* and the 1622 Memorial to Gregory XV). For her, there was no halfway house; her vision would come into being exactly as God meant it, or it would not be established at all. Thus, her Ignatian vocation did not allow her foundation to adopt the same lifestyle as the Ursulines, for this would entail restrictions which ran contrary to its Jesuit-like nature. Since work in the

---

[35] Alison Weber, *Teresa of Àvila and the Rhetoric of Femininity* and 'Little Women: Counter-Reformation Misogyny', in David Luebke (ed.), *The Counter-Reformation. The Essential Readings* (Oxford, 1999), pp. 143-62.

[36] BCA, B5, letter to Roger Lee, dated November 1615.

English mission was the *raison d'être* of her project, it could adopt the Ursuline compromise between cloister and apostolate only partially. Therefore, Ward had to move away from a traditionally-established conventual pattern in order to embrace the Jesuit model which suited her vocation more adequately: convinced that she was doing the will of God, she adopted a position which was as non-negotiable as it was earnest.

The Ursuline art of diplomacy

Conversely, it was the very diplomacy of its leaders which allowed the French Ursuline movement to gain such unprecedented success. When secular and religious pressures combined to push the small lay congregations towards their transformation into cloisters, most communities were prompt in joining the gradual process of conventualization. Toulouse, like the majority of French congregations, embraced enclosure willingly. Indeed, as early as 1607, their superior Marguerite de Vigier had of her own accord inaugurated a way of life in which her followers endeavoured not to leave their house on the Rue des Trois Rois Vieux; they welcomed boarders inside their buildings and opened some classrooms to day students, but relinquished all other aspects of their pastoral in the city, such as visiting prisoners or relieving the poor and the sick. This surprising step was taken for a variety of reasons, some of spiritual nature, as an homage to religious claustration, and others of a more pragmatic kind. Vigier's sensitivity to the gendered perceptions of her neighbours was one the main factors; in tune with the anthropology and the moral standards of her age, she knew that unmarried women living without a male *custos* could not fail but become the butt of public jokes and malevolent rumours, which would ultimately damage their reputations and leave them ostracized.

However, as their vocation gradually focused on education and their separation from the world became more complete, the *congrégées* did not abandon their apostolate altogether. While they chose to specialize as teachers within the walls of their house, they created the lay association of the *Dames de Sainte Ursule,* a sorority which was composed of married or widowed ladies who wished to be linked to the congregation without entering it formally. These women went through a two-month probation period before being fully received. They were headed by one of its own members, who was elected for a term of three years as superior; however, the ultimate authority belonged to one of the Ursulines, who was in charge of the lay company's overall supervision. [37]

Once a week, these emissaries of the world labouring in the city on behalf of the *congrégées* sought the spiritual counsel of their Ursuline sisters and kept

---

[37] ADHG, 221H-34, *Établissement de la congrégation et communauté de sainte Ursule, et règles d'icelle.*

them informed of their own actions. Assembled in the chapel every Thursday, they discussed religious themes and read devotional works together before practising acts of personal mortification and concentrating on mental exercises to advance their spiritual progress. The open confession of faults was an occasion for the penitent to receive public penance from her superior and humiliate herself publicly, in total accord with the traditional practices of conventual houses. In their daily routine, half an hour was to be reserved for mental prayers, and the *Dames* of the company were encouraged to make as much time as possible available for the reading of devotional works, upon which they should meditate. Those who could not do this were required to repeat the *Ave* and *Pater Noster* five times, in honour of the five wounds of Christ, reflecting upon His torments and the humiliations He had endured to save humankind. Such contemplation was an homage to an act of pure love and self-abnegation which represented the ultimate aspiration of the Ursulines.[38]

Thanks to this compromise, the Toulousain Ursulines limited their travels about the city streets and gained, through their voluntary semi-enclosure, some of the cachet of other respected religious institutions. By the year 1609, only five years after their settlement in the city, the house in the Rue des Trois Rois Vieux had attracted numerous boarders from wealthy families and even more day pupils from the ranks of the less socially-privileged local girls.[39] The community itself counted 27 *congrégées* and gave all the signs of a healthy religious congregation, the popularity of which increased steadily under the protection provided by Cardinal-Archbishop Joyeuse and *conseiller* Arnaud Bourret.[40] However, despite such seemingly favourable auspices, documents show that Marguerite de Vigier feared that the foundations of her work were not as stable as she wished. In that year, Antoine de Vigier (Marguerite's brother, of the Congregation of the Christian Doctrine) was sent as a representative to Rome; his brief was to present Paul V with the congregation's request to become an enclosed convent.[41] In other words, these independent lay *congrégées* wished voluntarily to relinquish their autonomy, submit to episcopal control, enter the state of religion and become cloistered nuns.

Why did the community want to become a convent when its initial form as a lay congregation allowed it a degree of independence and freedom of initiative which it would never have if it became a nunnery? Since the establishment's aim was to teach and evangelize all ranks of the female population, how could it propose to serve its educational and active vocation by becoming formally enclosed? Upon taking the habit, the Ursulines would become confined to their

---

[38] ADHG, 221H-37, *Mémoires*, f. 63.

[39] Unfortunately, numbers of boarders for that period are not available. The earliest register of boarders for the establishment on the Rue des Trois Rois Vieux is dated November 1771, ADHG, 221H-40.

[40] R. P. Parayre, *Chronique*, part 1, p. 128.

[41] ADHG, 221H-37, *Mémoires*.

convent and the house would be placed under male ecclesiastical control: therefore, claustration was bound to threaten their freedom of manoeuvre.

We will see that Marguerite de Vigier's plea for enclosure was the result of the interaction of many complex factors, not the least the prevalent reverence for the monastic ideal as the perfect path towards spiritual perfection and most complete union with God. Yet this was not the sole reason for requesting her community's elevation into religion, and this chapter will focus on another important factor: her sensitivity to the local circumstances of politics, culture and *mentalités*. To think that her appeal to enter religion contradicted her essential vocation would be to misunderstand or at least oversimplify the rich nature of the Ursuline brief; moreover, on a purely practical level, the acceptance of enclosure was in fact one of the most astute decisions Vigier was to take while she was at the head of the community. We have seen that, as simple *congrégées*, the Ursulines had been in sporadic conflict with the city's Catholic elite, whose support was so essential for their prosperity. Confrontations with influential local families may have dented her confidence, making her more acutely aware that her congregation was institutionally in breach of the Decrees of the Council of Trent. When girls such as Magdelaine Despanez and Françoise Rabonite joined the early settlement, they defied the received perception that young women should have either a husband or a cloister: by implication at least, they were questioning the early modern concept of womanhood in society. This new model of the unenclosed *religieuse* presented the city of Toulouse with an unresolved ambiguity with which even its most devout Catholic families felt ill at ease.

It is also possible that Vigier would have been aware of the difficulties facing the nearby community of Bordeaux. Founded in 1606 with the patronage of Cardinal Archbishop François de Sourdis (1575-1628), this congregation was severely threatened by local antipathy in 1609. Town officials and wealthy families were strongly opposed to this unrecognized institution which openly tried to recruit amongst their ranks. There were scenes of violence when parents hurled abuse at Ursulines and raided their house forcibly to remove their offspring from the buildings. When the people complained that the Ursulines were attempting to steal their daughters 'under some pretence of religion', Cardinal Sourdis had to intervene in order to restore decent neighbourly relations. Nevertheless, the people took their complaint to the local *Parlement*, where it found a sympathetic ear: officials ruled that the congregation was indeed a social threat.[42]

Toulouse's 1609 appeal for elevation into religion throws some light upon the seemingly paradoxical endeavours of the Ursuline congregation. The *Toulousaines* wrote their own account of the beginnings of their community in a manuscript book, covering the years 1604 up to 1621. For the year 1609 the chapter is eloquently entitled: 'How Mother de Vigier sent to Rome to ensure the

---

[42] MDPU, *Les Chroniques de l'ordre des Ursulines*, part 2, pp. 149-52.

future of the vocation by means of entering the religious state'. This title indicated that, on a practical level at least, the community envisaged Vigier's appeal to Rome as a means to save the foundation from potential danger. The manuscript explained:

> [she] feared that, one day, one of the devil's tricks might lead this company to be dissolved. Therefore, in order to ensure its future, she and the aforementioned young women resigned themselves to send a plea to Rome, asking for the Holy Father's intervention. They begged him to agree to the elevation of their house into a monastery of the Order of St Ursula.[43]

In this passage, the verb used in the French text is 'se résoudre de', which can be construed as meaning 'to resign oneself to doing something'; the term hinted that the foundress's decision was adopted partly as a means to safeguard the future of her house. It seems reasonable to infer that, had the congregation felt entirely safe and supported in its initial form, it might not have felt the need to apply for transformation into a cloister.

Finally, Parayre's explanation of this episode provides clear evidence that the chronicler himself understood the pragmatic aspect of the transition from lay gathering to convent; leaving aside for a moment the spiritual ideals which may also have entered into the equation, he acknowledged the change as a move in which Marguerite de Vigier responded to practicalities as well as to spiritual inspiration, ensuring the safety of her mission by seeking formal enclosure. He reported that Vigier had experienced a dream which filled her with an intense fear that her budding project, which she had nurtured for five years, should become the victim of potential opposition and be destroyed. Seized by the force of this sentiment, Vigier determined to transform her congregation into a convent, so as to secure its future. In the chronicler's words: '[she resolved] to elevate this congregation into religion, so as to secure it through this most effective of all means'.[44] Therefore, in the case of the Toulousain house, the purpose of conventualization was partly, and somewhat paradoxically, to serve its active educational vocation, since the *congrégées* aimed to safeguard their future by gaining papal approval.

---

[43] ADHG, 221H-37, *Mémoires*, 'Comme la mère de Vigier envoya à Rome pour assurer la vocation par la Religion': '[Elle] entra en appréhension que par quelque artifice du diable cette compagnie ne vint un jour à se dissiper; et désirant de l'assurer pour l'avenir, elle se résolut avec lesdites filles d'envoyer à Rome pour y faire intervenir l'autorité du Saint Père, lequel elles supplièrent de vouloir ériger leur maison en monastère de l'ordre de Sainte Ursule.'

[44] R. P. Parayre, *Chronique*, part 1, p. 129. In French: '[Vigier résolut] d'ériger cette congrégation en religion, pour l'assurer par ce moyen le plus efficace de tous.'

However, the papal understanding of a female religious house differed widely from that of the Toulousain petitioners. In 1609, the pope refused them the privilege of becoming a religious Order in their current form, since the Council of Trent, endorsing the decrees of Lateran IV, had prohibited the founding of new Orders.[45] Instead, the procedure was considerably delayed when Paul V asked the *congrégées* to submit to one of the pre-existing approved religious Rules. After deliberations, the women opted for the Rule of St Augustine, which prescribed a moderate type of asceticism which they deemed particularly suited to their active way of life. Subsequently, all French houses of Ursulines were to adopt this same Rule, which allowed them some discretion in the physical hardships of the monastic life.[46] In 1614, Antoine de Vigier was dispatched to Rome a second time and, finally, came back to Toulouse the bearer of a papal Bull elevating the Toulouse congregation to conventual status.[47] In this document, the pope recompensed the *congrégées'* 'humble begging': through its assurances of filial submission, undoubtedly aimed to placate the Holy Father, Ursuline rhetoric had struck the right chord. The pope granted the community's request 'out of a sense of benevolence', thereby demonstrating that the Ursulines' gentle and unassuming stance was more efficient at pleasing the Holy See than Mary Ward's open and straightforward approach.[48]

The literary style of Ursuline supplications appears, at times, positively cloying to the modern reader: the congregations stress their submission to male authorities as well as their own unworthiness, their insistence on their good intentions matched only by that put on their intrinsic female weakness. Judging by papal replies, which customarily used the vocabulary found in the pleas themselves, such a distinctive brand of feminine rhetoric ran through the Ursuline appeals to Rome, and Toulouse was no exception. The community was aware that, in order to obtain approval for their house, they would need to apply careful strategies to placate and win over the authorities on whom their future depended: it was therefore a tactical decision that led the *congrégées* to present Rome with a proposal which fitted the ecclesiastical opinion of women. In order to increase its chances of success, the appeal was phrased most carefully, time and again reiterating the requisite standard of female humility and begging for what it presented as an immense privilege, thereby demonstrating awareness of the women's 'littleness' and emphasizing their subjection to male authority.[49] In the case of the French Ursulines, the contrast was striking between the boldness of

---

[45] Norman Tanner (ed.), *Decrees of the Ecumenical Councils*, vol. 1, pp. 227-73.

[46] M. C. Gueudré, *Histoire de l'ordre des Ursulines*, vol. 1, p. 113.

[47] The Bull, dated 9 April 1614, was originally written in Latin, and the ADHG hold both the Latin version and its translation into French, see ADHG, 221H-25, item 20. For a transcript, see R. P. Parayre, *Chronique*, part 1, pp. 130-34.

[48] ADHG, 221H-25, item 20.

[49] ADHG, 221H-25, 20: '[Nous] avons été humblement suppliés de la part desdites filles d'ériger et instituer leur dite maison [en religion].'

these women's goals and the humility with which they endeavoured to suffuse the pleas they presented to Rome.

Yet as the ensuing sequence of events demonstrates, apparent meekness and subjection sometimes hide the firmest of resolutions. The Bull obtained in April 1614 was entitled *Bull of elevation of the congregated Ursulines into the religious Order of the Eremites of St Augustine*, and the very use of monastic vocabulary seemed to seal the alignment of these Ursulines to the norm of the enclosed life. The text specified:

> [The sisters shall] live under the yoke of religion, perpetual enclosure and regular observance, under the jurisdiction, visitation, and obedience of the local ordinary. [They shall] take the vows of poverty, chastity and obedience and, in addition, take care of [...] the instruction of girls, provided that the pupils live in the monastery, and keep the rules of enclosure.[50]

This passage is remarkably clear: Paul V changed the Toulousain Ursulines into nuns, thereby ordering them to keep their enclosure so closely as to teach boarders only, and this within the confines of the cloister. As a consequence, the foundation would retain none of its initial particularities. Its elevation into religion entailed its abandonment of all interaction with local girls: it seemed that the bid for papal approval had, unwittingly, brought about the suppression of the Ursulines' wide-ranging evangelizing mission.

Thus, although Marguerite de Vigier had succeeded in securing papal approbation, she had failed in obtaining the validation she had initially envisaged, as a participant in the Catholic mission of education in the Toulousain. The 1614 Bull indicated that the pope had not understood the congregation's wish to continue, albeit within the safety of the cloister, its teaching activities for day pupils. The Ursulines envisaged catechizing girls and living in religion in terms which were not mutually exclusive; on the contrary, these two ideals were to co-exist in their new way of life. Yet, the pope's protection came at the cost of the house's freedom to catechize all who cared to listen at their grill and to teach externs in their classrooms: it bore the unmistakable stamp of Tridentine tradition on female religious life. However, for the Toulouse *congrégées*, elevation into religion was by no means to be synonymous with the cessation of catechizing and teaching activities. Therefore, since the 1614 Bull was unacceptable to the

---

[50] *Ibid.*, f. 2, *Bulle d'érection des Ursulines congrégées en religion de l'ordre des ermites de saint Augustin*: 'sous le joug de la religion en perpétuelle clôture et observance régulière, sous la juridiction, visitation et correction et obéissance de l'ordinaire du lieu, et faire les vœux de pauvreté, chasteté et obéissance, et vaquer néanmoins à l'institution ou instruction des filles [...] (pourvu toutefois que ces filles observent les lois de la clôture durant qu'elles demeureront audit monastère)'.

congrégées, six out of the twenty-six sisters flatly refused to take the habit unless the Bull acknowledged their teaching duties towards day pupils.[51]

Indeed, most of the early members had felt drawn to the community because of its innovative profile which, unlike that of traditional convents, involved interaction with other women and the instruction of the local youth. For instance, Jaquete de Maynie (1588-1631), aptly named in religion *sœur* Saint Jean l'Évangéliste, had felt compelled to join the community in 1606, deeply convinced that its educational vocation was the community's main *raison d'être*.[52] Maynie was the leader of the six *congrégées* who, in 1614, saw the papal Bull of enclosure as incompatible with the Ursulines' original vocation. She refused to take the habit unless the Bull acknowledged the community's teaching duties toward the day students. In fact, the entire congregation delayed their entry into religion while Antoine de Vigier was again sent to plead with Pope Paul V. Before his return, one of the six protesters, whose name never appears in the record, had left the community, but the other five waited with their fellow sisters.[53]

At long last, a further Brief was issued which dissipated all doubt concerning the Toulousain Ursulines' right to teach day pupils. This *Papal Brief to add the institute of the Christian Doctrine to the monastic life*, dated 3 October 1616, bore a title which was as revealing as that of the preceding Bull. In it, Pope Paul V now agreed to the Ursulines' request to teach externs:

> [Let them teach] outside girls, even those who are married
> [...] but within the enclosure of the said monastery and in a
> place that is separate from the cells and living quarters of the
> said religious, where the aforementioned girls will be
> received freely.[54]

Thus, by 1616, the Toulousain Ursulines had obtained a supplementary papal Brief enabling them to teach not only their enclosed boarders but also local externs. These girls, often of lower social status, were officially allowed to enter and leave the convent to receive their lessons on a daily basis. Such an outcome was a tactical *tour de force*, through which the congregation formally accepted the patriarchal concept of religious women (enclosed and contemplative) and, in so doing, found themselves in a position to secure the safety of its active teaching initiative. As cloistered nuns approved by the pope, yet actually ordered by him to

---

[51] ADHG, 221H-37, *Mémoires*, ff. 44-7. The oldest of the initial 27 *congrégées* had died: Brigite Seysol, widow of nobleman Pierre Delpech, had joined Marguerite de Vigier in 1606, when she was already 80 years old. She died of old age in 1614.

[52] R. P. Parayre, *Chronique*, part 2, pp. 45-87.

[53] ADHG, 221H-37, *Mémoires*.

[54] ADHG, 221H-25, item 30, *Bref du pape pour joindre l'institut de la doctrine chrétienne à la vie monastique*: '[qu'elles enseignent] les jeunes filles du monde et même des mariées [...] néanmoins dans la clôture dudit monastère et un lieu séparé des cellules et habitations desdites religieuses, où lesdites filles seront librement reçues et admises'.

teach and catechize day students, the Toulousain Ursulines had thus become virtually invulnerable to opposition.

In this matter, although there is no doubt that the Ursulines of Toulouse were profoundly respectful of Catholic institutions and values, one could say the sisters had found a useful ally in stereotypical feminine subjection to patriarchal rules. They endorsed traditional female subjection to male authority in order to accomplish their self-appointed educational mission. In effect, they complied with the conservative decrees of Trent so as to be in a better position to transgress them from within. It was at this point only, seven years after their original appeal of 1609, that all the *congrégées* of Toulouse were prepared to become nuns. With the exception of the anonymous sister who left, they all entered the religious life and took novices' habits together in 1616; in the same year, seven further women joined the new religious community as lay sisters.

During the years it took Toulouse to complete the transition from a lay congregation to a religious establishment, the Parisian foundation in the Faubourg Saint-Jacques had petitioned for and speedily obtained papal approval in 1612, signalling the subsequent transformation of most Ursuline houses across France during the 1620s and 1630s and defining a working role for enclosed religious in the France of the Catholic Reformation.[55] Although the *congrégées* of Toulouse (and across France at large) had been obliged to abandon their unenclosed apostolate, they had nevertheless found a compromise which allowed them to remain an active female force within the Church.[56]

There is no doubt that the Ursulines' initial 1609 appeal for elevation into religion was the result of a correlation of factors, some of a spiritual nature, others of a more practical scope. To caricature this momentous decision simply as a tactical move designed to secure papal protection would be to strip the Ursuline philosophy of its rich complexity in which pragmatism and action were always interwoven with mystical pursuits and elevated piety. Yet, if the Toulousaines' desire to become nuns was as genuine as it was practical, it also presented them with an opportunity to plead with the Curia during the deliberations which followed the Bull and led to the 1616 Brief. Once granted papal recognition in 1614, the *congrégées* were astute enough not to accept its terms blindly but to negotiate a compromise which would allow them to be true to their catechizing vocation. In this way, they realized that their reception into the Church had granted them a degree of power which they could use to inaugurate a new form of female religious life, one which allowed daily interaction with the world in the form of its day students. Although they were cautious never to expose themselves to either clerical or secular criticism, they had learned the art of subtly using the humility and submission expected of women in order to serve their original educational purpose. By 1616, the community of Toulouse had concluded their

---

[55] Marie Andrée Jégou, *Les Ursulines du faubourg saint-Jacques à Paris*.
[56] Linda Lierheimer, 'Female Eloquence and Maternal Ministry', p. 17.

dealings with Rome and found an institutional voice for the dual essence of their vocation. In the process, the congregation had undergone major structural changes, but it had successfully negotiated its place within the Counter-Reformation movement. In contrast with the Institute of the English Ladies, the Ursulines provided the Curia with a compliant, obedient attitude. In the first instance, they requested papal approbation through the intermediary of male representatives. They then adopted a humble approach, accepting monastic enclosure to fulfil all the Tridentine requirements on women religious; the congregation had ensured that its plea would not be contentious, thereby guaranteeing its success.

By the 1620s, the French Ursulines and the English Institute, which had initially assumed comparable forms and pursued similar goals, had nevertheless achieved vastly different results. As they first busied themselves in the evangelization of local women and girls, the Ursulines had shown no signs of preoccupation about their designation. Their establishments corresponded to no recognizable category: they were neither convents nor traditional sororities. To them, these technicalities remained secondary to the practical pursuit of the congregations' catechizing vocation; however, they were soon forced to address the issue, as it became apparent that their enterprises risked being jeopardized by their discrepancies with the traditional, recognized form of conventual life for women.

Thus, after careful negotiations with Rome and their local ecclesiastical authorities, the Ursulines agreed to become enclosed, on condition that they were allowed to continue teaching externs; their formula, combining the spirit of Mary with the duties of Martha, corresponded to a particular brand of spirituality which was increasingly attractive to young women in seventeenth-century *dévot* France and, just as importantly, one which appeared quite safe in the eyes of both secular and ecclesiastical authorities. Although the gradual process of enclosure did not always go smoothly, most congregations embraced their entrance into religion peacefully, if not enthusiastically. As a result of this acceptance of enclosure, the Order grew to become one of the most successful in France by the end of the century and became the most reputable teaching religious institution in the country.

Mary Ward, on the contrary, repeatedly refused the confines of the cloister and chose to embrace, as fully as it was possible, the controversial model of the male Society of Jesus. Predictably, her project came to an abrupt end in 1631, when Pope Urban VIII issued the Bull *Pastoralis Romani Pontificis* suppressing the Institute, ordering the English Ladies to disperse and condemning the foundress as a heretic. However, despite the Bull of suppression, Mary Ward believed that, if she persevered with her schools (albeit in a lower key), their success would eventually bring the papacy to revise its judgement about the Institute as a religious institution, a female Society of Jesus. Thus, although most of her houses on the Continent were closed as a result of the papal decree, the

Redefining Female Religious Life

foundress, together with a small core of followers, chose to resume their activities in England, where they retired in 1639.

To all intents and purposes, she and her followers were continuing the work of the Institute, but they were not, strictly speaking, disobeying the Holy See; the Ladies, after the dissolution of their Order, were no longer perceived as a threat to the ordered structure of the Church. They functioned as laywomen, on a private basis, and did not represent a new form of female religious life, imitating the model of the Society of Jesus. Thus, in some ways, the act of suppression actually brought the English Ladies a new kind of freedom. After 1631, the development of small covert centres in England did not arouse the same degree of universal opposition as the Institute had done previously. Therefore, although they were forced to function on a more modest scale, the work of the English Ladies, in that sense, benefited from Urban VIII's Bull of Suppression. So long as they remained limited to areas deemed fitting for women's works, the Ladies (as individual proselytizers) did not meet with much opposition from within the ranks of the clergy.

It is clear that the English Ladies and the French Ursulines had different views upon the negotiability of their proposed vocations. If, in their responses to adversity, both Orders demonstrated some degree of gender awareness, they did not have the same conception of gender politics. By rhetorically emphasizing their submission, humility and obedience, the Ursulines had sought to deflect the boldness of their ambitions while stressing their feminine weakness, thereby proving that the sisters understood the frame within which they were required to work and adapted their requests for their audience. The Ursulines, like so many women across France resorted to the 'pragmatic stylistics' which we have seen Mary Ward abandon after the 1612 *Schola Beatae Mariae*. Mary Ward's endorsement of the patriarchal theory of the 'empty vessel' showed that she was not contesting the established conceptions of female frailty; yet, in an unexpected transvaluation of this misogynistic idea, she gained her very strength from this assumed weakness. Since Ward and her followers, as women, were fallible creatures, they trusted God rather than their own judgement, they were moved by Him, and therefore could not be wrong. Hence, Ward's apparent acknowledgement of her weakness rendered her position all the more inflexible.

On the other hand, the Ursulines used gender stylistics in an entirely different manner, giving in to ecclesiastical pressure when in danger and using a meek, placatory approach in order to endure the success of their negotiations. In accepting claustration, they lost much of the freedom they had enjoyed as *congrégées*, but gained stability and prestige. From that secure position, they were ideally placed to request the necessary adjustments to monastic rules in order to teach the youth. Thus, although they appeared much more docile than the English Ladies, the French Ursulines nevertheless managed to achieve their initial goal: to open free schools for girls and take part in the on-going movement of Catholic revival in France.

Chapter 4

Serving the Church in the Classroom

> Men must be occupied both at home and abroad, both in
> their own matters and the common weal. [...] As for a
> woman, she has no charge to see to, but her honesty and
> chastity. Wherefore when she is informed of that, she is
> sufficiently appointed.[1]

The general view according to which women needed no further knowledge than that required to be obedient daughters, virtuous wives and industrious housekeepers was one of the most essential pillars of patriarchy. Even those scholars who encouraged some degree of female schooling often expressed their own deep-seated misogyny in their works; their conceptions of women as intellectually and morally inferior reminds the modern reader that even authoritative figures such as the renowned Spanish pedagogue Juan Luis Vivès (1492-1540) - who, in 1523, had published his treatise on women's education, the *Institutione Christinae Feminae*, for the edification of Henry VIII's and Catherine of Aragon's daughter Mary - endorsed the typical androcentrism of their contemporaries. Educational differences between boys and girls were one of the expressions of a society in which female scholarly achievement and erudition seemed incongruous, since women's perceived lesser abilities naturally confined them to ancillary positions.[2]

Hence, no endeavour in Europe had, thus far, attempted to give the teaching of girls a real institutional expression. Both the French Ursulines and the English Ladies were to be amongst the pioneers of a formally organized movement in a seventeenth century which witnessed a subtle shift in attitudes towards female learning. By the time male pedagogues turned their attention to the gendered inequality of educational provisions and criticized the widespread failure to give girls parity of treatment with boys, these two Orders had been changing perceptions on the subject for around eighty years. Thus, when François Salignac de la Mothe Fénelon (1651-1715) famously lamented that 'nothing is more

---

[1] Juan Luis Vivès, *The Instruction of a Christian Woman*, in Foster Watson (ed.), *Vivès and the Renascence Education of Women* (London, 1912), p. 34.

[2] Suzanne Hull, *Chaste, Silent and Obedient: English Books for Women, 1475-1640* (San Marino, Cal., 1982); Pollock Linda, ' "Teach her to live under obedience": the Making of Women in the Upper Ranks of Early Modern England, *Continuity and Change* 4.2 (1989) 231-58.

neglected than the education of girls', he was voicing a concern which had already been identified and addressed by the apostolic women for quite some time.[3] Their schools had emerged as a response to a deep-seated need for female initiatives and were in demand on two fronts: on the one hand, their catechizing was essential to the success of the Counter-Reformation offensive while, on the other hand, their secular curriculum anticipated their society's reassessment of its views on female education.[4]

The English Ladies and the French Ursulines conceived schooling as their offering to the Church: it was, in their eyes, the most valuable contribution they could make to the on-going mission of Catholic recovery. In their effort to reach out to the female half of the population and strengthen the links of the Catholic Church with women of all backgrounds, they would have to a adopt versatile and comprehensive outlook not only on whom they resolved to teach, but also on their curriculum and on the methods they would adopt to be pedagogically effective. How did the first teaching nuns propose to serve the Church in the arena of the classroom?

Female education without social boundaries

Both congregations proposed a *modus operandi* which incorporated some new elements to an otherwise quite classic formula. The most traditional component in their schools consisted of the boarders - usually the daughters of the gentry or the nobility - who entered the boarding schools at a young age and received their education free of charge, although their parents were asked to pay for their pension. Of course, religious institutions had, in the past, been providing young women with some degree of education and for centuries well-to-do families had placed their daughters in the boarding schools of enclosed convents, there to be educated and prepared to re-enter elite society when they came of age. This, therefore, presented little novelty. However, the Ursulines and the Ladies offered a different approach: as part of the contemporaneous effort to re-Catholicize the masses, they aimed to teach not only wealthy boarders but also day pupils from humbler social backgrounds. In poorer strata of society, girls could neither afford to pay for lessons nor be spared all of their daily work, on which their families depended for their sustenance. It made sense, therefore, to open classrooms which would enable these young souls to benefit from some basic instruction at no cost to

---

[3] François Salignac de la Mothe Fénelon, *De l'éducation des filles* (1687), in *Oeuvres* (Paris, 1854) t. 4, p. 240. Fénelon wrote: 'Rien n'est plus négligé que l'éducation des filles.'

[4] See Kenneth Charlton, *Women, Religion and Education in Early Modern England* (London, 1999); Roger Chartier, Marie-Madelaine Compère and Dominique Julia, *L'Éducation en France du XVI° au XVIII° siècle* (Paris, 1976); Helen Jewell, *Education in Early Modern England* (London, 1998) and Georges Snyders, *La Pédagogie en France aux XVII° et XVIII° siècles* (Paris, 1965).

themselves or their families, while still allowing them to go about their lives in the world. It was important to reach beyond the boundaries of class and to address the much-bemoaned crudeness of the poor; therefore, families who could spare no money for a pension, parents who could not dispense with their daughters' labour were not condemned to be left out of this new educational programme but on the contrary represented the primary target of the teaching nuns' efforts.

The teachers' essential goal was not to train future novices in religion but rather to secure and strengthen the faith in girls who, in time, would be expected to marry and have families of their own. These were the most ignorant segments of society, where entire neighbourhoods had defected the Church and barely knew the foundations of Catholic doctrine. The raw and unsophisticated minds of the deprived youth were perceived as so many abandoned gardens which, with adequate fertilizing, nurturing and care, could provide rich soil and a plentiful harvest. Thus, disadvantaged girls would be offered a solid Catholic education free of charge, they would be 'externs': welcomed in the classrooms every morning in order to receive their lessons, they would be allowed to go home at mid-day before re-entering the classrooms for the afternoon sessions and returning to their families at night. These externs therefore continued to live with their parents and their attendance at school was designed to allow them to fulfil their roles in their family circle and to cause as little interference as possible.

In this respect, the constitutions of Toulouse are entirely representative of the national Ursuline spirit.[5] After stating that 'the principal aim of this institute is to instruct girls in Christian doctrine',[6] they solemnly prescribed: 'Since the primary aim of the sisters in this monastery is to instruct youth, [they] will keep open classes in order to teach girls for the love of God, without asking any payment either for their entrance or for their instruction'.[7] It was the teaching of local day pupils which differentiated the Ursulines from other religious schools of the period; through these, it was hoped, catechists would make contact with families of all walks of life, touching entire households every day. This flexible formula, allying boarding school with day classes, allowed them to reach a wide cross-section of female youth, instructing pupils from both well-to-do and humble social backgrounds.

But the effort was to go further than simply giving the people a wider scope of possibilities. These zealous pedagogues did not wait passively for interest to take hold: for so long as they were free to enjoy commerce with the world, the

---

[5] There are several copies of the Toulouse constitutions; I have used the manuscript in ADHG, 221H-28 bis, 5. When the text was damaged, I used the other manuscript in 221H-41

[6] ADHG, 221H-28 bis, 5, f. 3. The French text runs thus: 'Le principal but de cet institut est d'instruire les filles en la doctrine chrétienne'.

[7] *Ibid.*, f. 14: 'D'autant que la principale fin des sœurs de ce monastère est d'instruire la jeunesse, elles tiendront classes ouvertes pour instruire les filles pour l'amour de Dieu, sans leur faire rien payer pour l'entrée ni pour leur instruction.'

French Ursulines strove to address the entirety of the female population. Not content with simply receiving those who came forward and enrolled as their pupils, they walked through cities and towns trying to convince the undecided and reconcile the hostile. Then, even when they became religious and lost the mobility they had enjoyed as *congrégées*, they proved keen not to sever their links with those who were willing to hear their teaching. Since *internats* and *externats* were opened to young girls only, the nuns could no longer, in theory, educate adults. However, Parayre commented that members of the Order all across France continued to reach out to the world by standing at their grill every Sunday and feast day, to teach the women who had gathered there regardless of age or class. He explained that every Ursuline establishment in the country kept open classes for externs of every condition and quality but also evangelized women at the convent's grill which, he remarked, was patent proof of their zeal to teach.[8] His work dwelt upon the disparity of social condition amongst the catechists' audience, which ranged from 'girls of most delicate constitution [...] and of most considerable origin' to 'girls from all sorts of conditions' and 'servants and other working people'. Through the three outlets of the boarding school, the day classes and the admonitions they gave at their gates, the Ursulines touched a broad sample of society even as an enclosed Order.[9]

In essence, the Institute's design was remarkably similar to that of the French Ursulines. It sought to form versatile women whose religious education would be as sound as their secular knowledge, in order to equip them with the tools necessary to become strong upholders of the faith. Mary Ward thought of her schools as a sort of teacher-training ground, preparing girls for their prospective roles as Catholic mothers in charge of the education of the next generations of recusants in England. Her scheme was, in this way, a perfect educational expression of the centrality of the female-controlled household in English recusant Catholicism, above all in her own gentry class. Since Mary Ward's followers, like the Ursulines, opened public lessons to externs, their establishments in continental Europe were rather similar to those ran by the Frenchwomen and obeyed the same rationale. The foundress expressed her all-embracing vision in the 1616 *Ratio Instituti*, in which she exhorted her followers to 'be ready to teach and instruct any persons of their own sex, ever regarding in their pupils the value of their immortal soul, although these pupils should be of lower or humble birth'.[10] The 1621 *Brevis Declaratio* further developed this principle and explained that her followers did not target privileged portions of society only, but '[bestowed] themselves entirely for the salvation of all, be it of those who sojourn in cities and populous towns, be it of

---

[8] R. P. Parayre, *Chronique*, part 1, p. 24.

[9] *Ibid.*, p. 142: 'Elles s'occupent des filles de très délicate complexion [...] et de naissance très considérable [...] et après que pendant la semaine elles ont instruit dans les classes les filles de toute sorte de condition; elles s'occupent les fêtes et dimanches à instruire les servantes et autres gens de métier, qui ne peuvent pas y aller les autres jours.'

[10] BCA, B18, *Ratio Instituti*.

those who labour in country house and castles in the extreme forgetfulness of salvation'.[11]

Just in the same way as the Ursulines provided a pragmatic solution to the female education crisis in Catholic France, the English Institute offered much needed alternatives for recusant families of all social backgrounds. Conditions in early modern England made 'popish' schooling highly hazardous both for tutors and tutees.[12] On the one hand, the Established Church required teachers to swear an Oath of Allegiance to the crown, the persistent refusal of which was punishable by life-long imprisonment or even death: by the time the English Ladies began their work, 23 Catholic schoolmasters had already been executed between 1570 and 1610.[13] On the other hand, the expense of traditional methods of education, ranging from £11 to £20 per year, weighed heavy on families already burdened with penal fines. In such a bleak context, the Institute's policy to teach everyone free of charge provided parents with welcome financial relief and offered unrivalled opportunities for those who were eager to educate their daughters in the Catholic faith. Mary Ward's enterprise, therefore, was doubly valuable, since it proposed to run boarding schools on the Continent in parallel with some smaller, clandestine day schools in England, for those who preferred or had no other option but to stay in their home country.

The English boarders who entered Continental schools were, for the most part, expected to return to their homeland in order to marry and manage their own households. The Catholic education provided by the Institute aimed to train these young women to become pillars of the clandestine community, the female heads of recusant families, armed with the profound knowledge of Catholic doctrine which alone could enable them to remain steadfast in their faith. Catechesis was all the more essential since the English Ladies, like the Ursulines, considered their pupils as the Catholic teachers of the future. Moreover, it was not uncommon for teachers to go to great lengths in order to ensure the broadest possible scope for their religious instruction. The English Ladies, whose freedom of movement was never constricted by enclosure, did not limit themselves to educating the pupils who came to them either as boarders or as day students. Travelling between towns and villages, visiting prisoners, relieving the poor, helping the sick, assisting the bereaved, they reached out even to those who did not present themselves at their schools.

---

[11] BCA, B18, *Brevis Declaratio*.

[12] A.C.F. Beales, *Education under Penalty: English Catholic Education from the Reformation to the fall of James II, 1547-1689* (London, 1963) and David Cressy, *Literacy and the Social Order: Reading and Writing in Tudor and Stuart England* (Cambridge, 1980).

[13] 'An Act for the better Discovering and Repressing of Popish Recusants' (3 & 4 Jac. I. c. 4) and 'An Act to Prevent and Avoid Dangers which may Grow by Popish Recusants' (3 & 4 Jac. I. c. 5), in J. R. Tanner, *Constitutional Documents of the Reign of James I* (Cambridge, 1930), pp. 86-104.

This novel, far-reaching approach to female education appears to have captured the spirit of the age and responded to a pressing need both on the Continent and in England. Many documents from these two pioneering congregations show that French Ursulines and English Ladies enjoyed a great accomplishment thanks to the adaptable profile of their schools. Everywhere, the boarding establishments filled up with the daughters of reputable and influential families whilst the day schools attracted scores of underprivileged pupils who, for the first time, were offered access to some degree of learning. The Ursuline chronicles compiled by Mère de Pommereu testified that, in many cases, the schools' success was extremely rapid. Thus, in Dijon, in 1607, the Bishop of Langres had granted Françoise de Xainctonge a licence for her small corps of *congrégées* to teach local girls; this was ratified by the municipal authorities in 1608 and, as soon as the classrooms opened, they were full to capacity. The burgeoning congregation, which counted only five teachers, estimated the increase of pupils would legitimate employing around 20 of them. Soon, their premises could no longer accommodate the day and boarding schools and they were forced to sell their buildings in order to relocate to a much larger venue.[14]

Similar success stories abound, not only for Ursuline schools but also for those opened by the Institute, both in England and on the Continent. In a letter addressed to Urban VIII, Mary Ward mentioned the school she had founded only two years earlier in Vienna; in that city of contested religious allegiance, the foundress was proud to report that her day classes received up to 450 students of varied social make-ups, to whom were added large numbers of boarders from wealthy and influential families. Such credentials in a city which, she reminded the pontiff, 'contained many heretics and persons addicted to such vices as always go with consciences in which there is little fear of God', could not fail to testify not only to the great need for such female initiatives but also to the excellence of the Ladies' educational endeavours.[15]

Throughout her life, Mary Ward remained dynamic in her desire to touch others. When she returned to England in 1639, eight years after the suppression of her Institute, the Institute's London house was used as a Catholic centre for the sacramental and devotional relief of local recusants but did not as yet function as an educational centre. She immediately turned her attention to developing the establishment by founding an elementary school for Catholic girls, a project which faced many difficulties since, as she phrased it in a letter to her *consœurs* in Rome, the running of day classes in the capital seemed impossible 'without a miracle'. Yet, she believed that, if it could not teach, her Institute would have failed to fulfil its essential goal; in her own words, 'all else [would] be to little purpose'.[16] Fortunately for her, the Ladies' vocation answered a profound need in the recusant

---

[14] MDPU, *Les Chroniques de l'ordre des Ursulines*, part 2, pp. 160-2.
[15] BCA, B18, *Petition to Urban VIII*, March 1629, f. 4.
[16] BCA, B5, f. 132.

population of London and appeared to command respect in Catholic circles; thus, the much-desired school was soon in a position to open. Ward and her companions settled in their residence and were in high demand from friends and acquaintances to receive their daughters.[17] Recounting this episode, the *English Life* emphasized how Ward was successful in putting together a close-knit network of Catholic education and instruction which catered not only for the gentry but also for the humbler classes:

> Diverse [wealthy families] importuned her to make some young gentlewomen happy by partaking of her excellent education. Others her own charity moved her to take, because not only needy of that happiness, but incapable to have, but where there was like charity. So as notwithstanding the great danger of those times, she kept a great family. [18]

The London school became well established and benefited from a growing reputation in the domain of Catholic education for girls; as this passage testifies, the Institute never excluded the humbler sort from its apostolate but accepted that poor pupils were crucial elements in its scheme for re-Catholicization of England and represented the ultimate target of its Jesuit-inspired vocation.

Documents both from the English Ladies and the French Ursulines highlighted not only the novelty but the inherent value of teaching students from all walks of life; it was the first time female institutions were attempting to give girls an education which would strive to match that given to boys by male organizations such as the Society of Jesus. Before the first decade of the seventeenth century, the daughters of the underprivileged had never been considered worthy of the Church's efforts of evangelization and schooling on such a scale as that proposed by the new teaching congregations. In their rules and constitutions, the establishments of both denominations were constantly reminded that their vocations called them to integrate day pupils and boarders as equally worthy parts of their educational system. Their Rules specified that they should treat the poorer girls with as much respect and kindness as they did their wealthier counterparts. Episcopal archives in Augsburg show that the teachers were clearly required not to treat aristocratic children differently from those of more modest families. The schools of the Institute always claimed to uphold a regime in which children of all backgrounds would benefit from the same respect and the same education, and the teachers' rules exhorted them in those terms:

---

[17] M.C.E. Chambers, *Life*, vol. 2, p. 462.

[18] The biography known as the *English Life* was originally entitled *A Briefe Relation of the Holy Life and Happy Death of our Dearest Mother*; it is a posthumous work, written jointly by Mary Poyntz and Winifred Wigmore, Mary Ward's two closest followers, c. 1650. BCA, B12.

> They must strive diligently to maintain peace and unity as
> the greatest joy and blessing of the house; they are to treat all
> in the same manner, and with the same love and care, thus
> avoiding with all their might, hatred, quarrelling and
> dispute.[19]

The Ladies therefore promoted a sense of fairness and encouraged tutors to deal
with all pupils equally, since the souls of all these children were of identical value
in the eyes of the Lord.

Therefore, teachers tried to ensure order and harmony and to instil in their
students a deep respect for authority. Inspired in part by the Jesuit *Ratio
Studiorum*, they emphasized that girls should not be guided by fear of chastisement
but by a love of decency and a deep sense of propriety. Thus, the general
atmosphere in the classrooms should be one of trust and diligent obedience.
French Ursulines and the English Ladies saw their works with the day girls as their
own efforts to imitate Christ himself. The rules of the Ursuline congregation of
Paris specified:

> The sisters who are destined to the instruction of extern
> pupils must apply themselves to this task with redoubled
> affection since, in this occupation, their lives imitate even
> more closely that of the Son of God who, during his own life
> time, principally sought to instruct the poor and the
> ignorant.[20]

In the Ursuline convent of Bordeaux, Françoise de la Croix was delighted to see
that pupils came from far and wide to her school. Soon, her day classes became so
popular that she and her *consœurs* were quite overworked, but de la Croix rejoiced.
Catechizing was the essence of her vocation and the purest gift she could give to
the Church and to God; Pommereu reported: '[She] did not believe there was a
more noble exercise than to instruct the youth in the most solid virtues.'[21]   In
Evreux, Elizabeth Turgis (*sœur* de Saint Michel) applied herself more specifically
to the teaching of the day pupils and went to great pains to educate those whose

---

[19] Mary Roswitha Etscheit, 'The Place of Mary Ward in the Education of Catholic Girls
during Penal Times, in England and in German-speaking Countries, 1558-1688',
unpublished PhD thesis (University of East Anglia , 1986), in BCA, B33, chapter V, p. 11.

[20] *Règlements des religieuses de la congrégation de Paris, divisés en trois livres* (Paris,
1751), part 2, p. 158: 'Les religieuses qui sont destinées à l'instruction des écolières
externes, s'y doivent porter avec d'autant plus d'affection, qu'en cette occupation elles
imitent de plus près le Fils de Dieu: lequel pendant sa vie a voulu principalement instruire
les pauvres et les ignorants'.

[21] MDPU, *Les Chroniques de l'ordre des Ursulines*, part 2, p. 151: ' [Elle] ne croyait pas
qu'il y eut un plus noble exercice que celui de former cette jeunesse aux plus solides vertus.'

ignorance and limited academic abilities would have deterred a less committed pedagogue.[22]

Examples abound which illustrate the fervour of the initial apostolic drive. Marie de Liberos (*sœur* de la Trinité) was one of the initial members of the Toulouse house; a moving spirit of this congregation, she is described in its chronicle as the living expression of the Ursuline vocation which, she believed, manifested itself through her in the shape of the visions she experienced.[23] Liberos, whose pedagogical zeal was such that she was among the few sisters who periodically left Toulouse in order to help existing houses or found new ones in rural areas, claimed to see a lighted torch, a well-known emblem of pedagogy, burning by her side as she was entered the classroom. This torch represented her community's educational endeavours and the excellence of its Christian aim. Her *consœur* Catherine de Pins (1585-1664), in religion *sœur* de Saint Bonaventure, was so dedicated to her teaching brief that, according to Parayre, she declined to take her thirty-minute break each afternoon, but insisted on employing it to teach and help students individually.[24] As with Marie de Liberos, her efficiency helped to optimize Ursuline success in the region and, in 1623, she was sent to found a new community in nearby Auch.

Jaquete de Maynie, another Toulousaine, displayed the same concern for her educational and evangelizing vocation.[25] The daughter of one of the most noble and powerful families in the city, she had previously fallen prey to the distractions of the wealthy society in which she lived. Parayre described her as an idle young girl, full of social ambitions and delusions of grandeur. He wrote: '[her] Christian practices were not only dissipated [by her worldly pursuits] but altogether infected and corrupt'. He recounted the episode of her conversion as a miracle, saving her from the perils of dangerous 'books of fashion and profane stories'. In the chronicler's words, 'these thoughts possessed her so absolutely that they were strong enough, not only to distract her in her prayers and in all devotional practices, but also to make her abandon them altogether.'[26] Perhaps as a consequence of her own conversion, Jaquete de Maynie became one of the most active catechizers of the initial lay gathering. Her awareness of the Ursuline vocation as essentially educational led her to play a crucial role in ensuring that the community remained devoted to this brief even after the major structural changes which were to occur when the *congrégées* became nuns in 1616. To her, it was essential that, in embracing the cloister, her *consœurs* did not become entirely

---

[22] *Ibid.*, part 3, p. 289.

[23] R. P. Parayre, *Chronique*, part 2, pp. 338-375.

[24] *Ibid.*, pp. 26-44.

[25] *Ibid.*, pp. 45-87.

[26] *Ibid.*, p. 46: 'ses pratiques chrétiennes en étaient non seulement dissipées, mais encore infectées et corrompues'; 'ces pensées la possédaient si absolument qu'elles avaient assez de force, non seulement pour la distraire dans ses prières, et en toutes pratiques de dévotion, mais encore les lui faire quitter.'

devoted to the contemplative life of Mary but continued undertaking the duties of Martha.

This zeal for teaching was by no means the preserve of the Toulousain foundation; it is a recurring theme in Ursuline documents all across France, a fact which demonstrates that the sisters were globally aware and proud of their evangelical brief. The four volumes of death notices collated from establishments around the country by the Ursulines of the Faubourg Saint Jacques in Paris provide numerous examples of sisters set apart by particular fervour for their pedagogical responsibilities. For instance, in Périgueux, Marie Boyer (in religion *sœur* de Sainte Ursule) was praised for her dedication to her classes. In her obituary, her superior reported that she took no interest in keeping any contact with the world, save for the day girl, of whom she was first mistress for 34 years. Boyer's dedication for her post led the author of the death notice to reflect: 'she always practised her function with tireless assiduity and zeal, and she derived all her pleasure from being with these young innocents'. This teacher enjoyed such a fond relationship with her pupils that on the day of her funeral, countless students, present and past, gathered in the church to pay their respects, some crying quietly, others unable to contain their grief and weeping out loud, much to the astonishment of the companions of the departed tutor.[27]

Similarly, the necrology of Nicole le Doux (in religion *sœur* de Sainte Eufrasie) in Saint-Denis, mentions very little about her that is not related to her classroom activities: this Ursuline, it seemed, liked nothing better than to teach externs. Not only did she remain in the office of *maîtresse des externes* for an extraordinary length of time, she also spent much effort devising inventive methods which would ensure the pupils' full attention and effective learning. Moreover, le Doux strove to gain the girls' affections not for herself, but for her catechesis, so that learning became a pleasant and rewarding occupation even for the poorest pupils; to this end, she ensured her lessons were methodical and easy to understand and she regularly rewarded progress with some little stories which she composed herself, in verse.[28]

Thus, both Orders launched a movement which sought to give young women new opportunities in the field of secular schooling and religious instruction. One of the far-reaching novelties proposed by the French Ursulines and the English Ladies was the availability of educational provisions for females of all backgrounds, considering the furtherance of the faith and the salvation of souls before any preoccupation with social standing or wealth. In this respect, both congregations were spearheading the seventeenth-century pedagogical drive; but were the methods employed and the topics covered in their schools equally at the vanguard of the movement?

---

[27] BA, ms 4990- 80, Périgueux, 21 May 16?? (illegible), '[Elle] a toujours exercé cette charge avec un zèle et une assiduité infatigable; tout son plaisir était d'être avec ces petites innocentes.'

[28] BA, ms 4991-30, Saint Denis, 28 January 1693.

Pedagogy in the communities

Unfortunately, when compared with the astonishing wealth of documents detailing the administrative and religious life of the English Institute and of the French Ursulines, there is a relative paucity of archives regarding the actual pedagogical work undertaken in their schools in the early modern era. In particular, little is known about their curriculum or the teaching practice of individual establishments. In this respect, Toulouse seems once more representative of the rest of the Ursulines in the country: whereas there are 46 voluminous bundles of manuscripts to document the economic and religious life of the convent, little evidence has survived about the day-to-day running of the classrooms. The historian M. C. Gueudré remarked that this seemed to be the case for the majority of French communities.[29]

Amongst the documents which survived, the *Règlemens* of Paris illustrated some of the main features of Ursuline pedagogy; they can be assumed to provide a broad indication of the curriculum followed across the country since, despite slight variations on points of details, individual congregations usually shared a common core of essential *formulae*.[30] From these we know that any Ursuline could be a classroom teacher immediately after profession since the hierarchy was threefold only: its first element, the novices, became on profession either lay sisters or choir nuns. In all establishments, some of the latter doubled as tutors and teaching could therefore be considered as an office comparable to any other. Teachers could be of any age, although the *prefecte* (general headmistress) and the two *principales* (one overseeing the progress of the boarders, the other that of the day girls) should in theory be over 26 years of age and have at least ten years of profession behind them.[31] Such arrangements illustrated the houses' determination to run their schools in a professional way: the *prieure* could assign younger sisters to these posts only on obtaining a special licence from their archbishop, recognizing that their particular talents were precious enough to dispense with usual age requirements.

Such an organization was not adopted by the English Ladies. In the Institute, Mary Ward created a degree of specialization whereby teaching actually determined a member's status in the community. The 1616 *Ratio Instituti* explained that, in addition to novices, associates and professed Mothers, the structure included a fourth, separate element: the mistresses. The rank of mistress was higher than that of novice or associate, but lower than that of professed Mother. However, being a mistress was not simply a stage allowing the transition of novices to the state of Mothers; critically, it was a self-contained position of its

---

[29] See M. C. Gueudré, *Histoire de l'ordre des Ursulines*, vol. 2, pp. 8-15.

[30] *Règlements des religieuses de la congrégation de Paris*.

[31] ADHG, 221H-28 bis, 5, f. 15.

own. The mistresses' role was multi-faceted and the 1616 *Ratio Instituti* described it as follows: 'To learn and to exercise any duty, office, or employment [...] for the greater glory of God, the common good of our Congregation, or *for the service of our neighbour*', thereby placing the teachers' duties firmly into the sphere of the apostolate rather than that of contemplation.[32]

Regrettably, as in the case of the Ursulines, circumstances conspired to lead to the disappearance of many of the original documents regarding education in the English Institute. In 1697, one of Mary Ward's earliest followers, Barbara Babthorpe, collected in Munich all the papers concerning schools and archived them meticulously. However, a great many were destroyed in the Bavarian secularization of teaching establishments of 1810, leaving modern researchers with little early material regarding organization, pedagogy and curriculum; some copies have survived in local houses of the IBVM, but other irreplaceable manuscripts have been lost.[33] Nevertheless, there remain enough documents to piece together both the professional attitudes to teaching and the organization of the Institute's schools; even if details are scant about subject content, the rest of school life can still be discovered with some accuracy.

The educators underwent a novitiate suited to their office for six months at least, or a whole year when circumstances allowed, at the end of which they became full members of the Institute. This specialization was highly meaningful: far from being a duty like any other or an office held by a sister who remained primarily a choir nun, teaching had become defining in itself. Perhaps for the first time in the history of female education, and in a manner which was not fully conceptualized in the Ursuline psyche, it was possible to become a teacher *per se*. In the Institute, the mistresses were just that: teachers. They were not novices, nor lay sisters (associates) nor choir nuns (professed Mothers); they were separate from these categories and defined by their function as educators.

As was the case in many respects, efforts at standardization were to be the hallmark of late seventeenth- and early eighteenth-century pedagogy. Teaching methods and daily routines following a strictly planned schedule were developed and applied in Christian schools across Europe, often based on the model instigated by the Society of Jesus. The basic pedagogy of the French Ursulines and the English Institute was directly influenced by the innovations of Ignatius and, in particular, both congregations adopted the Jesuit model of the *decurions* in order to cope with crowded classrooms. For this purpose, they nominated some of the more advanced girls to act as overseers, each in charge of a group of ten fellow students. Generally a *decurion* (or *dizainière*) was responsible for ten externs whom she supervised every day, thereby considerably lightening the main teacher's workload and ensuring the smooth running of lessons.

---

[32] BCA, B18, *Ratio Instituti*, ff. 8-9, emphasis mine.

[33] See Marion Norman, 'A Woman for all Seasons: Mary Ward (1585-1645), Renaissance Pioneer of Women's Education', *Paedagogica Historica* 23.1 (1983), p. 126.

In Paris, each *dizainière* ensured that, every morning, her group gathered by the exterior classroom door a few minutes before it opened. She made her 'pupils' stand in pairs in an orderly fashion and in silence. When the doors opened, she led her group to its bench, distributed books and generally made sure they were all set up when the teacher entered.[34] This division of classes into ten-strong groups allowed pupils of similar abilities to learn together, while a *régente* was appointed to supervise a maximum of forty pupils, moving around four sub-groups in her classroom; should more pupils fall under her responsibility, the Superior would allocate another sister to help her in her duties.[35]

Once the problem of managing classrooms was dealt with, there remained issues relating to the manner in which students ought to be taught. The central skill in the Ursulines' and the Institute's schools was reading, since this would enable girls to become familiar both with the Scriptures and with devotional works. In both Orders, learning to read followed the well-established pattern used both in religious schools and in those run by local neighbourhoods. In the classroom, all the pupils used the same book at any given time; the mistress in charge spelt out each word of a passage of a few lines, before reading out a longer piece of one or two pages. As she read, she took great care to pronounce clearly, observe all relevant pauses and accentuate properly, since she was setting the example to be imitated by the learners. Meanwhile, all the pupils followed her reading, enunciating each word clearly to themselves. Next, the teacher asked one pupil to repeat the entire extract aloud, then another would read it again.

The process of learning was thus based on initial imitation of the teacher's reading, then on repetition of the newly deciphered passage. It was therefore most important that the tutor's performance was of high standard, since it would determine all of her students' ability to read without perpetuating her own mistakes. The issue of language has to be considered here. In France, most pupils from poor backgrounds would speak the local *patois* amongst themselves, and were required to converse in French only in the formality of the classroom (a situation which endured until the early decades of the twentieth century in many rural locations). They were highly unlikely to have any knowledge of Latin, and indeed, even amongst the urban elites which generally benefited from at least basic vernacular education in French, music and arithmetic, Latin remained a rare achievement. The Ursulines sought to remedy this situation and taught their pupils to read in Latin, before even contemplating reading lessons in the vernacular.

At first, this practice may appear puzzling; since evidence shows that communication between sisters, teachers and pupils was carried out in French, it might have been expected that Latin would follow only when the students reached a sufficient level of proficiency in reading French, a language with which they

---

[34] *Règlements des religieuses de la congrégation de Paris*, part 2, pp. 178-9.
[35] ADHG, 221H-28 bis, 5, f. 3.

were all orally familiar. So why did pupils learn to read the Roman language first? This practice had been standardized across the kingdom simply because its pronunciation was more consistent: whereas in French many letters were not pronounced, in Latin, each letter was pronounced and each syllable was equal to the sum of its letters. It was, therefore, a much more accessible language to decipher.[36] Moreover, Latin was the vehicle of the main writing of the Catholic Church and it was thought essential that young women should be able to read such works appropriately. Incidentally, the teaching of the Roman tongue often stopped there; if reading it was deemed essential to one's salvation, there was no question of writing it or speaking it fluently, since such achievement far surpassed the expected needs of both students and teachers.

While knowing how to read was considered to be an instrument of salvation enabling girls to become acquainted with scripture and pious works, writing was seen in a different light: both skills did not go hand in hand but were understood as two unrelated accomplishments. Moreover, writing demanded additional equipment, such as desks, knives, quill pens, paper, inkwells and powder, all of which were costly. The difficulties of making and storing the ink, as well as the fashioning of quill-pens, made the teaching of writing a demanding task. Consequently, only girls who had already mastered the skill of reading were permitted to learn to write and, at least initially, the only day pupils who were allowed to put pen to paper would be those who were anticipated to need that skill in later life.

Once more, Ursuline pedagogy relied heavily on initial imitation and subsequent repetition of a model set out by the teacher. Pupils were taught to sharpen their quill pens and to keep their paper and their clothes neat. Then they were instructed in the way to hold a pen between the thumb and the forefinger, using the middle finger as a rest. When the students' posture and technique were deemed satisfactory, they then learned to form letters tidily by copying lines. Teachers provided their classes with models of letters, which the pupils would reproduce as faithfully as possible. The first letter to practise was the vowel *o*, followed by *i*, then *e*, *a* and *u*. Each one of these vowels had to be reproduced perfectly from the model before the pupil could move on to the next letter. Consonants also followed a pre-set order, starting with *m* and *n*, then *b, d, l, f, g, h, c*, until the entire alphabet was acquired. When learners had proved their ability to write perfectly formed individual letters, they were then allowed to link them, with lines such as *uuuu* and *mmmm* first, before moving on to complete words. It was only when the practical techniques of writing were mastered that spelling could be considered by the practice of dictation.[37] Similar methods were also employed by the English Ladies: we know that the school founded in Hammersmith, for

---

[36] S. Roux, *Méthode nouvelle pour apprendre à lire parfaitement bien le Latin et le Français* (Paris, 1694).

[37] *Règlements des religieuses ursulines des la congrégation de Paris*, part 1, p. 75.

instance, used a primer known as *Dyche's Spelling Dictionary* and the pupils were asked to propose words to test one another's progress.[38]

In both Orders, senior students had also access to arithmetic, which occupied a place of minor importance in the curriculum and remained basic. Using *jettons* or counters, pupils were taught to add, subtract and multiply using both Roman and Arabic numbers before they could calculate on paper. The teaching of this skill usually acted as a brief training for managing household accounts or a family business and did not aim at any advanced proficiency in mathematics. In the Ursuline schools, some of the abler pupils might have been allowed to become familiar with the basics of arithmetic, but the Rules specified that such pupils should be the exception rather than the norm, and their arithmetic remained limited in any case.[39] This was also the case in most of the Continental schools of the Institute where there is no mention of arithmetic in most class timetables until the start of the eighteenth century. Henriette Peters, however, has unearthed the curriculum of the school in Pressburg in Slovakia which, she conjectured, was drafted in 1628. This showed that the classes were divided up into four forms and, although arithmetic was not available in the first two forms, it became optional in third form where pupils could chose between Latin grammar, various handicrafts or basic arithmetic. These options could all be pursued further into the fourth form.[40]

As the English Ladies and the French Ursulines developed their own individual teaching particularities, it becomes possible to differentiate between the educations they provided; their secular curriculum mirrored most clearly the essence of each Order and illustrated its strengths and weaknesses. After the transformation of their congregations into enclosed convents, Ursuline schools in France became more limited to the topics deemed appropriate for education in the cloister. Conversely, the English Institute's imitation of the Society of Jesus and its independence from any conventual Rule allowed it to transgress those gender-defined boundaries and follow the Jesuits even in the topics it taught. Thus, the Orders' teaching echoed their institutional differences.

Ursuline pedagogy across France enjoyed only a limited margin of adaptability and innovation; teaching methods remained strictly standardized according to rules designed to avoid personal initiative. Any private enterprise in diversification or innovation on the part of the tutors amounted to a breach of obedience and was viewed as the manifestation of undue self-will on the part of the teacher concerned. The nuns' advances in key areas of pedagogy, therefore, remained carefully checked by the episcopate and the Ursuline constitutions show

---

[38] BCA, 2, Hammersmith, A, 37.

[39] *Règlements des religieuses ursulines de la congrégation de Paris*, part 1, p. 85.

[40] Henriette Peters, *Mary Ward*, pp. 451-2.

this tension between the promotion of female education and the enforcement of Church control over female initiatives.[41]

Male authority, power and jurisdiction contained Ursuline schooling within the limits of what was, at the time, deemed proper for female education. Mistresses were expected to adhere exactly to the order of exercises, never changing, adding or omitting anything without the advice of the *principale*, who orchestrated every detail. Such innovations as would nowadays pass for trivial - for instance, the reversing of the order of exercises without permission - were faults which warranted censure and to which the guilty sister would have to confess to the community.[42] Thus, all changes were condemned as the potential bearers of novelties, which could upset or jeopardize the order of the cloister. A panel of officers ensured observance of the convent's rule: priests, as canonical superiors, were available to hear possible complaints and the archbishops of the archdioceses in question ultimately dealt with any improper teaching, be it of an unsuitable matter or manner.

The Institute, however, escaped some of the constraints which the Ursulines had accepted when they gained religious approval by becoming a convent. If its boarding schools in England were somewhat restricted in their activities because of their clandestine nature, they were much freer to recruit in larger numbers and diversify in their programme of study on the Continent, where they offered a curriculum which was far from being limited to religious instruction or the inculcation of basic secular knowledge and essential domestic skills. In their efforts to imitate the Society of Jesus even in their programme of study, the English Ladies offered teaching in modern languages and in Latin at a level which was more akin to male higher education than to that available at female establishments. To Mary Ward, such an emphasis on modern languages made perfect sense, since most of the houses of the Institute were founded in various European countries. Thus, where the French Ursulines limited their language teaching to French and Latin, a more varied *palette* was necessary for the Continental schools of the Institute, if only to allow sisters and students to interact, both amongst themselves and with their local neighbourhoods. Thus, in addition to English and Latin, the houses in St Omer and Liège taught their boarders French, those in Rome, Naples and Perugia taught Italian and those in Munich, Vienna, Prague, Pressburg, Cologne and Trier taught German.

Although the increasingly important place given to French reflected its prominence as the language of refinement, it was Latin which, above all, occupied a privileged place in Mary Ward's idea of her Institute's education. Her enthusiasm for it further demonstrates her desire for a humanist academic foundation modelled on Jesuit lines and her dedication to excellence was illustrated

---

[41] Linda Lierheimer, 'Female Eloquence and Maternal Ministry', p. 241.
[42] *Règlements des religieuses de la congrégation de Paris*, part 1, p. 20.

in a letter she wrote to Winifred Bedingfield, (1610-66) then Superioress in Munich, in order to congratulate her on 'the unexpected progress of [her] Latin schools'.[43] Ward derived great joy from the fact that her schools were highly successful at teaching Latin. In that same letter, she wrote: 'All such as are capable invite them to it [...] no talent is so much to be regarded in them as the Latin tongue.' Since a deeper knowledge of Latin represented the cut-off point between elementary and advanced education, Mary Ward was aiming at a new type of learning for women, one which was akin to that provided by the Jesuits for their male students. She and her followers had started to address the issue of female schooling in a new way.

Yet, as she concentrated upon her usual pragmatism, Ward failed to take traditional boundaries into account and overstepped the mark of feminine modesty in education in the same way as she had done in institutional and vocational matters. The Institute's schooling never deviated from its self-appointed path of expediency: the knowledge and the abilities taught there were those deemed necessary for their pupils, whether they were usually esteemed suitable for women or not. For instance, in December 1627, she wrote to her companion, Winifred Campion, then acting as Superioress in Naples:

> I would have Cecilia, and Catherina begin out of hand to learn the rudiments of Latin; fear not their loss of virtue by that means, for this must and will be so common to all as there will be no cause of complacency, [...] what time can be otherwise found besides their prayer, let it be bestowed on their Latin.[44]

The foundress believed that Latin was a highly valuable skill for her pupils and she braved the common assertion of the period, which held that knowledge bred pride and arrogance in women, in order to provide her students with all the erudition they might need in later life. So by including the learning of such topics, the members of the Institute consciously took female education beyond the accepted boundaries established in the Europe of their day.[45]

In order to glean information about the education provided in the small schools running in England, one can turn to the obituaries of some of the members of the Institute who had themselves been pupils in their youth. Some of these necrological articles refer to the sisters' knowledge of Latin, German and French; the register of Hammersmith made special mentions of Mary Austin and Cecilia Cornwallis (1656-1723) who were both said to be competent in Greek, Hebrew and astronomy, a most unusual and ambitious programme for women at that time, when it was generally assumed that teaching unnecessary - elevated - topics such

---

[43] BCA, B5, letter 41, f. 68, 16 July 1627.
[44] BCA, B5, letter 46, f. 73. The girls' surnames are not provided.
[45] *Ibid.*

as Greek would serve only to feed a woman's pride.[46] Proficiency in Greek implied a certain familiarity with the classical scholars' art of rhetoric, an art with a political purpose and which remained thus far the preserve of male scholars; indeed, rhetoric provided learners with the power of eloquence and argumentation, the efficient and convincing use of speech to win debates and sway one's interlocutor through logical demonstration. Women with such gifts therefore flouted the Pauline injunction to remain silent in public; yet, seen from the Institute's sensible point of view, these skills were most useful for proselytizers, in order to convince those who were hesitant and even to convert their opponents.

Mary Ward never relented in imitating the Society of Jesus and her school syllabus clearly reflected this intention. One of the most revolutionary aspects of the Institute's teaching was to incorporate dramatic performances as part of the curriculum. Since drama was part of Ignatian schooling, it was included in the Institute schools too. Thus, her schools caused a scandal when they put on theatrical plays acted by their pupils and, in September 1619, the Jesuit General Muzio Vitelleschi was compelled to enquire into allegations that a member of the Society, John Falkner, had directed several theatrical plays which had been performed by the pupils of the school in Liège.[47] The foundress was unquestionably ahead of her times in upholding her belief that women were, in most regards, as capable as men. This outlook on femininity shaped her work to its very core, nowhere more so than in its teaching and in its faithful copying of the Jesuit *Ratio Studiorum*.

Later, in the heat of the debate which raged in the years 1621-1622, the Benedictine Robert Sherwood (1588-1665) presented a petition against the English Ladies in Rome. Amongst his accusations, the charge that the Institute produced what he called 'immoral plays' was highly prominent.[48] No doubt this aspect of girls' schooling was tremendously novel, considering that it was dispensed by a religious community and not taught by a private tutor in a family home. In Munich, the pupils were expected to perform a little celebratory play on special feast days and holy days, as well as for the clothing of postulants or to celebrate a visit by an important person. Such performances, held for a restricted public, gained the Institute's schools a certain renown and captured the interest of influential aristocratic and bourgeois families.

One of the particularities and, indeed, unorthodoxies of Mary Ward's schools was that they were instigated and managed entirely by women, for women, without any more male intervention than was absolutely necessary. True to her vocation, Mary Ward ensured that her schools followed the Jesuit model as closely as it was possible in a female establishment. Such similarities between the Institute and the Society of Jesus were sometimes uncomfortable for the Jesuits. After the

---

[46] BCA, C45, Register of Hammersmith and St Mary's in York. Cecilia Cornwallis succeeded Frances Bedingfield in the post of Superioress of Hammersmith in 1672.

[47] Henriette Peters, *Mary Ward*, p. 254.

[48] *Ibid.*, p. 342. The petition was written sometime between December 1621 and May 1622.

English Ladies had opened a school in Liège in 1619, some members of the Society of Jesus drew up a short questionnaire in an attempt to determine its form and its aims. The third question concerned the teachers and their activities: 'Do [the English Ladies] themselves intend to teach music and languages, or will these be taught by a master?' Ward replied in the name of her followers: 'Our desires are to be able among ourselves to teach such as we bring up, both language and music, that we need not have other masters. To this end, we wholly apply some of our own to gain perfection in these.'[49] There is a distinctly recognizable determination in the foundress's answers, one typical of the spirit which has rendered her so attractive to the modern historian.

Given the situation in England at the time, however, it was difficult for the English Ladies to carry out their educational tasks without attracting the attention of government officials. Therefore, the very nature of their organization required not only a low profile but a degree of adaptability and resourcefulness that was not necessary, and indeed not encouraged, for the French Ursulines. Once the members of the Institute had secured a relatively safe settlement, there remained the problem of providing teaching material, such as books, works of devotions, catechisms and quills, paper, ink and other indispensable commodities. Pedagogical material had to be procured from abroad and Catholic religious objects smuggled in with extreme caution. When working in England, Ward became much more safety-conscious and chose to write most of her correspondence in lemon juice, so as to be invisible to spies who might intercept it. Moreover, she used coded language to mask all references to Catholic practice, in order to avoid detection of her project for a school in the capital.[50] In a 1639 letter, she wrote:

> Commend the best success [of this school] to God and seek
> to provide samplers [i.e. Catholic objects] [...] Without
> samplers we should do nothing and here are none to be had
> nor must we seek them of any here, also plays [i.e. spiritual
> books], all [that] can be had without notice or the least
> suspect, also meditations. [51]

The impossibility of a regulated and unchanging daily routine is further illustrated by the fact that the members in England could never hope to settle anywhere permanently. No community was ever safe from the pursuivants and hasty relocations were as vital as the Ladies' ability to perform several roles at the same

---

[49] BCA, B9, *Various papers* (this is a copy of the 1619 questionnaire kept in Brussels, Archives Générales du Royaume; Archives Jésuitiques, Province Gallo-belgique).
[50] BCA, B5, f. 132: Clarifications between square brackets should facilitate the reading of this quotation; the code interpreting 'samplers' as Catholic objects and 'plays' as spiritual books is provided in the archives of the Bar convent.
[51] *Ibid.*, f. 132.

time. Constant change, not immutable order, was the lot of the Institute on English soil.

Hence, Mary Ward believed in gender equality in matters concerning the availability of education; what is more, she also believed that the range of topics taught in girls' schools should not be limited by prejudices against the learned woman but, on the contrary, expanded to provide a more fully-rounded individual. In terms of education, as in terms of religious involvement, she considered her contemporaries' notion of woman as restrictive and endeavoured to free her pedagogy, and her Institute at large, from male control wherever she found it unfair. This was a testimony to her determination to imitate the Society of Jesus.

Preserving traditional elements

The true core of the women's vocation was to give the so-called 'weaker sex' a degree of schooling it had generally been denied. Just as the Catholic Reformation had focused on teaching boys, opinion in both secular and religious circles had evolved little on the subject of the schooling of girls before the seventeenth century. It was still generally believed that excessive feminine learning posed a potential threat to the patriarchal order, since knowledge gave women some means of self-assertion. It was feared that, when girls were taught to handle the tools of their salvation, they were also presented with the temptation of abusing them. Even when writing towards the end of this century of change, self-proclaimed champion of female education François Salignac de la Mothe Fénelon expressed a view which illustrated the scope and limits of the early modern philosophy of teaching girls:

> Above all, you should inspire girls with the sober and temperate wisdom recommended by St Paul; make them wary of the trappings of novelty, which their sex naturally tends to love; let a salutary horror warn them against all singularity in religious matters.[52]

Although they advocated a modicum of learning as an instrument of salvation, pedagogues envisaged this as entirely different from male education. To them, sharing the same erudition across gender boundaries would have been nonsensical: why teach a woman to be a man? Thus, schooling was based on fixed gender assumptions, according to which male and female learners would be equipped with skills adapted to the demands of their roles and stations in life. The teaching

---

[52] François Salignac de la Mothe Fénelon, *De l'éducation des filles* (1687), in *Oeuvres* (Paris, 1854) t. 4, p. 276: 'Surtout inspirez aux filles cette sagesse sobre et tempérée que saint Paul recommande; faites-leur craindre le piège de la nouveauté, dont l'amour est si naturel à leur sexe; prévenez-les d'une horreur salutaire pour toute singularité en matière de religion.'

directed at a female audience should therefore be a much simplified version of that dispensed to male pupils, in order to correspond to that period's notion of woman and of both her capacities and her expected place in life. In a word, it was meant to enhance feminine skills on a practical level. Consequently, schools offered curricula which were designed to train girls in all the essential virtues of respectable women; they provided 'the inculcation of a way of life', where women were taught how to behave and think according to their rank.[53]

Although the lessons run by the French Ursulines and to an even greater extent those managed by the English Ladies presented some notable innovations, no evidence has yet been unearthed which would demonstrate a 'modern' view on women's learning, one which would claim *complete* parity with that of men. Although they gave girls' schooling its first institutional expression, Ursulines and English Ladies remained representative of their society and their documents echo the timeless patriarchal opinions which were still expounded about learned women in early modern Europe. Thus, they were in a sense comparable to Fénelon who, although lamenting the lack of education for young women, nevertheless remained entirely aware of the intrinsic difference between the sexes, a difference which he deemed as physiological as it was socially-constructed. The bishop of Cambrai understood education as gendered:

> [women] do not have to govern the state, go to war, or enter the sacred ministry; therefore, they can do without certain types of specialised knowledge that belong to politics, to the military arts, to jurisprudence, to philosophy and to theology.[54]

This was a definition which the French Ursulines and, to a lesser degree, the English Institute, would have endorsed; indeed, their particular aim was not to produce erudite girls who would amass knowledge for its own sake, but rather to inform girls of their duties and roles as Catholic women. The lay syllabus, therefore, was tailored to suit the pupils' expected stations in life, but never to provide them with an opportunity to rise above them; it covered a wide scope of topics, ranging from reading and writing to good house-keeping, imparting the amount of secular knowledge which was deemed necessary for the students' social obligations.

Even such pioneers as the first French Ursulines and English Ladies could not help but be a product of the anthropology of their time; therefore, as they gradually acquired knowledge, their pupils were simultaneously taught to keep within their own measure. The inculcation of feminine virtues - as these were

---

[53] Elizabeth Rapley, *The Dévotes*, p. 155.
[54] François Salignac de la Mothe Fénelon, *De l'Éducation des filles*, t. 4, p. 240: 'Elles ne doivent ni gouverner l'État, ni faire la guerre, ni entrer dans le ministère des choses sacrées; ainsi, elles peuvent se passer de certaines connaissances étendues, qui appartiennent à la politique, à l'art militaire, à la jurisprudence, à la philosophie et à la théologie.'

understood in the post-Reformation Church - constituted a crucial element of female Catholic schooling. It was implicitly understood that both the learners and their teachers, as women, were conscious of their limitations and would willingly remain within the boundaries which patriarchy had ascribed to female capacities.

In this respect, the English Ladies followed the established pattern. Like the Ursulines, and indeed most Catholic congregations with an educational brief in early modern Europe, they also emphasized the traditional standards of female behaviour as the essential guardians of pupils' virtues. The fifty-third point of Ward's 1612 *Schola Beatae Mariae* illustrated this conventional stand on moral education. It summarized the principal aims of the staff as such: 'the mistresses [...] will teach a sense of duty, Christian doctrine, good morals'.[55] To this common stem, the *Schola* added gender-specific requirements and addressed the education of girls by endorsing, on the whole, the received ideal of feminine perfection. The pupils were exhorted to behave as perfect models of proper female social behaviour, to:

> Conduct themselves peacefully in everything, curb passions,
> restrict inordinate desires, obey parents, turn away from the
> levity of girls; observe virginal maturity, correct in time the
> defects of nature, control themselves in all matters, show
> respect by rising to elders.[56]

Such traditional views on female education are all the more worthy of note considering that Mary Ward's innovations were deemed highly controversial in her own time and continue to strike us today by their modernity.

Yet the Institute's teaching, particularly as described in the early Plan *Schola Beatae Mariae*, retained elements of a traditional nature and inculcated the virtues advocated by the patriarchal consensus of the period as intrinsically female. Industry, for instance, should always be preferred to idleness, and order and cleanliness were championed to preclude untidiness. Likewise, the qualities of reserve and discretion should become second nature in a pupil in order to prevail against curiosity and gossip – two faults believed to be particularly common in young females. More importantly, the triumvirate of the most holy virtues in women, chastity, humility and obedience, was praised and recommended daily as the crown of any virtuous wife.

Similarly, Ursuline teaching stressed the importance of propriety and the school in Toulouse recorded using a manual entitled *A Summary of the Duties of a Good Housewife and of those of a Daughter towards her Parents*.[57] The Ursulines, like the English Ladies, taught students who were destined to varied types of life in

---

[55] BCA, B18, *Schola Beatae Maria*, item 53.
[56]*Ibid.*, item 54.
[57] ADHG, 221H-28 bis, 5, f. 9, *Un Abrégé du devoir d'une bonne mère de famille et d'une fille à l'endroit de ses parents*.

the future, preparing them to excel equally in their understanding of Catholic doctrine and in their knowledge of the virtues and duties of their sex. Both Orders hoped their pupils would, in turn, influence their families and later bring up their own daughters in accordance with the principles of the Catholic faith and the composure required of respectable housewives.

Thus, needlework, though a 'profane' occupation, was considered a worthy and essential skill, embodying the essence of femininity in the patience, application and industry it required. Both the Ursulines and the English Ladies taught it as one of the fundamental practical skills required in a well-rounded young woman. The Institute's 1612 *Schola Beatae Mariae* also indicated that its pupils were taught sewing and embroidery as well as spinning and curtain making.[58] However, the types of needlework taught remained of a humble and simple sort, avoiding all fancy designs or other niceties which might give rise to sentiments of pride or vanity.

Silence was also perceived as a necessary virtue in respectable women and therefore, from the youngest age, idle chatting between students was keenly discouraged. Such pervading sense of propriety and cloister-inspired virtues meant that teaching was concerned even with the physical posture of the girls as they learned. When studying and sewing, they should remain seated in the perfect pose, with their backs straight, their legs together and their feet planted together neatly on the floor. When not holding books and needlework, they should keep their arms properly folded. They were taught to look in front of them, their eyes slightly cast down, so as not to be distracted by their neighbours; when looking at their mistress, they should avert their gaze a little to one side. Girls' schools, clearly, endeavoured to train pupils whose inner virtues were expressed through the perfection of their physical demeanour: their upright morality was mirrored in the straightness of their backs, their humility in their downcast eyes and their propriety in their posture.[59]

Moreover, conservative attitudes were still visible in the schools run by the French Ursulines and the English Ladies. Teachers were always careful not to impose the presence of the usually poor day students upon their wealthier boarders; schools were organized so as to preserve safe separations between groups and each category of pupils was taught as a unit, in separate classrooms. *Prima facie*, class-consciousness in the Ursulines and in the Ladies was not only the product of early modern conceptions of society, but also derived directly from the women's own family background. Since most of them came from the aristocracy or the gentry, with a few from the bourgeoisie or below, they reproduced the patterns of early modern social consciousness, for lack of deliberate detachment from those hierarchical categories. Class consciousness remained present even at the core of

---

[58] BCA, B18, *Schola Beatae Mariae*, item 53.
[59] Roger Chartier, Dominique Julia, and Marie-Pierre Compère, *L'Éducation en France du XVIe au XVIIIe siècles* (Paris, 1976), p. 115.

an Institute which aimed to be accessible to all, as can be seen in recommendations that aristocratic pupils should never be reprimanded, let alone chastised, in front of their social inferiors. Even in schools which claimed to offer unprecedented opportunities for the poor and to broaden the scope of female schooling not only in its content but in its outreach, educating all girls in an inclusive fashion, the divisions which characterized their society still operated.

Such policies made good sense and were partly the result of entrepreneurial pragmatism which endeavoured to please influential families (whose support the congregations desperately needed) by preserving their social privileges even inside the classrooms. Concretely, the sisters had to guarantee the safety and wellbeing of their richer patrons if their establishments were to remain viable; the inconveniences which could arise from the gathering of such a broad social spectrum of pupils under a common roof had to be kept to a minimum. Numerous anecdotes show that this surfaced in the everyday experience of the school, whether of the English Ladies or the French Ursulines. In the Toulousain house, for instance, Marguerite Boyer (*sœur* de Saint Benoît, died 1652) contracted so much vermin from her day girls that, to avoid the contamination of the whole community, her teaching habit had to be burnt.[60] Lice, fleas and viral infections were legion in the open classrooms of the *externats* across France. In Paris, Charlotte de Louvencourt (*sœur* de l'Annonciation) caught smallpox when teaching the day students, a condition which left her disfigured for the rest of her life.[61] Although she reportedly felt honoured to suffer in the service of the Church, one can only imagine the consequences if the disease had been allowed to affect the boarders; a daughter's scarred face could all but ruin a family's chance at a profitable marriage alliance when she returned home. Separation, therefore, was meant to ensure a degree of safety, not only for the boarders but also for the schools' reputation

The Ursulines' care of social propriety led them to develop a system within which separation applied even amongst the day pupils themselves. Thus, the Parisian *Règlemens* encouraged teachers to spare the 'girls of condition' any distasteful experiences by sitting 'the poorest and uncleanest girls' at a distance from them. This social division of the day classes, though intended to be discreet and kind to the sensitivities of the poorest students, nevertheless testified that early modern class awareness was an integral part of the collective psyches of these communities.[62] Since the future of the houses relied heavily upon the support of influential and wealthy families, common sense dictated that the sisters preserved

---

[60] R. P. Parayre, *Chronique*, part 3, p. 313.

[61] MDPU, *Les Chroniques de l'ordre des Ursulines*, part 3, p. 92.

[62] *Règlements des religieuses de la congrégation de Paris,* part 2, p. 166: 'Elles prendront garde à ne pas mettre les filles de condition proche des plus pauvres et mal propres, pour ne leur point donner de dégoût: ce qu'elles feront pourtant avec discrétion, afin que les pauvres ne se croient pas méprisées.'

social etiquette within the classrooms in an attempt to strengthen their links with those circles.

Teaching the Catholic doctrine

There was one factor in which pupils received exactly the same treatment, regardless of whether they were poor or wealthy: they all benefited from the same lessons in Catholic doctrine. Indeed, neither the Ursulines nor the members of the Institute considered the accumulation of secular learning as the principal aim of their schools; although lay instruction formed an integral part of their curriculum, their particular brief was to evangelize, to produce strong Catholic characters guarded by all the virtues of their sex and anchored in their knowledge of the faith. Since in France, and particularly in heavily Protestantized areas such as the Midi, the Ursulines were actively involved in the Catholic battle to re-conquer the minds and hearts of the populations, lessons in doctrine were most prominent within the daily curriculum, and despite some minor regional differences, French Ursuline schools all functioned according to a similar pattern, placing the lesson in Catholic doctrine as the climax of the day's instruction, at the end of the afternoon, usually from 3.00 to 4.00. Moreover, the primacy of this particular class was signified by the fact that it was not taught by a *maîtresse* but by the *principale* herself.

In agreement with Salesian philosophy, the Ursulines underlined the importance of knowing the *Credo*, *Ave* and *Pater Noster* in Latin but insisted that such recitation had no salutary qualities unless the meaning of the prayers was understood. Therefore, they partook of the *dévot* spirit when they ensured that their pupils became familiar with the essence of each prayer in French, in order to make the act of praying a personal and engaging communication with the divine. Like François de Sales, they stressed that deep piety did not spring from the mechanical repetition of religious *formulae* learnt by rote, but from a personal understanding of the liturgy. Therefore, the *Pater Noster*, *Ave* and *Credo* were taught both in Latin and in French, as a way of ensuring that the girls understood their meaning. Theoretical lessons focusing upon the Ten Commandments, the seven deadly sins and the cardinal virtues were often followed by *exposés* through which the pupils learned the basic Catholic creed as well as the means to do good and avoid evil. The children were also taken to Mass daily and prepared for the sacraments of confession and communion. In fact, the religious education of wealthy boarders and humbler day pupils was identical: since the catechism was the axis of the schools, it was taught to all in a uniform manner, culminating with Sunday classes.

Similar principles applied to the English Ladies' schools, where catechism was also at the centre of the programme: in the later part of the afternoon, pupils received half an hour's religious instruction and, on Fridays, from 1.00 to 3.00, they recapitulated what they had learned in this topic during the week, before hearing 45 minutes of catechism. According to the traditional practice of teaching Catholic doctrine, students first learned and recited by rote a series of questions and answers on the Creed. However, in order to ensure the full comprehension of each subject, the pupils later took part in a discussion on a religious theme and questioned one another in matters of faith and spirituality. This encouraged the transfer of theoretical knowledge into the practical sphere. It enabled the pupils to become familiar with religious and spiritual issues and allowed them to become proficient in the art of using their learning in appropriate circumstances outside the context of a classroom.

If the inculcating of Catholic doctrine was the *raison d'être* of both these congregations, it also constituted its most difficult challenge. Aware of the Pauline injunction (1 Tim 2, 12) that women should not teach, they had to remain within the boundaries of acceptability. Indeed, seventeenth-century conceptions questioned women's ability to educate others, since speaking in public flouted humility and the intrinsic weakness of the female intellect might lead them to teach falsehoods. Moreover, the blurred frontier between teaching and preaching meant that tutors should be careful not to step from the domain of acceptable private teaching into that of public preaching, which remained an exclusive male preserve. As Lierheimer argues, it was essential for both Orders to differentiate clearly between the two activities in order to legitimize and protect their mission.[63]

Thus, the Ursuline congregations across France were advised to dispense Catholic doctrine strictly according to their catechism manuals, avoiding any personal input which could resemble preaching. Though they were valued catechizers, the sisters were discouraged from developing the charisma of orators.[64] The model to be followed was Pius V's *Catechismus ex decreto concilii tridentini ad parochos* (1566), the official manual responding to the Council of Trent's concern with catechism. This functioned as a teacher's guide and was designed for the clergy's use; it was soon complemented by the Jesuit Roberto Bellarmino's *Brief Christian Doctrine* (1598) addressing catechism with the young or simple learner in mind. However, in many dioceses such as that of Toulouse, although male missionaries were very active on the ground, teaching in the vernacular and simplifying texts so as to ensure complete understanding, they were not so efficient at producing a printed guide for local catechists.[65] Indeed, the diocese of Toulouse published its first catechising manual in 1685 only.

During those years without guidance, one of the *régentes* in the Ursuline school of the city took it upon herself to compile her own textbook, a method ensuring some degree of consistency in the sisters' practice and making Catholic doctrine accessible to pupils. The anonymous author explained:

---

[63] See Linda Lierheimer, 'Female Eloquence and Maternal Ministry', particularly chapter V, 'Teaching or Preaching? Ursuline Apostolate and Women's Public Speech', pp. 236-88.
[64] *Ibid.*, p. 263.
[65] H.J. Schroeder, *Canons and Decrees of the Council of Trent*, pp. 197-8.

> The reason [for writing this manual] lies in the necessity we had to teach, every day for a whole year, classes in Christian doctrine to young or unsophisticated minds. In order to instruct them, we were compelled to write short, clear and methodical lessons and we could not find those elsewhere.[66]

Thus, in order to teach local girls, the text presented a simplified version of the Catholic faith, in the Jesuit-like format of questions and answers. Pragmatically, the author used her daily classroom experience to manufacture this tool, which she reserved for her fellow teachers' private use only. The manual was tailored exactly to suit the type of audience which attended the school's lessons. However, the *régente* did not innovate in any way: her simplified version of Christian doctrine proceeded according to the received format of the catechism of the Council of Trent. It was methodically divided into six parts: the first and the second explained the *Credo* and the *Pater* and *Ave* respectively. The third part dwelt on the commandments, the fourth on the sacraments and the fifth upon the capital sins and the cardinal virtues. Lastly, the sixth part gave instructions for the various holy days of the year. Within each part, or lesson, she started with an imagined dialogue, where she answered all the questions she expected from the learners. Then she explained the day's lesson in a more discursive manner, concluding with a vivid example to fix the main message of the lesson in the girls' minds.

Diverse influential patrons eventually persuaded the anonymous sister to submit it for publication in 1695, for the edification of others.[67] The work was praised by two Jesuits and three Augustinian fathers and by the Toulouse Vicar-General Crozat who recommended its use for the benefit and edification of other female teaching congregations. One of the Jesuits wrote in his reference: 'Such a useful book must not remain for the exclusive use of the Ursulines. It is important that it should be given to the public.'[68] His opinion was confirmed by that of his *confrère*, Michel Mourgues, who wrote in his approbation: 'It seemed to me that this Catechism can be used by all sorts of people.'[69] This was ample proof that, by 1695, the Ursulines were indeed a force to be reckoned with in the Toulousain movement for the recovery of Catholicism. The compilation of their catechetical manual was a testimony to the community's educational commitment. Indeed, it

---

[66] *Instructions sur les principes de la doctrine chrétienne pour l'usage des écoles des religieuses ursulines de Toulouse* (Toulouse, 1695), avertissement: 'L'occasion n'est autre que la nécessité de faire tous les jours durant un an des leçons de la Doctrine Chrétienne à des esprits jeunes ou grossiers, pour l'instruction desquels on fut obligé d'en dresser de courtes, claires et méthodiques, n'en trouvant point de telles ailleurs'.

[67] *Ibid.*, avertissement.

[68] *Ibid.*, in the approbation by J. Gisbert, SJ, *Professeur Royal de Théologie* at the university of Toulouse: 'Un livre aussi utile ne doit pas être pour le seul usage des religieuses ursulines; il est important de le donner au public'.

[69] *Ibid.*, approbation by Michel Mourgues, SJ, *Professeur Royal* at the university of Toulouse: 'Il m'a paru que ce catéchisme peut être d'usage pour toute sortes de personnes.'

proved that the establishment in the Rue des Trois Rois Vieux envisaged teaching as a career, a vocation that they addressed in a professional way, so as to give female schooling one of its first academic expressions.

Thus, the congregations' chosen *formulae* did differ, since Ursuline pedagogy remained in keeping with the contemporaneous norms of female education, whereas Mary Ward's followers took teaching resolutely beyond those established boundaries, believing as they did that advanced schooling was beneficial to women as well as men. However, both the Ursulines and the Ladies of the English Institute envisaged female education in the same way. According to them, knowledge was not to be pursued for its own sake, but rather as a means of perfecting oneself and offering one's endeavours to God. As such, schooling functioned as a two-way process: on the one hand, the members of the congregations worked towards their own salvation by using the classroom as the terrain of their apostolate. On the other hand, their pupils were enabled to read, write and improve their minds, which ultimately gave them the opportunity to become closer to God. Education, therefore, was the ultimate tool which allowed these women to take a full part in the drive for Catholic Reformation. Despite retaining the paternalistic values which defined woman's place in early modern society, both the French Ursulines and the English Ladies nevertheless opened the way for a new system of institutional education for women, and their schools were immensely successful as a result.

Consider the evangelical, missionary activity of both groups. The Ursulines were far more effective in this field because they worked from within their enclosure, therefore not overtly threatening patriarchy. ELs on the other hand deliberately elevated scruits — a factor that helps explain their different fates.

Chapter 5

Pushing the Boundaries of Female Ministry

For it neither becomes a woman to rule a school, nor to live amongst men, or speak abroad, and shake off her demureness and honesty, either all together, or else a great part; which if she be good, it be better to be at home within and unknown to others folks, and in company to hold her tongue demurely, and let few see her, and none at all hear her.[1]

The achievements of both the Institute's and the Ursulines' schools were remarkable for their time. Although they mostly remained within the sphere which the Catholic Church had traditionally defined as suitable for female activity, providing assistance for the communities around them and undertaking the teaching of girls, these new congregations were professing the educational apostolate as their main vocation. They envisaged this systematically, on a scale comparable to that of the education of boys by the male Orders, opening it to students outside the usual forum of conventual boarding schools. It was the first time that women from religious institutions viewed catechizing and teaching girls, inside and outside their buildings, as a defining trait of their vocations.

The rapid multiplication of French Ursuline communities and of the English Institute's branches in England and on the Continent was a manifestation of the growing involvement of women in the seventeenth-century Catholic mission; it was also symptomatic of a shift in women's perception of their own roles. As they became increasingly influential in the Catholic movement of recovery, lay women, both in France and in England, grew more aware of the importance of their positions in the network and saw their vocations take a turn towards missionary activities. In fact, it was arguably in this field that both Orders were perceived as truly pushing the boundaries of acceptable female endeavours.

The English Ladies and the French Ursulines epitomized unprecedented aspirations for women; what remains to be ascertained is whether their

proliferation of & ELs importance of women in perception of their roles &

[1] Juan Luis Vivès, *Instruction of a Christian Woman*, in Foster Watson (ed.), *Vivès and the Renascence Education of Women* (London, 1912), p. 55.

establishments, which seemingly announced dramatic changes in female religious life, actually did transcend gender norms at any time or push their roles beyond those which were traditionally deemed acceptable for women. Did the French Ursulines and the English Ladies ever turn from being the 'guardian angels' of Catholicism into the 'amazons of Christianity'?[2]

Active yet non-controversial: women keeping to their own sphere

In England, the government's repression of Catholicism provided women with opportunities to transcend traditional role-distributions and to apply their skills practically where they were most needed, without incurring the censure which usually accompanied female enterprise. As pragmatism was progressively preferred to the compartmentalization which characterized the early modern Catholic Church's insistence on role-definition, some recusant laywomen effectively became agents in the English mission and worked alongside the missionary priests. Thus, the specific circumstances of English recusancy and its covert nature allowed lay women to play active roles which were crucial to the survival of the Catholic community; in this case, somewhat ironically, the Protestant repression empowered women in the mission.

When the Ladies in England focused their work on the maintaining of the faith and the relieving of recusants, they rendered themselves valuable allies to the on-going mission and were all the more appreciated as they were not perceived to overstep the limits of feminine propriety. In so doing, Ward's followers managed to use circumstances to their advantage; since the clandestine nature of the English mission meant that traditional strictures towards female participation in the apostolate was relaxed, the women (so long as they did not antagonize the priests with whom they worked) enjoyed a latitude which would not have been as acceptable in France, for instance, after the Assembly of the Clergy received the Tridentine decrees in 1615.

The organization of a recusant centre succouring existing Catholics in England demanded a high level of discretion and organization in order to ensure that the resources available were equally accessible to all. Thus, when working in England, Mary Ward usually kept two priests in her house: one of these provided for the spiritual needs of those who lived there, while the other was on hand to visit the poor and the sick in the neighbourhood. In order to help the priests, the foundress and her followers would often go out to meet the people themselves, assisting them in their examinations of conscience and instructing them on how to make a good confession. The Ladies, in fact, took charge of all the preliminary stages leading to the sacrament of confession. On the one hand, such work promoted the priests' safety: it saved considerable time and allowed them to

---

[2] To use R. P. Parayre's words, *Chronique*, part 1, p. 22 and p. 140 respectively.

proceed directly to their sacerdotal duties, thereby reducing the length of their stay in any one place and making their movements more difficult to track. On the other hand, the increased pace of the clergymen's work also allowed them to minister to a greater number of people each day, thereby making the entire operation much more efficient. The *Briefe Relation* testified that, thanks to these apostolic aides, 'the priests [would] avoid the danger which a long stay would have brought them, and they would have more time to employ in such functions as alone belonged to their character'.[3]

When they prepared women and children for confession and communion, the English Ladies were arguably taking on some of the functions of the clergy; however, in the context of the clandestine recusant network, their intervention was appreciated or, at least, it was not impeded either by the priests themselves or by the laity. One of the crucial factors which gave Mary Ward's followers such a degree of latitude in their apostolate was that, in England, they worked from within the privacy of recusant homes, or from that of their own Catholic centres. This degree of latitude was extended further after the 1631 suppression of the Institute, since their lay status freed the English Ladies from clerical control and from the constant threat of enclosure. As secular individuals in England, because they did not teach in public but applied their quiet industry to families and individuals, their contributions remained of a suitably feminine, domestic nature. Therefore, they were not perceived to be trespassing the preserve of the clergy or to be usurping the public roles of priests.[4] Perhaps more importantly, these activities were limited to serving the recusant community rather than extended to converting Protestants; the women were not making new Catholics, but simply ministering to existing ones. Though somewhat dramatized by the constant threat of government pursuivants, their duties were still in line with those traditionally associated with female endeavours. Their succour remained mostly palliative, hence appropriate for women: therein lay the key to general acceptance from both lay and religious Catholics.

Despite the relative paucity of evidence documenting the educational work of the Institute at large, we know a little about the English establishments founded, after Mary Ward's death, by Frances Bedingfield in Hammersmith and York in 1669 and 1686 respectively. One of the striking traits of these centres was that, living amongst a constant element of danger and persecution, they rarely entered the realm of truly missionary action. Indeed, the Ladies in both locations focused on receiving the daughters of recusant families in their schools, while tending to the needs of their kin. Risky though this occupation might be in a Protestant country, it still remained pastoral rather than proselytizing in nature. The difference was essential: these schools maintained the faith where it was already present but did not specialize in the conversion of Protestants, a much

---

[3] BCA, B12, *Briefe Relation*, f. 20.
[4] See Linda Lierheimer, 'Female Eloquence and Maternal Ministry', p. 285.

riskier activity which was perhaps better suited to the endeavours of individual proselytizers.

The house in Hammersmith, which started with three members, rising only to a modest fourteen by 1703, illustrates the nature of the Ladies' undercover establishments.[5] It came under suspicion during the troubles of the Oates Plot, and a raid of the premises was reported in January 1679 in the capital's newspapers. One article recounted that: 'upon search they found divers children of several persons of quality, and three or four women to attend them'. It described the incident in further details: 'This house went under the name of a boarding school yet we are told [...] that under that pretence there is a private nunnery maintained to educate children of several of the Popish nobility and gentry in the Romish Superstition and Idolatry.'[6] All books, teaching material and religious objects were immediately seized and the chaplain, together with the house superior, Cecilia Cornwallis, were ordered to appear the next day before the Commission of the Peace. This report, which caused a sensation at the time, demonstrated that some Catholic communities were managing to remain lively and well organized despite the anti-popery regime.

In fact, the establishment in Hammersmith was run in a manner comparable to that of the more traditional Ursuline convents in France. Although a secular community, the Ladies lived together in what the reporter likened to a 'private nunnery'; they observed a regular routine which kept as many aspects of traditional monastic life as possible under those circumstances. Moreover, they combined their religious observance with the teaching of boarders in their 'boarding school'. In addition, this report revealed that influential members of the recusant community resorted to the house in Hammersmith to ensure the Catholic education of their daughters, which indicates that the Ladies enjoyed strong links with their neighbours who, no doubt, had recourse to their chapels and the services of their priests regularly.

Nine years after this well-publicized raid, Frances Bedingfield took steps to reinforce the Institute's educational mission in the North of England, where Mary Ward had spent the last years of her life. In 1678, she attempted to re-found a school in Heworth Manor, where the foundress had lived and worked from 1642 until her death in 1645, but her efforts were defeated by the renewed wave of anti-Catholicism which swept the realm in the aftermath of the Popish Plot. Her high profile as a known Catholic led to her arrest and imprisonment in York Castle, where she remained for no less than seven years, until after the accession of the Catholic King James II in 1685. Yet, undeterred, Frances Bedingfield resumed her

---

[5] Frances Bedingfield left Hammersmith as soon as she had secured the foundation. The initial three sisters who worked there from 1669 were Mary Austin (no dates), Cecilia Cornwallis (1656-1723) and Elizabeth Henslow (no dates).

[6] BCA, 2, Hammersmith, A 8. Transcript of an article in the newspaper entitled 'The Domestic Intelligence or News both from City and Country', n°55, dated 13 January, 1679-80.

activities in the North as soon as she was released; in 1686, she resumed work on her project of a house in Yorkshire, which had been interrupted by her imprisonment.

Eventually, she bought a house outside Micklegate Bar, in York, where she established a school and a community of English Ladies.[7] This establishment, which is known today as the Bar Convent, quickly became a highly successful boarding school, which received no fewer than 190 girls in twenty-four years, between 1686 and 1710. However, like its Hammersmith predecessor, the York foundation appeared to concentrate its efforts on the continuance of a Catholic tradition where it was already thriving. While recusants, and particularly their daughters, were given a degree of support and a pastoral infrastructure which was without precedent, the Institute's members in York functioned as catechists and helpers, securing and affirming the faith rather than propagating it.

These activities appear rather timorous when contrasted with the ambitious claims of the 1621 *Institutum*, which described the company as a valiant missionary force of quasi-military resolve in its battle against Protestantism; could one attribute such reserve to the Ladies' fear of persecution? Although an obvious consideration, this was probably not strong enough to count as the main reason for such caution, especially since circumstances in England were, by that time, becoming less dangerous and the Institute benefited from the protection and support of the new king and of the dowager Queen Catharine. Indeed, the political situation had been more tolerable for some time and already, in 1683, the Duchess of York and wife of the future James II, Maria Beatrice, had extended her patronage to the English Ladies, bestowing upon them a large house in Whitefriars Street in London, to which the king subsequently made a yearly grant. The documents relating to this period of growth regard the re-opening of the poor schools in London as a complete triumph for the evangelical work of the English Ladies.[8] Three hundred Catholic children were allegedly received there from the very start, and the day schools were said to have attracted so many pupils that the house could not provide enough teachers to staff it.

This tendency towards the maintenance of the faith in the parishes rather than its active propagation was also a dominant trait in most urban Ursuline foundations in France. If we continue to consider the example of the Toulouse community as generally representative of the national picture, evidence indicates that the Ursulines' diplomacy and politics helped them to secure their position both with the municipality and the local clergy in the first few years of their settlement. The women's road to recognition was paved with negotiation and compromise, but their placatory attitude was key to their success. By endorsing gender definitions to pacify local clerical and secular authorities, they had gained the trust of both and

---

[7] M.C.E. Chambers, *Life*, vol. 2, p. 513.

[8] BCA, C1, the Cramlington papers, ms 2, f. 1.

were soon considered as one of the most renowned elements of the Catholic movement of recovery in the city.

In Toulouse, as elsewhere, the Ursulines were the ideal partners of the Church in its efforts to strengthen its links with local people. The clergy's struggle was twofold: on the one hand, the Huguenots (particularly in southern France) had proved determined to resist the Catholic effort, and missionaries found it difficult to make conversions in some regions such as Guyenne, for instance. Although the combat against existing Calvinism was believed to be beyond the concerns of the Ursulines, whose cloistered life rendered missionary activities apparently impossible, the sisters were precious allies in the Church's endeavours to stop it from spreading to wavering Catholic populations. Through the medium of their lessons, numerous young students were solidly educated in the principles of the faith and therefore better armed against what they perceived as the persuasive sophistry of Protestant preachers.

Like all main Ursuline houses in the first half of the century, the Toulouse foundation not only attracted high numbers of pupils, boarders and novices but also was extraordinarily active in starting branches outside the city.[9] In that time, Toulouse made 21 smaller foundations, mainly in Brive-la-Gaillarde (1608), Limoges (1620), Bayonne (1621), Béziers (1632), Auch (1623), Grenade (1626), Villefranche-de-Rouergue (1627) and Pamiers (1644). Of its first 50 members, twenty were, at various points, sent to rural neighbouring areas, either to start new congregations themselves or to assist others in the settlement of fledgling houses. Thus, Toulouse acted as the centre of a developing network, selecting its most able sisters in order to foster new establishments and supervise the quality of the schooling they provided.

As early as June 1608 (a mere four years after their settlement in Toulouse), the congregation founded its first rural branch. Under the patronage of M. Antoine de Lestang, *conseiller du Roi* and *Président en la cour du Parlement de Toulouse*, *sœurs* Catherine de Capdeville (1586-1653) and Jeanne Grisonne (no dates available) left Toulouse for Brive-la-Gaillarde, just as Marguerite de Vigier and Françoise de Blanchet had left Avignon less than four years earlier to found their congregation in Toulouse.[10] However, in the first few months of their settlement, Catherine de Capdeville and Jeanne Grisonne suffered from ill health, and adverse circumstances rendered them unable to hold any day classes or undertake any physical labours. It is a testimony to Toulouse's dedication to education that the community decided to continue with the project. As far as their superior Marguerite de Vigier was concerned, any branch of Ursulines which did not teach externs was, in effect, not serving its essential *raison d'être*. She

---

[9] Pierre Hélyot, *Dictionnaire des ordres religieux ou histoire des ordres monastiques, religieux et militaires et des congrégations séculières de l'un et de l'autre sexe, qui ont été établies jusqu'à présent* (Paris, 1848), vol. 3, p. 773.

[10] On the foundation of the establishment in Brive, see ADHG, 221H-3. The biography of Catherine de Capdeville can be found in R. P. Parayre, *Chronique*, part 2, pp. 375-93.

therefore replaced Capdeville with Marie de Liberos, who was reputedly one of the Order's most fervent teachers and catechizers.

We have seen that Marie de Liberos (*sœur* de la Trinité), symbolized the educational vocation of her congregation through her visions of a lighted torch when she entered the classroom.[11] In April 1609, she went to Brive-la-Gaillarde with Marie de Raymond (in religion *sœur* de l'Incarnation), and her dedication to teaching was as efficient there as it had been in Toulouse and attracted large numbers of Catholic pupils.[12] In this way, Marie de Liberos extended the Ursuline educational vocation of Toulouse, the provincial centre of Catholicism, to the less privileged town of Brive-la-Gaillarde. Her lessons allowed the local Catholic girls to benefit from both a secular education and a religious instruction they may not have otherwise received.

The impact of the school was such that families were soon sending their daughters to be boarders there; in addition, Catholic wives, mothers and widows became lay helpers of the community and several young women postulated to become Ursulines themselves. Parayre wrote that 'in very little time, her virtue and her doctrine were known everywhere, her day classes were very full and so were the boarders' and the applicants' quarters, for she attracted them from everywhere'.[13] Thus, the Brive establishment remained a healthy and successful house of *congrégées*, catering for local Catholics in an unenclosed form until November 1620. Then, in this year, Bertrande de Tatoûat (*sœur* de Saint Jérôme, d. 1670) was dispatched from Toulouse in order to supervise the establishment's transformation into a convent, to bring it in alignment with its mother house in Toulouse.[14]

However, despite its obvious educational drive, the establishment in Brive is not overtly depicted in documents as militant proselytizing campaign. First of all, it was not initiated by the Ursulines themselves, but commissioned by one of the members of the *Parlement* of Toulouse. Moreover, even when the Ursulines settled in Brive, there is no evidence that they went beyond their typical brief, catering for the Catholic population which already lived in town: their mission was more concerned with maintaining the faith than it was with propagating it in non-Catholic circles. In this new foundation, the Ursuline sisters can be construed more as the 'guardian angels' than as the 'amazons' of Catholicism.

There were countless examples like that of Brive-la-Gaillarde, and it was their dedication to simple teaching and catechizing which consolidated the Ursulines' position in the Church. Through such non-threatening yet highly effective activities, they gained the trust of the clergy and forged a solid reputation

---

[11] R. P. Parayre, *Chronique*, part 2, pp. 338-375.

[12] *Ibid.*, pp. 320-28.

[13] *Ibid.*, p. 370: 'dans bien peu de temps sa vertu et sa doctrine, fut répandue de tous côtés, la classe se trouva fort remplie, et la maison des pensionnaires ou postulantes; car elle les attirait de toutes parts.'

[14] ADHG, 221H-15, f. 230, and R. P. Parayre, *Chronique*, part 2, pp. 163-171.

as dependable keepers of the faith. This is illustrated in an episode which records how a young nun, having escaped from one of the city's other convents, asked an urgent audience with the archbishop.[15] She declared that her convent's confessor, a clergyman named Abadie, whose erudition and piety were held in high esteem around the city, had surreptitiously become a Calvinist. He had surreptitiously abused his position of trust as the nuns' religious director to pervert their minds, sow the seeds of doubt in many and even successfully convert the women who held the most influential posts in the community, including the *supérieure* and the *maîtresse des novices*. With the two most crucial offices in the house now held by *Huguenotes*, the entire convent was in peril. Novices in training were taught Calvinist doctrine, while the professed nuns who remained Catholic felt intimidated by their Protestant *supérieure*; factions were forming, causing discord in the cloister. The crisis was all the more acute since one of the *sœurs portières* had also been converted, thus jeopardizing the safety of the entire convent by putting its enclosure at stake and scandal was sure to ensue.

Faced with this emergency, archbishop Charles de Montchal (1628-1651) resolved to turn to the establishment of Ursulines on the Rue des Trois Rois Vieux. On 25 January 1647, he asked their superior, *mère* de Saint Augustin,[16] to send three of her sisters to manage the government of the endangered convent and undertake its reform. She chose Isabeau de Gramont, *sœur* Sainte Croix de Bartelemi,[17] to act as the convent's new *supérieure*; to help her, she appointed Marie de Madron (*sœur* de l'Annonciation)[18] as *portière* and Françoise de Bertier (*sœur* de l'Assomption)[19] as *maîtresse des novices*. The superior of the 'perverted' convent, her *portière* and her *maîtresse des novices* were sent to stay with the Ursulines. Thus, while the three Ursuline sisters were reforming the endangered establishment and ensuring its return to good order, the main three Protestant nuns were staying at the Rue des Trois Rois Vieux where the sisters endeavoured to win them back to the Catholic faith.

The decision to use Ursulines to re-establish doctrine and order in a convent whose spirituality had been influenced by Calvinism was proof of the degree of trust the archbishop bestowed upon them as teachers of doctrine. It illustrated the sense of harmony that united the Toulousain Ursuline community and the local episcopate who considered their faith strong enough not to be weakened when faced with Protestant doctrine. In this case, the Toulouse community was commanded by its male superiors to exceed its usual role of educators of local youth. The sisters had in effect been promoted to the rank of

---

[15] *Ibid.*, part 1, pp. 144-145. Unfortunately, neither the runaway nun nor her conventual community is named. See also M. C. Gueudré, *Histoire de l'ordre des Ursulines,* vol. 2, pp. 557-58.

[16] ADHG, 221H-15, f. 197, Catherine de Roquelaure, born in 1601.

[17] *Ibid.*, f. 221, Isabeau de Gramont was born in 1597 and entered the Ursulines in 1616.

[18] *Ibid.*, f. 208, Marie de Madron, born in 1597; she entered the house in 1616.

[19] *Ibid.*, f. 28. Françoise de Bertier, born in 1610, entered the establishment in 1626.

reformers, far beyond the typical roles of female communities within the Catholic Church.

However, it is worth underlining the fact that the sisters were vested with this new role only within the carefully controlled environment of the convent. Both communities in this instance were subject to the supervision of episcopal authorities and their progress could be monitored at any given time by the local ordinary. Therefore, though symptomatic of the high degree of trust which linked the community to the male Church authorities, this incident cannot be used to identify the Ursulines of Toulouse as decision-making proselytizers since, despite being assigned the reform of a community and the conversion of Protestants back to the Catholic faith, the Ursulines were never left to their own devices in the process. Nor did they enjoy complete freedom of initiative; throughout, they acted in conformity with the roles they had been given by archbishop Montchal. Far from being independent 'amazons', the Ursulines continued to fit within the approved sphere of female activity in the Church.

In a somewhat similar vein, but showing more individual enterprise, Catherine Canterel (in religion *sœur* de Saint Augustin) saved her convent of Amiens from Calvinism when, as superior, she became suspicious of the good character of their new spiritual director. Despite this clergyman's excellent reputation in the town where he was reportedly 'perceived as an angel', a learned and devout paragon of virtue, she exposed him as one who had 'betrayed his faith and his character to become a minister of the false religion'.[20] Thanks to her vigilance, Catherine Canterel kept her community safe from the 'corruption' of Protestantism and, by extension, prevented the endemic propagation of the new doctrine to its pupils. This incident demonstrates that Ursuline sisters could be depended on in matters concerned with the preserving of the faith.

However, there was a more decidedly missionary trend to Catherine Canterel's spirituality. Before the episode of the Protestant confessor, she had always relied on the Jesuits to provide the spiritual direction of her *consœurs*. This personal preference, she noted, was vindicated in the aftermath of the incident, when she resolved not to accept any confessors other than those belonging to the Society of Jesus, upon which she looked as the height of Catholic perfection. Canterel's links with the Jesuits were extremely strong, and she maintained a particularly fruitful spiritual relationship with fathers Brebœuf, Le Jeune, Ragenau and de Caen, all high profile missionaries in Canada.[21] Her interest in the mission to convert the Canadian Indians, then commonly called the '*sauvages*', continued throughout her life and, though she never physically left her convent, she spiritually embraced a world-wide, missionary ideal.

---

[20] MDPU, *Les Chroniques de l'ordre des Ursulines*, part 3, p. 418: 'cet homme trahit sa foi et son caractère pour se faire ministre de la fausse religion'.
[21] *Ibid.*, p. 421.

Transgressing the boundaries of gender norms: female missionaries

Sœur de Saint-Augustin was not the only one to feel an affinity with missionary ventures; although enclosure prevented the Ursulines from travelling freely across continents unless specifically mandated to do so by their bishops, they appear to have retained a keen interest in the Christianization of far-away lands. The French colonization of Canada presented missionaries with unparalleled opportunities to catechize and convert natives; the sheer number of Ursulines who put their names forward to be delegated to the Canadian enterprise testified to the Order's active outlook: the teaching nuns were truly seeing themselves as an integral part of the wide-ranging movement of the Catholic mission. Their desire to be actively involved was such that in 1635 Paul Le Jeune, the Jesuit Superior in Quebec, confessed to being amazed at how many nuns had appealed to him to be sent overseas.[22]

In effect, the Ursuline vocation and its institutional expression were ideally suited to such a mission, since they allowed interaction with girls and undertook both secular and religious instruction. The most famous Ursuline missionary is of course Marie Guyart (1599-1672), in religion Marie de l'Incarnation, the foundress of the Ursuline movement in Quebec.[23] She and her two companions enjoyed privileged relations with the Jesuits, and they were given the supervision of six young native girls as soon as they arrived in 1639. Immediately, Marie de l'Incarnation set about the instruction and the conversion of local girls and women; she was purposeful and methodical and there was very little to differentiate her from male missionaries in her activities. True to the spirit of post-Tridentine evangelization, she learned Algonkin and Huron before turning her attention to Iroquois. She intended to communicate with this tribe, the fiercest adversary of French settlers and, having finished writing her Algonkin dictionary, she wrote another in Iroquois, as well as a catechism in that language.[24]

In Canada, where religious enclosure was by necessity greatly relaxed, Marie de l'Incarnation and her *consœurs* benefited from a degree of geographical mobility and organizational freedom which was impossible in their homeland. In the face of adversity, they turned their hand to all that was required, thereby prioritizing human need over the strict observance of canonical law for female religious. There were numerous instances when their activities were more akin to

---

[22] Reuben Gold Thwaites (ed.), *The Jesuit Relations and Allied Documents*, 73 vols. (Cleveland, Ohio, 1896-1901), vol. 6, p. 142.

[23] See Dom Guy Marie Oury, *Marie de l'Incarnation 1599-1672* (Tours, 1973). Also Roger Paul Gilbert, *Marie Guyart, folie de Dieu: récit témoignage* (Montréal, 2003); Françoise Deroy-Pineau (ed.), *Marie Guyart de l'Incarnation: un destin transocéanique, Tours 1599-Québec 1672* (Paris, 2000).

[24] Charles Sainte-Foi, *Vies des premières Ursulines de France tirées des chroniques de l'ordre* (Paris, 1856), pp.163-222.

public preaching than they were to private teaching, and this caused recurring friction between the women and some of their local clergy.

When she died, Marie de l'Incarnation had written her autobiography, which was later published by her son, Claude Martin. Martin was acutely aware of the pioneering nature of his mother's activities in the mission and tried to justify them by somewhat downplaying their audacity: he drew a clear distinction between preaching and teaching and insisted that his mother's work should be viewed as the latter. Whereas priests were true apostles, he claimed, women were merely 'apostolic women', the guardian angels of the faith, helpers moved by the spirit of the mission as far as their sex permitted. As Lierheimer argued so well, 'by downplaying the apostolic actions of Marie de l'Incarnation and highlighting her apostolic spirit, Martin could argue that she did not attempt to appropriate a role the church reserved for men'.[25]

Yet, such a degree of involvement in the Canadian mission was to remain exceptional, and most Ursulines were denied any contribution other than the one which they could offer from the shelter of their French cloisters. Indeed, Quebec was the theatre of constant tensions between female zeal and official reluctance. The Church and the state were both concerned for the safety of nuns in an hostile country where wilderness, the elements and violent raids from native tribes contributed to the fragile state of all new settlements. The achievements of extraordinary women such as Marie de l'Incarnation remained but a distant dream, an aspiration at the most, for the teaching nuns in the old world. Yet this attraction for missionary work undertaken outside the walls of convents continued to be a feature of the Ursuline apostolic spirit even into the eighteenth century. In Toulouse, a long letter addressed to *sœur* Hyacinthe in 1740 demonstrates the community's links with the missionary efforts in the East,[26] and although most of the sisters were not destined to lead a life of active conversion of 'heretics' and 'savages', this did not necessarily imply that their interests never transcended the traditional gender-definitions which limited their work to private, unassuming female teaching.

Examples abound of sisters who would have wished to become part of this much more missionary movement. In Lisieux, Marie Godebit, in religion *sœur* de Sainte Magdelaine, was a fervent supporter of the conversion of Canada; this personal attachment to the mission in foreign lands was construed as a defining trait of her character, so much so that it found its way into her obituary, where it was reported that 'her zeal for the salvation of souls drove her to offer her prayers

---

[25] Linda Lierheimer, 'Preaching or Teaching? Defining the Ursuline Mission in Seventeenth-Century France', in Beverly Mayne Kienze and Pamela J. Walker (eds.), W*omen Preachers and Prophets through Two Millennia of Christianity* (London, 1998), p. 220.

[26] *Relation de la conquête du Mogol par Thamas-Koulikan, et de la façon de vivre des dames Mahométanes; écrite par un missionaire francais qui est dans le royaume de Bengale, à Mad. de S. Hyacinthe, religieuse Ursuline à Toulouse* (Toulouse, 1740).

for the conversion of Canada, begging God to give strength and efficiency to the words of those who work for the salvation of these poor peoples'.[27] Godebit found much pleasure in reading news of the progress of the Canadian missionaries and actively sought to procure as many accounts as she could. One of her *consœurs* in Evreux, Elizabeth Turgis (in religion *sœur* de Saint Michel) volunteered to be part of the Ursuline effort in New France; however, after some deliberations, she was informed that the French settlements there already counted enough religious women and that the rough conditions of that country did not, as yet, allow for the arrival of others. Disappointed, Turgis did not lose her missionary impetus but tried to view her lessons with the day pupils as her own downscaled mission; she called the *externat 'son cher petit Canada'* and likened the girls in her classes to the *'petits sauvageons'* across the Atlantic.[28]

If, for most sisters, the far-away missions were to remain inaccessible, they could nevertheless apply a proselytizing spirit to their work in France. The Ursuline contribution to the Counter-Reformation, therefore, went further than the simple maintenance of the faith where it was already present: it triggered the conversions of many. Their success was such that their eulogist Parayre termed them the 'amazons of Christianity'.[29] Elizabeth Turgis is representative of many of her *consœurs* who, like herself, felt passionately about the conversion of non-Christians.

An even clearer missionary impulse surfaces in the papers of the Ursuline branches which bloomed some distance away from the larger cities in which the influence of the bishop was more immediately felt. Documents abound that indicate a surge of activity on the part of some individual sisters, usually in establishments located in more rural areas of the country, further from the direct influence of the episcopate. Some had ambitious agenda which seemed surprising for the representatives of an enclosed order. Their object was the re-Catholicization of those who had left the Church and the conversion of Protestants. This type of active evangelization can be illustrated by the branch founded in June 1644 by the Toulouse house in the smaller town of Pamiers, which had become a Huguenot stronghold in the Wars of Religion. Anne Dubois (1604-1670), in religion *sœur* de la Visitation,[30] and Claire Durdes (died 1663), in religion *sœur* de Saint François,[31] were sent to Pamiers to start a convent and a school of Ursulines there in 1644.

---

[27] BA, ms 4990-56 - Lisieux, 2 May 1686: 'Son zèle pour le salut des âmes la portait à offrir ses prières pour la conversion du Canada, demandant instamment à Dieu qu'il donna force et efficace aux paroles des personnes qui travaillent au salut de ces pauvres peuples.'

[28] MDPU, *Les Chroniques de l'ordre des Ursulines*, part 3, pp. 288-90.

[29] R. P. Parayre, *Chronique*, part 2, p. 140.

[30] *Ibid.*, part 3, pp. 79-165.

[31] *Ibid.*, pp. 2-16.

The choice of these two sisters as the founders of a new community in itself testified to the mother house's desire to ensure high standards in its fledgling branches. Indeed, Anne Dubois was well known for her intense spiritual life and for the inspiring qualities of her piety. Claire Durdes, in contrast, was renowned for her erudition, her familiarity with both the Scriptures in Latin and the works of St Augustine, and above all her dedication to the duties of the classroom. In the religious establishment in the parliamentary city, she had been *maîtresse des pensionnaires* and *maîtresse des novices*. However, she also entertained relations with the outside: she was appointed to the *parloir* to help secular women in their preparations for general confession. Later, she acted as the supervisor of the lay *Congrégation des Dames de Sainte Ursule*, the secular counterpart of the convent, undertaking of the apostolic works the enclosed sisters could no longer see to; she met these women on a weekly basis at the church grill. In this way, Dubois embodied the contemplative side of the Ursuline essence, while Durdes personified its teaching element: the fact that they were chosen as a pair to found the house in Pamiers demonstrated Toulouse's clear determination to perpetuate its dual vocation at the highest level.

The initial steps of the creation of this new Ursuline establishment did not promise much in the way of a missionary impulse where the women would progress beyond their allocated roles. In fact, restrictive hierarchical formalism made the procedure painfully bureaucratic; whereas new foundations urgently needed the help of experienced supervisors and teachers, the procedure of transferring nuns from one congregation to another was a complex and lengthy affair which required a license from the archbishop or the vicar general. Official authorizations bore testimony to the Catholic Church's unease with the mobility of nuns; after a brief appreciation of the teachers' work, they pointedly enjoined them to respect their claustration and spend as little time as necessary out of doors. This entire process was to be scrupulously observed in reverse when the sisters wished to return to the mother-house. Events at Pamiers illustrate Archbishop Charles de Montchal's reservations over the movement of the sisters:

> We allowed you to leave your convent in this city [of Toulouse] in order to found a house of your Order in the town of Pamiers. God having blessed your work there, you have shown the desire to come back and received the appropriate license from Monseigneur the Bishop of Pamiers. [...] Therefore, we now allow you to return to the college of St Ursula of this town [...] taking great care not to wander elsewhere and to return with all the decency and modesty befitting your profession.[32]

---

[32] ADHG, 221H-15, f. 78. Licence written on 13 January 1651: 'Dieu ayant donné bénédiction à votre travail [...] à l'établissement du collège de votre ordre dans la ville de Pamiers pour lequel nous vous avions permis de sortir de celui de cette ville, et nous ayant témoigné le désir que vous avez d'y retourner et fait savoir que vous en avez reçu la licence

Despite the obvious need of a Catholic school to educate the local youth, allowing a nun to go from one convent to another remained a slow and inefficient process. Such difficulties illustrate the hardships experienced by a female Order trying to combine the observance of the conservative Tridentine laws and its active work in support of the missionary offensive urged by the same Council.

The new house was intended to give the existing Catholic female population of Pamiers the benefit of Ursuline education, as well as providing a focal point for female piety in general.[33] Wives and mothers could use their chapel, whilst young girls had the opportunity to enter their novitiate or simply to benefit from their teaching. However, Claire Durdes's personal zeal led her to transcend her duties as an Ursuline pedagogue and take on a role which far exceeded the boundaries of the traditional feminine sphere. As the superior in Pamiers, she imprinted her personality on the work undertaken at her house: her weekday classes were soon full, and the lessons in Catholic doctrine which she gave on Sundays and Holy Days were so well attended that she decided to split the pupils into two groups, each with its own teacher, one taking the youngest girls whilst another undertook the instruction of their elder sisters. Moreover, Claire Durdes's catechism attracted so many women that, to avoid incurring the censure which was bound to meet her exhortations, she procured a special licence, permitting her to instruct the women of the town. This document expressly allowed listeners to gather in the lower choir of the church in order to hear her speeches, which an unusually supportive Church deemed fruitful enough to be worthy of protection.[34]

When she instructed the local people at her convent grill in this way, Claire Durdes blurred the boundaries between private and public speech; although she was still working within the conventual enclosure, her teaching at the grill addressed a much more varied audience than the usual pupils attending her classes and instantly filtered to the outside world, thereby transferring her lessons into the public domain. Durdes was, in effect, a preacher in Pamiers. According to Parayre, she catechized up to 80 women at a time, who were joined by numerous local men; soon her lessons became more popular than those of Père de Saint Denis, who had been appointed by the local bishop to teach Catholic doctrine. This may have been a subject of embarrassment, even of displeasure, for the local episcopate, who might have considered that Durdes was usurping roles which were essentially male. Indeed, she was flouting both the Pauline prohibition to teach in public (I Tim. 2:12) and the Tridentine interdiction on preaching. Thus, she was stretching the Ursuline vocation to its limits and often verged on what the Church

---

de Monseigneur l'Évêque de Pamiers [...] nous vous avons permis et permettons par ces présentes [...] de revenir au collège de Ste Ursule de cette ville [...] sans vous divertir ailleurs et avec la décence et modestie convenable à votre profession.'
[33] ADGH, 221H-15, f. 183.
[34] R. P. Parayre, *Chronique*, part 3, p. 15.

may have construed as objectionable practices, had they not, in practice, been confined within the limits of the house's enclosure and undertaken under the protection of an episcopal licence.

What was even more daring was that Claire Durdes did not merely maintain the faith of willing Catholic listeners but also worked towards the conversion of non-Catholics. When in Toulouse, she had already converted eight 'debauched' women who all became nuns as a result of her good counsel; in Pamiers, she converted four young *Huguenotes* who later became Ursulines themselves.[35] Her individual success in proselytizing was a vital feature of the Ursulines' mission in the erstwhile pronouncedly Protestant rural region surrounding the city.

Obviously, the congregation of Toulouse was not alone in producing sisters with such active missionary spirit: evidence of Ursulines operating the conversions of Protestant and deviant women abound. Antoinette Micolon (*sœur* Colombe du Saint Esprit) opened a school of *congrégées* in 1614, in Ambert; in the early stages of her work, she and her *consœurs* were not yet bound by enclosure and were able to interact with the local people, to whom they taught the basics of the Catholic doctrine. From the beginning, Antoinette Micolon transgressed the boundaries of private female teaching when, on Sundays, she addressed gatherings of up to 60 women in the local poultry yard. She was quite obviously speaking in public, thereby disobeying that most important of Pauline injunctions; moreover, she was following the practice of the male missionaries by choosing to speak to these simple women in their local dialect, Auvergnat. Not only did she teach large groups of women in a public place with all the gusto of a trained orator, she also stood on a chair in order to be heard more clearly. This method was expedient and efficient: according to her memoirs, the women were avid learners and were rapidly changed from ignorant imbeciles into devout women, with an adequate knowledge of the Catholic doctrine. The entire town seemed willing to reform, many women became Ursulines themselves; in the wake of such devout revival, a new monastery of the Récollets was opened. Micolon had definitely moved outside the female sphere of private domesticity and usurped all the distinctive attributes of a preacher.[36]

The chronicles and documents of nearly every congregation in France are punctuated with examples of Ursuline teachers taking their brief further than was intended in the Bulls which defined them as enclosed nuns. In Nevers, Angèle d'Anvantois (in religion *sœur* de Sainte Croix) gained a reputation for making converts through her powers of persuasion; the *Chroniques* highlight her success in what Mère de Pommereu termed 'hazardous enterprises for one of her sex and age'.[37] D'Avantois's missionary spirit was always a strong motive force in her life.

---

[35] *Ibid.*, p. 17.

[36] Henri Pourrat (ed.), *Mémoires de la Mère Micolon*, pp. 98-100.

[37] *Ibid.*, part 3, p. 234: 'des entreprises hasardeuses à son sexe et à son âge'.

Indeed, even before she had decided upon entering religion, the young woman had attached her services to syphilitic prostitutes whose health and salvation had been jeopardized by their trade, and brought them back to God before they died.

In Poitiers, Marguerite Poisson (in religion *sœur* du Saint Sacrement) struggled to fill her boarding school but had much more success with the day students, who came to her in large numbers. The tutor valued these classes even more highly than those of the more privileged boarders, since she saw them as an opportunity to allow her teachings to reach beyond the convent into the world. Since most day pupils discussed their lessons with their families when they returned home, the piety of the convent was likely to receive a hearing even in poorer families thanks to the open classes. One such day girl is said to have sown the seeds of doubt in her Protestant grandmother, which led eventually to her conversion to Catholicism. Marguerite Poisson also converted a young *Huguenote* who, despite her family's outrage, entered the Ursuline community and convinced another five Protestant girls to follow in her wake. She next applied her efforts to a lady of notorious ill repute, whose atheism was allied to her all-consuming addiction to 'infamous vice'; in this case, however, although the woman abandoned her ways and entered the Ursuline house in Angers, the conversion was only a partial success, since her virtue was soon found to be tainted and she was condemned to a prison term in another convent of the Order.[38]

Others were successful public speakers: Perette de Bermond, one of the founding stones of the Ursuline edifice in France, established a small congregation in Moulins, in 1616. There, she began to teach the catechism on Sundays and feast days in the chapel where, each week, a growing numbers of people of both sexes and various social conditions gathered to hear her. Her success was such that seats were reserved in advance and that latecomers had to be turned away, as if for popular sermons or for a public spectacle. However, her story is one which encountered the censorship which Claire Durdes and Antoinette Micolon had escaped: in 1623, the public nature of her lessons became too uncomfortably close to that of preachers and the male superiors of her establishment prohibited the continuation of such an unfeminine practice.[39]

Yet, in the eyes of the Church, the conversion of Calvinists or deviant characters was not the responsibility of an Ursuline sister; one incident related in the Toulousain papers highlights the importance of conforming with seventeenth-century gender norms and provides an example of what Rapley described as men's 'constant state of vigilance, always alert to the other sex's efforts at usurpation'.[40] Françoise de Rabonite once again illustrates this point. As one of the initial members of the community (which she had joined in 1607), her later years as an

---

[38] *Ibid.*, pp. 471-73.
[39] MDPU, *Les Chroniques de l'ordre des Ursulines*, part 2, p. 173.
[40] Elizabeth Rapley, *The Dévotes*. p. 3.

Ursuline demonstrate the popular reserve and the general mistrust towards women who undertook remarkable and unusual work. In 1632, she was sent to become the *supérieure* of the Ursuline house in the Protestant town of Béziers, about 105 miles to the south east of Toulouse. There, she taught Catholic doctrine just as any sister would, but crucially, she chose not to limit her evangelizing to young girls or even to women of good repute. Parayre wrote of the 'general moral reform' she engineered in the town; on the one hand, Rabonite made it her particular brief to galvanize the religious zeal of polite society but on the other hand she also strove to win back the souls of women who were deemed lost to the faith. Her attempts to reform the whole town were far-reaching and knew no social bounds, touching men and women, the rich and the poor, the literate and the illiterate.

This Ursuline deliberately set out to become publicly known through her admonitions in order to attract as many people as possible to her grill, where she interacted with Protestants and even with well-known prostitutes, and where she was successful in converting some of them to the Catholic faith.[41] By gaining a public voice, she presented an unusual profile which was in sharp contrast with that of the humble and silent nun; Rabonite's aim was to get the town talking about her, she did not seem to shrink from becoming some sort of local curiosity since, as she saw it, this kind of notoriety incited many to come and hear her speak. She also had regular discussions with the local clergy, during which she advised them. The roles were all but reversed when this nun, in effect, became the spiritual director of priests in all but name. However, as soon as she outgrew the gender-defined limits of her vocation by undertaking a systematic mission of conversion in the public arena, Françoise de Rabonite was making enemies.

On the one hand, when she tried to win back *Huguenotes*, she automatically antagonized the rest of the considerable population of Protestants in Béziers. On the other hand, she also irritated many Catholics when she exceeded the limits of a typically Ursuline brief by trying to reclaim prostitutes. These were tasks for male priests and a woman was not trusted to undertake them, since her own constancy was perceived to be endangered by meddling with women of little virtue. Her outreach was also impinging upon the public sphere in a way which was not appropriate for a religious woman; even spatially, this was symbolized in the fact that this proselytizer stood at the *grille* of her house, right on the fringe of its enclosure and in effect transgressing its boundaries by addressing the outside. Thus, Françoise de Rabonite had not only transgressed her Ursuline brief, but she had also taken on the preaching attributes of a priest.

The opinion in Béziers was that she had overstepped the mark by undertaking the difficult and dangerous task of conversion, instead of focusing on the more feminine task of educating girls. Her success demonstrated a certain power of persuasion, a skill of militant eloquence which far outgrew the Tridentine definitions of female teaching and catechesis; this was interpreted as a blatant lack

---

[41] R. P. Parayre, *Chronique,* part 2, pp. 103-4.

of modesty, as a defiant display of autonomy and will which flouted all early modern ideals of female virtue. It is therefore not surprising that such a character, who had found her public voice and dared to address the world directly, should have been condemned as sexually incontinent: soon, Françoise de Rabonite became the object of local calumny. It began with accusations of a moral nature, questioning her relationship with one of the priests with whom she had regular contact; her reputation and her virtue were marred. Allegations about her sexual licentiousness derived directly from the public nature of her activities: it was as if the transgression of spatial boundaries had come to symbolize the transgression of moral codes. A woman whose message was public was by extension a public woman; the spatial and social mobility of her perceived preaching evoked her frivolity and put into question both her honesty and her humility. The freedom and the fluidity of her ministry represented the looseness of her morals, the insubordination of her mind and the perversion of her soul. In time, her detractors accused her of being *'une illuminée'* and even a witch.[42] Much saddened by this criticism, she travelled back to Toulouse where in 1653 she returned to enclosure and observed a lifestyle more consistent with the Tridentine idea of female religious life; she died there eight months later.

The Ursulines found themselves at the core of an unresolved dilemma in the Catholic mission. On the issue of female teaching and the female voice in the Church, Ursulines such as Marie de l'Incarnation, Antoinette Micolon or Françoise Rabonite occupied a precarious position. As helpers in the evangelical drive of male missionaries, their educational vocation was both respected and valued. Yet, when their teaching and catechizing resembled that of priests, the Ursulines became the very embodiment of the diminishing divide between teachers and preachers. If proselytizers neglected to signal their positions clearly, either by obtaining a licence or by defining their activities as domestic, their zeal inexorably incurred censure. In this way, somewhat paradoxically, the restrictions of the cloister served the catechizing purposes of the Ursulines, whose missionary spirit found an unlikely ally in monastic observance: enclosure itself.

Indeed, claustration granted propriety and episcopal support to a kind of public catechesis which would otherwise have met with immediate condemnation. The Ursuline compromise was successful because it allowed sisters to interact with seculars without however venturing outside their monastic enclosure. Working from within their walls (which embodied the moral prescriptions of the age towards women), most Ursulines simply allowed their message to cross over to the world via the intermediary of their pupils. In doing so, they were obeying the papal Bulls which ordered them to teach day girls: they were in no way exceeding their brief and they were perceived as dutiful, humble teaching nuns. In this context, they were allowed to achieve the mass education and catechization of girls on a scale which had never been possible before. On the other hand, when

---

[42] *Ibid*, p. 114

individual members of some communities took it upon themselves to enlarge their brief in order to address issues of public ministry and preaching, they faced universal condemnation: a public voice was the mark of a woman who did not know her place, the sign of one who did not respect rules. The free flow of a verbal message became amalgamated with moral looseness, a sign of incontinence and unruliness. In this way, the activities of Pamiers and Béziers confirm Lierheimer's findings about the complex relationships between enclosure and freedom and indicate that the cloister, though restrictive in some respects, in fact allowed the expansion of the Ursuline educational apostolate.[43]

The difficulties emerging from such a normative moral scale did not apply to English recusant women to the same degree. In comparison with the organized and rather orthodox religious enterprise of *dévotes* such as the French Ursulines, the very nature of English recusancy did not allow for the strict allocations of differentiated roles between men and women. From the start of the English mission, Catholic priests working its field had come to depend largely on recusant women who played crucial parts as the organizers of Catholic networks. The example of Dorothy Lawson (1580-1632) of St Anthony's, near Newcastle-upon-Tyne, illustrates the degree to which the traditional divide between lay and religious, male and female, was often over-ridden in England. Lawson worked in the English mission with her confessor, the Jesuit William Palmes (c. 1595-1670), who wrote her biography in 1646. Despite being a renowned recusant, she managed to maintain an active Catholic centre under her roof. She used her personal high profile as a nonconformist to throw spies off the scent: although she harboured priests in her own house, she pretended to go out to Mass elsewhere and, by drawing the spies' attention to her mysterious journeys, masked the presence of priests working under their very noses.[44]

William Palmes described her as a lay proselytizer, whose house was at the hub of a buoyant missionary network and without whom operations would have collapsed altogether. Dorothy Lawson's role went further than that of the traditional recusant housewife: in addition to harbouring priests, helping her Catholic neighbours and catechizing her household, she became an alternative priest. On occasion, Palmes confessed, she made him almost redundant. Her expertise at midwifery allowed her to fulfil roles which were extremely close to those of priests, providing her neighbours with much valued moral support and physical protection during the frightening times of childbirth, using relics and making cordials to alleviate their suffering. In the not uncommon cases of emergency when the infant's life was in danger, she performed some baptisms

---

[43] Linda Lierheimer, 'Female Eloquence and Maternal Ministry', p. 287.
[44] Palmes, William, *Life of Mrs Dorothy Lawson of St Anthony's near Newcastle-upon-Tyne, in Northumberland,* ed. by G.B. Richardson (Newcastle-upon-Tyne, 1855).

herself and helped those mothers who, on their deathbeds, wished to become reconciled with the Catholic faith.

Vignettes such of this one bear much relevance to the history of the members of Mary Ward's Institute, since these women had grown up in the same English context, where women and their priests were closely linked by a relationship of interdependence. They had become habituated to a set of circumstances in which common sense and expediency prevailed over canonical prescriptions; the urgency of their situation shaped their vision of woman's role in the mission in a manner which was bound to be poles apart from that of the southern Curia in Rome. In England, the complementary nature of the work undertaken by recusant women on the one hand, and by the missionary priests on the other, contributed to the blurring of traditional roles. Women would often reconcile others to the Catholic faith and prepare them to be received into the Church and, although they could not confer the sacraments themselves, they effectively brought about the conversions which could then be made official when a priest became available. According to her English biography, Mary Ward's work had become so notorious in effecting such conversions that it attracted the archbishop of Canterbury's attention. As a consequence, a search warrant was issued for her capture, accompanied by a physical description of her person. The *Briefe Relation* recounted how:

> there was information given to NN: then Bishop of
> Canterbury, of the much evil (as they termed it) she and hers
> did, in so much as a particular search was appointed for her,
> and a precise description of her person set forth, and to make
> the better appear the enormity of her crime, the Bishop said
> she did more hurt than six Jesuits.[45]

Quite naturally, the Institute in England embarked on more than works of a pastoral nature: it followed a vocation which had a missionary trend running at its very core. The education of the daughters of established Catholic families represented one aspect only of the Institute's intended project, which was also strongly inclined towards the conversion of Protestants, thereby transcending the accepted sphere of feminine teaching. The 1616 *Ratio Instituti* defined the Institute's vocation as an international one, since Ward's ideal was essentially to transform the English mission into one which catered for women in the same way as it did for men, and to enable recusant women to organize efficient networks of female catechizers. It was in order to do so that the Institute adopted the working methods initiated by male agents and had colleges on the Continent but also pockets of missionary action on English soil. Expert Henriette Peters has argued that the usual straightforwardness of the text faltered with regard to the Institute's

---

[45] BCA, B12, *Briefe Relation*, f. 21. This was in the year 1618, and the archbishop of Canterbury was George Abbot (1611-1633).

activities in the English mission, as though trying to dissimulate activities which were likely to arouse hostility. However, it is hard to discern any feat of casuistry in *Ratio Instituti*.[46] One of the last paragraphs defined the Institute's endeavours in the English mission in a manner which cannot be interpreted as ambiguous:

> Others of our Society [...] are likewise labouring in England in conjunction with us [...] and send here noble young virgins to be educated, and others of more mature years to be prepared for holy religion, while they save others from the jaws of the imminent death of heresy and vice.[47]

This extract used the word 'Society' for the first time, a choice of vocabulary which could not be accidental. It was intended to promote the foundress's vocation to 'Take the Same of the Society' and informed Paul V about the way in which the Institute functioned in 1616. Houses of English Ladies on the Continent received girls who travelled from England, either to complete their Catholic education under their tutelage or to be prepared for entering existing convents. These English girls were recruited and assisted in their travelling abroad by members of the Institute who lived in England for this purpose. The text even hinted that, far from limiting themselves to the consolidation of the faith, the Ladies who worked in England often laboured actively for the conversion of Protestant women.

In the *Ratio Instituti*, the paragraphs concerning England were strategically placed to introduce and to conclude the Plan, in a position to remain at the forefront of the reader's mind. Had it been the author's intention, as Henriette Peters argued, not to draw attention to the Institute's work in England, these paragraphs would have been inserted towards the middle section of the text, where they would appear less conspicuous.[48] Thus, as early as 1616, the *Ratio* was attempting to present the papal authorities with a clear picture of Ward's vocation, which proposed nothing less than to establish a female Institute on the model of the Society of Jesus, taking on the same type of missionary activities.

This active proselytizing was further vindicated and emphasized in Mary Ward's introduction to her 1621 *Institutum*, in which the English Ladies were defined as 'soldiers of God', working alongside male missionaries for the conversion of Protestant England. Ward's military imagery, borrowed directly from the Jesuits, expressed the brand of militancy she envisaged as an essential part of her work:

---

[46] Peters, *Mary Ward*, p. 200; the author finds the text an 'almost embarrassed exposé of their effectiveness in England' and believes the paragraph regarding England to be 'almost as an appendage, as it were'.

[47] BCA, B18, *Ratio Instituti*, f. 17.

[48] The text is analyzed in Peters, *Mary Ward*, pp. 199-203.

> Whoever wishes to serve beneath the banner of the cross as a
> soldier of God in our Society, [...] is a member of a Society
> founded primarily for this purpose: to strive for the defence
> and propagation of the faith and for the progress of souls in
> Christian life and doctrine, leading them back from heresy
> and evil ways to the faith, to a Christian manner of life.[49]

The text then proceeded to remind postulants that life in the Institute would be
arduous, taxing their physical and spiritual resources to their limits; the military
metaphor continued, portraying the Ladies as soldiers in a battle, perhaps, even, on
a crusade: 'After they have enlisted through the inspiration of the Lord in the
militia of Jesus Christ, they ought to be prompt in carrying out this obligation
which is so great, being girded for battle day and night.'[50] All in all, Mary Ward's
Institute had in mind a much wider scope of action than that usually attributed to
women, even in the circumstances of the English mission.

The *Briefe Relation* explained that when she was in England, Ward
herself met the poor people in the streets of London under cover and attempted to
win them back to the Catholic Church:

> Our dearest Mother employed herself, sometimes in her own
> clothes, using sometimes familiar conversation, other times
> authority amongst the common and poor sort. [She] would
> put them in doubt of their own error and then lay they light
> before them [...]. God so blessed these her endeavours, as
> many, and persons of note, both for the quality of their birth
> and malice and perverseness of their Heresy were
> converted.[51]

Running parallel to the organized houses in London and later in the North, even
smaller temporary cells allowed the Institute to penetrate the fabric of English
society in a more discreet and covert way. In areas where a school was not
practical or simply too dangerous, some members of the Institute worked from
inside the homes of supporting recusant households, often as single, anonymous
individuals. In a manner similar to that of the missionary priests, an English Lady
would typically live with a family, under the guise of a member of the household.
The narrative of Sister Dorothea, of whom we know nothing except that she was
one of the lay members working in England, provides a vivid insight into this type
of work. In her report, Sister Dorothea described her activities near Ipswich, in
Suffolk, and revealed how she not only catered for existing recusants, but also
busied herself working towards the conversion of Protestants.

---

[49] BCA, B18, *Institutum*, f. 19.
[50] *Ibid.*, f. 23.
[51] BCA, B12, *Briefe Relation*, f. 20.

In the early 1620s, Sister Dorothea established a small centre under the protection of the Catholic Lady Timperley of Hintlesham Hall, near Ipswich, who was the only person to know her real identity. She worked under cover, teaching the children of local Catholic families while also helping adult recusants with pastoral work:

> I dare not keep schools publicly [...] but I teach or instruct children in the houses of parents, which I find to be a very good way, and by that occasion I get acquaintance, and so gaining first the affections of their parents, after with more facility their souls are converted to God. Besides teaching of children, I endeavour to instruct the simple and vulgar sort, I teach them their Pater, Ave, Creed, Commandments.[52]

Sister Dorothea spent a large proportion of her time helping the poor, caring for them in their times of sickness and generally doing good works. However, she left posterity without much information regarding the contents of her curriculum or even her pedagogical methods.

Significantly, she chose to focus on her missionary work of conversion in her report and she described her activities as a proselytizer in considerable detail. First, she presented her efforts to alienate conforming families from the Church of England. In those times of anti-Catholic persecution, many were not entirely ready to commit themselves to recusancy, for fear of the consequences. However, she applied herself to the pastoral service of such families, thereby gradually persuading them not to attend Anglican services regularly, or at least to refrain from communion there. She reported converting nine people, but encountering difficulties when trying to find a priest in order to receive these new converts into the Church officially. She often had to walk miles on foot to meet with the nearest priest; sometimes, she could do no more than wait for months before she could secure one.[53]

Success as a Catholic evangelizer brought her to the notice of Protestant authorities: the Church court issued a sentence of excommunication and it was only her care in preserving her anonymity which saved her in this crisis. Since villagers and officials knew her simply as 'Dorothy', the absence of a family name prevented the local minister from taking any further action. However, the immediacy of danger in her missionary occupations did not dampen her spirits for long. She soon became the guest of a local gentlewoman who had recently become a fervent Catholic, but whose mother and husband remained very reluctant, and had both taken the oath of allegiance to the king.[54] The husband had been critically ill for some time when Dorothea arrived and she persuaded him to talk to a priest

---

[52] M.C.E. Chambers, *Life*, vol. 2, p. 27.

[53] *Ibid.*, p. 28.

[54] Sister Dorothea never names this family, possibly in order to prevent detection should her account by intercepted by government officials.

on his deathbed. Unfortunately, he died before she returned with the Jesuit but, although she was saddened by this missed opportunity to reconcile this man, Dorothea saw in his family's bereavement a chance to touch the souls of the entire household. She applied herself to their service, cleaning and keeping the house for them whilst gradually speaking of religious matters. She took care, however, never to mention that she was a member of Mary Ward's Institute; her approach was more subtle, striving not to cause the family any alarm by revealing their unwitting association with a member of such a controversial group.

It seemed she had judged well, since in a short space of time, she claimed to have brought about the conversion of four members of the household. Later, a chapel was installed there and Sister Dorothea was able more openly to catechize the new Catholics, while she helped to organize the house as a fully-fledged recusant centre:

> It pleased God to give so good success to my poor
> endeavours that when I would have departed to my poor
> people, after I had been with them about six weeks, I could
> by no means get away. The Father of the Society, who by
> my means came acquainted there, [...] told me how much he
> was edified to see the good I had done and was like to do.[55]

This passage shows how individual members of the Institute worked in England in a manner entirely comparable with that of missionary priests. Although Sister Dorothea was not qualified to receive people to the Church formally, she converted and instructed them until she could procure a priest who could perform the official reconciliation. Indeed, she underlined the complementary nature of her work with that of the priests. At a time when clerical ranks were divided about the English 'Jesuitesses', she found that on English soil she could work hand in hand with missionaries and enjoy mutual support in their alliance in the common cause of the Catholic Church. Thus, although she could not dispense the sacraments, her work in Suffolk was obviously of an active missionary nature and therefore transcended early modern conceptions of womanly religious roles.

Sister Dorothea's account illustrates the kind of tasks which were to lead to the Institute's condemnation in 1631 because they were overtly taking place outside the established forum of religious enclosure. The Ladies' teaching and catechizing activities were the result of a self-motivated and independent enterprise which functioned outside the control of the episcopate and outside the secluded space of conventual classrooms. A contemporaneous report described the Ladies' activities eloquently:

---

[55] M.C.E. Chambers, *Life*, vol. 2, p. 32.

> Mistress Ward is become mother General of no less than 200
> English damsels, being most of them Ladies and Knights'
> daughters, who live in their Colleges at St Omer, Liège, and
> Cologne, and from thence are [to depart] for England to
> convert their country. [...] But now she is daily expected in
> England, to take account of her she-Apostles' labours.[56]

Even to onlookers, Mary Ward's disciples were not helpmeets, aides, or simply apostolic women: they acted as fully apostles. As such, they were, like the male clerks regular, undertaking works of conversion in the spirit of the direct followers of Jesus. Despite their gender, they were aspiring to be seen as the direct followers of Christ, thereby not only blurring the border between female teaching and male preaching but altogether obliterating it.

Thus, unlike the Ursulines for whom the intrinsic limitations implied by enclosure were largely compensated by the 'bargaining power'[57] they thereby obtained, the English Ladies' physical and institutional freedom actually worked against their ultimate success as an institution. It was because the Ladies catechized outside the traditional female arena of the enclosed boarding school that their endeavours were categorized as public preaching, in contrast with those of the Ursulines which, although essentially similar, were more readily seen as private teaching. As they outgrew the sphere of humble domestic maintainers of the faith, they became involved in works of conversion which were deemed highly unsuitable for women in seventeenth-century Europe.

The Ladies became aware of the dangers associated with their perceived preaching very early on and they defended themselves in official documents, such as a Memorial addressed to Cardinal Borghese in 1615:

> The one who is the enemy of every good thing, however,
> instigated some members of ecclesiastical and religious
> bodies to undermine the Ladies' good name, whereby with
> unfounded slanderous rumours these people strongly
> maintained that the Ladies preached in pulpits and squares
> and publicly disputed "de rebus divini". Many other such
> whimsical accusations were made, all of which are
> irreconcilable with our customs and far from our thoughts.[58]

They felt this point was important enough to be reiterated in their 1629 petition to Urban VIII, in which they repeat the same declaration almost word for word.[59]

Ward's closeness to the Jesuit mission working in England was as apparent on the ground as in the text of her various Plans. Moreover, the English Ladies' apostolate was not to stop there, for they (further emulating the Jesuits)

---

[56] James Wadsworth, *English Spanish Pilgrim*, p. 30.

[57] Linda Lierheimer, 'Female Eloquence and Maternal Ministry', p. 287.

[58] BCA, B5, item 28 ff. 2-3, *Memorial to Cardinal Borghese*, 29 February 1625. My italics.

[59] BCA, B18, *Petition to Urban VIII*, 1629, f. 2.

envisaged their mission on a world-wide level. Thus, in the 1621 *Institutum*, the members of the English Institute vowed to obey the pope should he send them 'among the Turks or any other infidels, even those who live in the region called the Indies, or among any heretics whatever'.[60] This clause, of course, encompassed the English mission itself, but also envisaged a universal mission of Catholicization in which the Ladies wanted to participate as actively as the male missionaries.

Therefore, the foundress's vocation as expressed in the 1621 *Institutum* marked a departure from the more localized and perhaps humbler endeavours of the Toulousain Ursulines. Whereas both communities had started with the common aim of catechizing women in their immediate *milieux*, Mary Ward's imitation of the Society of Jesus outgrew such geographical limitations and led her to envisage her vocation on a universal level. This would have crucial bearing upon the history of the Institute, as it took its mission beyond the immediate needs of the English Catholic community to open houses across Europe. An Institute of women educating girls in Catholic doctrine at local level (as the pragmatic response to a pressing need) resembled the French Ursuline establishments very closely and was unlikely to attract ecclesiastical opposition. However, by 1621, the *Institutum* openly presented a completely different image of Ward's definitive vocation: it aimed to develop an international Institute modelled on the Society of Jesus, pursuing the same goals and functioning with the same structures. This significant change explains why two communities which aimed at the same essential target were, in the end, subjected to dramatically different fates.

Hence, in matters of evangelization, as in matters of female schooling, the English Institute took its innovations one step further than the Ursulines ever did; however, this was not as a result of any radical discrepancy in their definition of their educational vocations; rather the disparity emerged from the different ways of working which the Institute and the Ursulines had chosen. Indeed, when the French Ursulines resolved to embrace enclosure as a means of securing their congregation's future, they accepted the limitations implied by physical confinement and male ecclesiastical control. On the other hand, Mary Ward had seen enclosure and conventual observance as irreconcilable with her Ignatian design; as a consequence, her Institute was able to take both its education and its apostolate beyond the established boundaries which defined the acceptability of female religious endeavours. Thus, in their commitment to reconciling Martha and Mary, both congregations chose different paths, which in turn allowed the English Ladies to become what they termed 'Soldiers of God', female missionaries who worked, to the best of their abilities, on a par with missionary priests. Conversely, although the Ursulines were never allowed to threaten patriarchal classifications on such a scale, their 'maternal ministry' functioned efficiently from within the

---

[60] BCA, B18, *Institutum*, f. 22.

enclosure of their convents, and their diplomatic tactics contributed towards taking Ursuline piety out of the cloister and into the world.[61]

---

[61] See Linda Lierheimer, 'Female Eloquence and Maternal Ministry'.

Chapter 6

Serving Martha and Mary:
Modus Vivendi

> The religious life which embraces the exercises of both the
> active and the contemplative life and which relates
> contemplation to the instruction of the people has a nobler
> and more excellent end than the one which is limited to
> contemplation or to action only.[1]

The English Ladies and the French Ursulines followed vocations which transformed the traditional model of female religious life and revolved around the delicate balance between contemplation and action. This dual vocation was at the very core of both Orders' *raison d'être*. They both aimed to catechize girls outside the usual forum of religious boarding schools, but still considered themselves intrinsically part of the Church and felt entitled to recognition as religious women. Although they opted for a life which was dramatically different from the silent contemplation of the secluded cloister, they saw themselves as brides of Christ offering their lives to God. They vindicated their right to teach day girls and to have a modicum of contact with the world, but they were essentially nuns: for the Ursulines, this was rendered official by the progressive adoption of the Augustinian Rule and of conventual enclosure during the course of the century. For Mary Ward's followers, the adoption of the Ignatian Rule, although unrecognized by the Curia, signified their commitment to a religious way of life. The convent walls were replaced metaphorically by the fortress of their probity: though they were physically free of restraints, their hearts were enclosed in the safety of their religious integrity. Thus, their goals and their ideals remained comparable even after both congregations had opted for different means to achieve them.

    This chapter turns to an analysis of the communities' preferred paths: it is through the specific ways of life they adopted that we can distinguish the embodiment of their different concepts of themselves. The English Ladies remained unenclosed in imitation of the Society of Jesus, the Ursulines accepted

---

[1] Parayre, *Chronique*, part 1, p.21: 'la religion qui embrasse les exercices de la vie active et contemplative, et rapporte la contemplation à l'instruction du peuple, à une fin plus noble et ensuite plus excellente que celle qui s'arrête à la seule contemplation où à la seule action'.

claustration in order to secure their educational apostolate, but both preserved elements of a traditional conventual custom which they adapted to enhance and to serve their pedagogical vocations. The French Ursulines and the English Ladies managed to reconcile both the duties of Mary and those of Martha, regulating their daily routines so as to allow spirituality and teaching not merely to co-exist but also to enrich each other. It is through their *modus vivendi* that this chapter will find an illustration of the communities' new dialectic of action and contemplation.

Religious women first and foremost

The first house of the Institute had settled on the Continent in 1609. In the main street of St Omer, then called the Rue Grosse, it served a dual function: on the one hand, it housed a congregation of women living according to religious principles, while on the other it acted as a school educating Catholic girls. In September 1612, in a petition asking for the support of Archduchess Isabella, the English Ladies explained the reasons for their foundation in the city:

> Seeing the necessities of the Catholics in England and the difficulty they lie under of bringing up their children in the Catholic faith, which cannot be done in that kingdom without great risk to the children and parents [the English Ladies] have settled themselves [...] in the town of St Omer.[2]

The boarding school in St Omer provided Catholic education for the daughters of recusant families whose parents were wealthy enough to send them on the costly journey across the Channel and to afford regular boarding fees.[3] Since the structure in this first foundation was later used as a model for the houses which were gradually founded across Europe, it seems legitimate to focus on the St Omer establishment in order to illustrate the Institute's *modus vivendi*.

In a document dated 1612, bishop Blaes presented an overview of the religious establishments which prospered in his city of St Omer; he wrote: 'One of the aforementioned houses is full of young English Ladies. About thirty or forty of them are gathered there and they also live under some form of monastic life.'[4] Blaes made no mistake in comparing the settlement with more traditional monastic houses: his observations are confirmed by the Institute's own documents, revealing some striking similarities with the typical early modern systems at work in

---

[2] BCA, C18, f. 6; also quoted in M.C.E. Chambers, *Life,* vol. 1, p. 273.
[3] See Marion Norman, 'A Woman for All Seasons: Mary Ward (5185-1645), Renaissance Pioneer of Women's Education', *Paedagogica Historica* 23.1 (1983), p. 129.
[4] As quoted in M.C.E. Chambers, *Life,* vol. 1, p. 272. Bishop Blaes's text was originally in French: 'Une des dites maisons [...] est remplie de jeunes filles Anglaises, s'y retrouvent illet de trente à quarante lesquelles vivent aussi sous quelque forme de vie monastique'.

European convents at large.[5] A brief look at the Institute's Plans will illustrate the extent to which it preserved the most fundamental structures of orthodox religious establishments in terms of personal hierarchy and allocation of duties as well as division of time and space.

As far the members themselves were concerned, the familiar patterns of monastic hierarchy were adopted and described in the 1612 *Schola Beatae Mariae* and the 1616 *Ratio Instituti,* and more crucially, they were not abandoned in the more radical 1621 *Institutum.* There were three degrees of religious membership corresponding to the three stations of novice, lay sister and choir sister found in traditional convents. Because of the evangelical vocation of the Institute, and in order to ensure that members were temperamentally suited to this active mission, the probation period for prospective members was longer than in most nunneries: novices therefore spent two years in this so-called 'first degree' of membership. The 'second degree', according to the *Ratio Instituti,* was represented by the lay sisters who, after their novitiate, became fully professed members of the Institute but focused on the domestic running of their houses and acted as the servants and helpers of the rest of their communities. Once bound to the Institute by their vows, they were known as 'Associates' or 'Assistants'.[6] Third came those who, during their novitiate, had shown aptitude for the specific brief of the Institute and who, on profession, formed the highest element of the hierarchy when they became professed Mothers.

In this respect, although its taxonomy varied slightly from the norm, the Institute adopted a recognizable, monastic-like structure which divided the community into novices, lay and professed sisters.[7] Hierarchy, in this aspect of the communities' lives, was retained without changes and served to identify members according to the groups to which they belonged. The only significant difference between the Institute and more orthodox, recognized Orders was the powerful supervisory office of Mother Superior General, which Mary Ward borrowed from the Jesuit model and which added an extra layer of government to her project

When turning towards the variety of offices which ensured the adequate management of the houses, yet more similarities with traditional religious communities become apparent. For instance, the English Ladies used the same repartition of duties as that encountered in Continental convents.[8] Therefore, unsurprisingly, each house was headed by a Mother Superior who was elected by the community for a renewable three-year term. Next in line was the Mother Substitute who shared her workload, overseeing the running of the house when the Superior could not attend in person. The four aptly named consultors advised the Superior and her Substitute, keeping them in touch with the community's preoccupations. One of the four consultors doubled as the admonitor, whose duty

---

[5] M.C.E. Chambers, *Life*, vol. 1, pp. 268-74.
[6] BCA, B 18, *Ratio Instituti*, f. 14.
[7] *Ibid.*, f. 8.
[8] BCA, B 18, *Schola Beatae Mariae*, ff. 8-14.

was to act as the community's first port-of-call, should the Superior be the object of complaints.

Other offices all echoed almost exactly the monastic structure found in traditional female religious houses: for instance, the novices were supervised by the mistress of the novices, whilst the chapel and devotional objects were, as in any established religious community, the preserve of the sacristan. Moreover, the model of the convent was also paralleled in the house's administrative management. Finances were in the hands of a bursar and a secretary was responsible for keeping precise records and minutes of meetings, decisions or elections. Thus, the usual role distribution of recognized religious communities was mirrored in the system of government of the Institute: in fact, where categorization helped to define roles and duties, the English project proved as hierarchical as any traditional cloister

Moreover, Mary Ward's foundations also observed a routine based on the monastic *horarium*. The English Ladies rose at 4.00 and attended to their rooms, before meditating for an hour between 4.30 and 5.30. Then between 5.30 and 8.00, they gathered together to hear Mass, say their vocal prayers and attend spiritual readings. From 8.00, they worked at their respective offices until 9.45, when they carried out their examination of conscience. At 10.00, they ate and enjoyed a long recreation. At 12.30, they reconvened for spiritual readings and at 1.00, they attended to their own duties once more. At 5.00 they stopped work to say their vocal prayers until 6.00, when they had supper and recreation. At 8.00, they recited the Litanies of Our Lady and the Saints, examined their consciences and were given the points of meditation for the next day. The house then retired to bed at 9.00.[9]

Thus, the Institute's hierarchy and its daily routine closely resembled the received patterns at work within established female religious communities. The parallel with the Ursuline lifestyle in particular becomes even more marked when both communities' school government is considered. The house in St Omer and the branches which subsequently used it as their model in continental Europe had much in common with the Ursuline convents and their boarding schools: in both Orders, the boarders' timetable were very similar and teaching practice was influenced by the Jesuit *Ratio Studiorum* (1599). Young boarders rose at 6.00 every morning and spent an hour dressing and saying their morning prayers. At 7.00, they heard Mass and then went to breakfast before starting their lessons at 8.00 every weekday. Lunch was served at 10.15 and followed by recreation; at 12.00 the lessons were resumed until 4.00 in the afternoon, when pupils went to Vespers and took refreshments before the Office and the rosary were said at 5.00. The day finished with supper and free time at 6.00 and concluded with evening prayers at 8.00. There were no classes on Thursdays, when the boarders were

---

[9] *Ibid.*, f. 34.

allowed an extra half hour's sleep and employed their free time usefully at skills such as needlework or individual study.[10]

In this way, the Institute's schools were imbued with a considerable sense of order and an atmosphere somewhat akin to that of a monastery, where each hour of the day corresponded to a specific task, according to a regular pattern. An important part of this routine was occupied by religious instruction and every day the boarders took part in the same devotions as the Ladies. These were comparable to those observed by nuns in enclosed convents, though considerably shorter in duration. One of the main differences between the daily school routine of the English Institute and that of Ursuline schools in France lay in the exclusion of the lengthy choir service from its regulations.

In France, the Ursulines' evolution from a lay apostolic congregation into a teaching religious order proved a successful compromise. Their position, strengthened by the respectability and prestige conferred by the propriety of the cloister, gradually made possible the reception of the daughters of influential families who, thus far, had shrunk from the potential instability of an uncloistered establishment.[11] Ursuline claustration was in keeping with Tridentine decrees and remained faithful to the formula of female religious life; the Order adopted a threefold structure which was comparable with that of traditional cloisters. Communities were composed firstly of young novices, secondly, of lay sisters (who acted as the servants of the house) and, thirdly, of choir nuns. Like in most monasteries, each group lived in its own quarters, in adjacent but separate parts of the building and unnecessary interaction, particularly between professed sisters and novices, was sharply discouraged.[12] Life was minutely regimented; each sister occupied, according to her rank in the hierarchy, a particular office, the duties of which were recorded in detail in the establishment's constitutions. Time and space were similarly subjected to strict regulation, so that conventual routine left nothing and no-one unoccupied, even for a moment.

Like any other religious Order, the Ursulines followed a highly hierarchical system; at the head of each house, the *prieure* ensured that the convent lived in scrupulous observance of the Rule of St Augustine and respected its constitutions. She was elected by the choir nuns for a term of three years which, according to the constitutions, ought not to be renewable in consecutive terms in order to ensure diversity of government and prevent autocracy; on this point however, practice often fell short of theoretical precepts and successful *prieures*

---

[10] BCA, B39, Marion Norman, *Mary Ward as Educator*, typescript pp. 10-11 and Mary Roswitha Etscheit, 'The Place of Mary Ward in the Education of Catholic Girls during Penal Times, in England and in German-speaking Countries, 1558-1688', unpublished PhD thesis (University of East Anglia , 1986), in BCA, B33, chapter V, p. 6.

[11] See Linda Lierheimer, 'Redefining Convent Space', p. 213.

[12] ADHG, 221H-28 bis, 5, f. 51'

frequently found themselves re-elected on several consecutive occasions.[13] The *prieure* or *supérieure* was assisted in her office by the equally essential *souprieure* who, also elected for a term of three years, was expected to undertake all that her superior would ask of her and even act in her place in cases of extreme illness or sudden death. The sister *admonitrice* acted as the mediatrix between the head of the community and its members; should her *consœurs* formulate grievances which the superior ignored, it was her unenviable task to report her to the local ordinary or to request a formal visitation.[14] This religious nomenclature was completed by the four *discrètes,* chosen from amongst the most trustworthy sisters of the community to advise and counsel the *prieure* and *souprieure* whilst keeping them informed of the communities' routine. Thus far, the parallel with the organization of the Institute is almost complete, with the *prieure* and the *soupieure* standing for the superior and the substitute and the English admonitor and consultors being mirrored exactly by the French *admonitrice* and the *discrètes.*

Numerous other powerful officers oversaw the administration of the establishment and organized its devotional life. Finances were the preserve of the *procuratrice,* whilst the *secrétaire* kept a record of all deliberations, decisions or elections. The *sacristaines* looked after the chapel and the altar, furnishing and decorating them as befitted a religious congregation; the *maîtresse des novices* was in charge of the novices' tuition in religious discipline and Catholic doctrine and generally oversaw their entire novitiate, while the *maîtresse du chœur*'s influential post allowed her to decide upon the readings and the liturgy she wanted to be read out by the *semainière,* who was changed on a weekly rota. Besides directing the community's life of prayer, she also regulated all the timetable and chores of her *consœurs* according to the calendar.

Like in any other religious establishment, each Ursuline was given a specific post so that no aspect of life was ever left to chance; hence, amongst others, the *apothicaire* looked after her *consœurs*' health, the *lingère* supervised their laundry and the *dépensière* bought food supplies.[15] Thus, in a manner typical of seventeenth-century convents and indeed of early modern society at large, Ursuline houses followed a highly hierarchical structure and allocated precise functions to particular denominations. For each aspect of life, there was an office and a customary procedure to follow and in this structural allocation of duties, English Ladies and French Ursulines remained very similar.

However, enclosure had been an essential condition for the transformation of the lay congregations of Ursulines into recognized religious establishments and this, of course, introduced contrasts with the Institute. Unlike the English Ladies, the women who accepted this change renounced any physical involvement in the world; breach of this engagement would bring the guilty sister to religious justice,

---

[13] *Ibid.,* f. 60.
[14] *Ibid.*
[15] *Ibid.,* f. 38.

to be punished adequately not only by her superior but by ecclesiastical decree also. Added to official retribution were the devastating consequences of public opprobrium, which would be quick to spread from the offender to her entire community. According to the constitutions of the Toulousain house, for instance, the Ursulines could leave the premises only when in actual danger of their lives. The text set out the few legitimate reasons for leaving the convent:

> The Sisters will take a fourth vow of enclosure; they shall not leave the convent under the pretext of disease or any other cause whatsoever, except for the ones expressly mentioned in Pope Paul V's Bull. These are: if they suffer from leprosy or contagious disease, in case of fire, flooding or war, or else in order to be employed for the foundation or the restoration of some monastery, and this only with a written license from Monseigneur the Archbishop or his Vicar General.[16]

When in August 1615 Toulouse's Vicar General Jean de Rudelle visited the Ursulines to assess the suitability of their house for its elevation into a nunnery, his report praised their lodgings, which he described as 'surrounded on all sides with high walls, and properly enclosed'.[17] His description of the garden was eloquent: 'at the centre of the said house, there is quite a pleasant little garden, in which we have not been able to make out that the neighbours could see [the nuns] in any part of the house'. The enclosure was indeed a literal reality, a distinct separation between the 'outside' and the 'inside'.[18] Whatever the dissimilarities encountered by visitors in various establishments across the kingdom, the Ursulines' great care over the enforcement and subsequent preservation of complete enclosure was an absolute constant: similar comments can be found in countless visitations reports, and although it has to be acknowledged that the French turn of phrase tended to be very formulaic, the very fact that reports go into such detail about the adequacy of the enclosure of the convent they assessed is testimony to the fact that Ursulines took claustration seriously.

In the Toulouse constitutions, the importance of this issue was illustrated by the imbalance between the sections of the book. Not only is the chapter dealing with enclosure the lengthiest and the most detailed, it is followed in the next

---

[16] ADHG, 221H-17, f. 19: 'Les Sœurs feront un quatrième vœu de clôture et ne sortiront pour quelque maladie, cause ou occasion que ce soit, si ce n'est en cas portés par la Bulle du pape Paul Cinquième, savoir si elles sont atteintes de lèpre ou maladie contagieuse, ou en cas de feu, inondation des eaux, et hostilité, ou bien pour être employées pour l'érection ou restauration de quelque monastère, et ce avec la licence par écrit de monseigneur l'Archevêque ou de son grand vicaire.'

[17] ADHG, 221H-4. Jean de Rudelle's report, dated 25 August, 1615: 'laquelle maison est entourée de tous côtés de hautes murailles, bien close.'

[18] *Ibid.*: 'au milieu de ladite maison un petit jardin assez agréable, par lequel nous n'avons pu discerner que d'aucune part de ladite maison les voisins les puissent voir.'

chapter by an elaborate description of the limitations and the strict surveillance imposed upon any communication with the outside world.[19] The *parloir* consisted of a grilled reception foyer for occasional converse with visiting relatives; they were fitted with double iron bars and grills topped with spikes, and shut with tin-plate in which small holes had been drilled. The only opening was a small window which a nun might open to speak to relatives, though only with the mother superior's authorization and under surveillance. Thus, the *parloir* acted as a separate territory, allowing exchanges between the cloister and the world, whilst not belonging fully to either; in essence, it was a kind of frontier. A similar device was used in order to keep the sisters separated from the public during High Mass, which was celebrated in the chapel; there, the Ursulines and their boarders were confined to one small section of the building which they accessed through their own chapel door. They were physically and metaphorically kept enclosed by a grill which allowed them to receive the sacraments through its bars while keeping them apart from the priest and the rest of his congregation, thereby symbolizing their separation from the outside world.

Of course, extreme caution was observed on the subject of men's entering the cloister. In the case of workmen called in for occasional repairs, sisters and pupils must under no circumstances look at or talk to them. The normal procedure to receive visitors prescribed that a little bell would indicate their visitors' presence at the door. All nuns would then gather inside the low choir and remain there while the *prieure*, accompanied by the four *discrètes* arrayed in their cloaks, went to meet the guests at the door and showed them in. The entrance of men in the houses of religious virgins was always to be problematic, and the chapter on claustration dealt with this most sensitive of issues at length, making particular provision concerning the admission of male clerics. In the event of severe disease, the father confessor could exceptionally be authorized by the *mère prieure* to enter the convent walls and bring the Blessed Sacrament to the suffering sister. He could also hear the sick nun's confession, but only once a fortnight. The text revealed the extent of the suspicion and fear aroused by the presence of any men among the nuns: 'The father confessor or any other visitors, when entering the cloister, will go only where they must, without straying into any other rooms.'[20]

This phrase is not without recalling the terms used in the episcopal licences which were required to allow Ursulines to venture outside their convents. The sisters were not to stray beyond their enclosure and their spatial movements were limited and controlled. Conversely, however, the cloister was their haven, a space where they were free to circulate but where others - the agents of the world - required monitoring and saw their movements restricted. Extreme caution seemed necessary to preserve the safety of the brides of Christ and was further legitimated

---

[19] ADHG, 221H-41, chapter 9, 'De la clôture' and chapter 10, 'Des parloirs'.
[20] ADHG, 221H-28 bis, 5, f. 20: 'Le père confesseur ou autres qui entrent dans le monastère n'iront qu'aux lieux nécessaires pour le sujet de leur entrée sans se divertir ailleurs.'

by the growing number of scandals which had arisen, from the fourteenth century onwards, because of improper behaviour and laxity. Occasions when a nun found herself romantically involved with a man, whether he was a priest or a workman, were far from rare and the stigma attached to pregnancy, elopement or apostasy were to be avoided at all cost.[21]

Ursuline houses were not solely places of regular Catholic worship but also educational establishments. As we have seen, the new foundations, like many older Orders, welcomed students in a separate wing of their buildings dedicated especially to the *pensionnat* alongside the three quarters allotted to the various categories of nuns (namely the novices, the choir nuns and the lay sisters). On a model which was common to most cloisters in early modern Europe, the boarders lived there for the entire duration of their education; although the majority of them would not necessarily wish to become religious once their schooling was complete, they were nevertheless expected to obey the regulations of the convent. Whether it was in the convent or the *pensionnat*, time was as carefully regulated as space and occupation; as far as possible, the Ursulines followed a routine which resembled that of most enclosed convents in the seventeenth century.

The nuns would get up at 4.30 in the morning and gather in the choir at 5.30 to spend an hour listening to the *semainière* who read some selected passages for meditation. From 6.30 until 7.30 they said Prime and Matins, before applying themselves to the duties of their respective offices from 7.30 to 9.00; during that time, the novices (who obviously did not hold any office) reviewed their morning's meditation and worked on their exercises. At 9.00, the sisters heard Mass and at 11.00 they had lunch, followed by grace, the litanies of Our Lady, prayers and an hour's recreation. At 1.30, the *semainière* read out extracts from a selected devotional book and at 2.00, the sisters retired to their cells for an hour to say the Rosary and either meditate, read or sew. Vespers were at 3.00 and followed by half an hour of prayer. At 4.00 the sisters returned to the occupations of their respective offices, before meeting again at 5.00 for their evening meal and half an hour's recreation. After Compline and the Divine Office at 7.30, the nuns examined their consciences and retired to bed at 9.30.

The boarders observed an equally regular pattern. They rose later than the sisters, usually at 6.00 and said their prayers; from 7.00 until 8.00, they read under the supervision of their *maîtresse*. Lessons began in the classrooms at 8.00, usually with reading or, for the more advanced, a little writing. At 9.00 they joined the community at Mass before breaking for lunch and recreation, reconvening at 1.00 for reading, writing at 2.00 and Christian doctrine at 3.00. Lessons finished at

---

[21] See Graciela S. Daichman, 'Misconduct in the Medieval Nunnery: Fact, Not Fiction', in Linda L. Coon, Katherine J. Haldane and Elizabeth W. Sommer (eds.), *That Gentle Strength. Historical perspectives on Women in Christianity* (Charlottesville and London, 1990).

4.00 and the pupils did their homework before going to dinner at 5.00. Like the nuns, they examined their consciences at 7.30 and went to bed at 9.30.

Being a boarder in such an institution also implied years of claustration for the young *demoiselles* who, while they lived inside the building, should have no more contact with the outside world than the nuns themselves. At least in the theory of constitutional texts, the *pensionnaires* were required to sever all links with their relatives and friends during their time in the school; they enjoyed no more leniency than the nuns themselves, with their contacts with the outside limited to the strict minimum and confined to the *parloirs*. The constitutions of Toulouse explained the situation in detail:

> Boarders above ten years of age will not be able to leave and enter again without a written license from Monseigneur the archbishop [...]. Nevertheless, when their parents wish to see them outside the enclosure, they will be allowed to go out into the exterior parloirs.[22]

Thus, the reality of enclosure meant that complete severance from the world was required even of the youngest inmates during their stay; neither the nuns nor the boarders had any knowledge of the life of the city - they lived in complete isolation from secular society.

The pupils were therefore in a situation comparable to that of the novices: although they lived in the same establishment as the professed nuns, they were restricted to their own quarters and came into only limited contact with them. Just as the novices were under the supervision of their *maîtresse des novices*, they were supervised by a *maîtresse des pensionnaires* (also sometimes called *principale*) who monitored their progress and generally oversaw life in the boarding school. In order to avoid the distractions occasioned by the *pensionnaires* and so as to preserve the 'spirit of Mary' in the convent, exchanges between the sisters and their charges were kept to a minimum. Outside services in the chapel, the pupils never came into contact with either non-teaching nuns or novices: they interacted only with their teachers and with their *maîtresse*. The *pensionnat* remained locked at all times and the girls were not permitted to enter the sisters' quarters without a valid reason, and then only under supervision. In a system which categorized individuals according to their status, it was vital that lay pupils and religious tutors were not allowed to mix.

The presence of boarders within the convent was therefore not allowed to disrupt the convent's routine. Indeed, despite sharing the same monastic observance as their religious mentors, the girls nevertheless represented a foreign

---

[22] *Ibid.*, f. 11: 'Les pensionnaires âgées de dix ans et au dessus ne pourront sortir pour rentrer sans la licence par écrit de Monseigneur l'archevêque [...]; néanmoins, lorsque leurs parents les voudront voir hors la clôture, elles pourront sortir dans les chambres des parloirs extérieurs.'

body inside the convent. The constitutions made provisions for the organization of school life *intra muros* by ensuring that this constant element of secular presence did not upset the house's religious observance. The text specified that the Ursulines should take the responsibility of accepting only as many boarders as was easily practicable:

> The sisters [...] will not take charge of more boarders than their regular institute will permit, lest the continual occupation occasioned by these girls [...] should cause them to lose the spirit of Mary, without which they cannot fulfil their vocations with dignity.[23]

This was an eloquent reminder that an Ursuline was by no means an ordinary teacher, engaged in education for its own sake; she was, first and foremost, a religious woman working in the service of God. Her educational vocation was intrinsically linked to her spirituality. Exact observance and the constant reminder of the sisters' dual vocation were essential to the harmonious balance of the Ursuline lifestyle, honouring both the duties of Martha and the spirit of Mary.

The dual essence of the Ursuline vocation was stated clearly in the establishments' constitutions, which set out to distribute the religious offices held by the sisters in their capacity of nuns whilst providing an equally clear allocation of posts for those involved in classroom activities. This categorization of roles and duties permeated the entire fabric of Ursuline life and mirrored the systematic allocation of space and time. In Toulouse, the constitutions insisted that their main purpose was to enable the sisters to live according to their chosen Rule of St Augustine, in a manner which would 'combine and maintain the institution and instruction of girls with monastic observance and religious austerity'.[24] They bore the mark of the establishment's dual essence, even in their title: *Constitutions du collège et monastère des religieuses de Sainte Ursule de Toulouse*. The house had the double function of convent, with a contemplative and monastic observance and college, with an active teaching brief. The purpose of the constitutions was to ensure that the house achieved equilibrium between both aspects of its twofold nature. They defined the Rule of St Augustine and the provisions that had been made to reconcile the teaching of girls with monastic observance and religious austerity.[25]

---

[23] ADHG, 221H-28 bis, 5, f. 4: 'Les sœurs [ne pourront] se charger de plus grand nombre que leur institut régulier ne pourra permettre, de peur que [par] les occupations continuelles que leur donneraient ces filles, elles ne perdent l'esprit de Marie, sans lequel elles ne peuvent s'acquitter dignement de leur vocation.'
[24] ADHG, 221H- 41, f. 3: 'accorder et maintenir l'institution et instruction des filles avec l'observance monastique et l'austérité de la religion.'
[25] ADHG, 221H-41, f. 3.

The organization of a community according to its teaching duties implied that some compromise had to be made with the religious life in order to satisfy the nuns' educational vocation. It was impossible for teachers to attend all eight services, day and night; they therefore obtained partial exemption from the daily Office, and they were allowed to practise their devotions privately, in their own time. Acts of mortification were also, to a degree, incompatible with the teachers' way of life. Moreover, they were exempted from certain austerities such as extended fasts, since their health was considered a practical priority. The constitutions clarified those points:

> On every teaching day, the *régentes* will have half an hour of recreation both before and after their classes; they will be allowed to eat something in the mornings before they start teaching, and will be exempted from saying the little office of Our Lady. [...] They will abstain from meat only and will be exempted from fasting. This also applies to the *maîtresses des pensionnaires*.[26]

To a degree, Martha's portion dictated the necessary alterations to Mary's. The demands of the classrooms made good health an obvious condition of effectiveness and so led the Ursulines, in theory at least, to abandon practices of physical mortification. Indeed, the ecstasies occasioned by extended fasts, though they formed part of the mysticism which characterized the contemplative orders, ran contrary to the Ursulines' more immediately practical aim of educating the young. Priority was given to educational apostolate over contemplative devotion, and the school became a central part of their ethos.

The Ursulines lived a rigorously regimented life, which ensured the harmonious combination of these seemingly paradoxical functions, with some of the enclosed nuns teaching in the boarding school, an occupation not uncommon in early modern cloisters. The novelty, however, lay in the extension of the nuns' teaching brief to their day pupils, who usually lived in the neighbouring area, did not belong to the religious establishment and did not partake either in its enclosed life or its regular practice.[27] Their daily entrance required some amendment to traditional conventual rule and more specifically to the convent's monastic enclosure. Indeed, the nuns who taught the day students came into daily contact with these emissaries of secular society, a situation which appeared to defy the contemporaneous definition of female religious life: Ursuline establishments were cloisters, the high walls, heavy doors and barred windows of which signified their

---

[26] ADHG, 221H-28 bis, 5, f. 15: 'Les régentes auront tous les jours de leçons une demi-heure pour se divertir avant d'enter en classe, et après en être sorties; elles pourront prendre quelque chose le matin avant d'entrer en classe, et seront exemptes de la récitation du petit office de Notre Dame [...] elles ne feront qu'abstinence de viande et seront exemptes de jeûne, ce qui sera aussi observé par les maîtresses des pensionnaires.'
[27] Linda Lierheimer, 'Redefining Convent Space', p. 211.

separation from the world. Yet, the enclosure was breached each day, since the convents also doubled up as day schools, open to all the girls who cared to be instructed there.   In a society where the world was conceived in terms of systematic attribution of roles and duties, where individuals were neatly pigeon-holed into pre-defined categories, how did such a two-headed monster become sufficiently well organized to gain general approval? Perhaps more importantly, did the sisters manage to balance their contemplative and active duties equally, or did they give priority to one particular aspect of their vocation?

Integrating the educational apostolate into religion

Although the sisters did not actually breach their vow of enclosure, the teaching of day girls implied that the convent opened its doors daily and allowed an exchange between the inside and the outside.   This minor infringement of the rule of enclosure was enough to allow the catechizing of hundreds of girls but presented potential threats to the integrity of the convent's religious observance. Therefore, regularity would become the very epitome of the Ursuline *modus vivendi*, the prime guarantor of order and harmony both in the cloister and in the classroom. As a consequence, the Parisian Rules warned: 'It is necessary, [...] in order to avoid the disorder and confusion usually entailed by a multitude of people and occupations, that all things be well structured, and that all the offices of those who are thus employed be regulated.'[28]   In this way, the order and regularity which suffused the *modus operandi* of the convent also pervaded the daily management of its school.

The office of the *portières* thus took on a new importance. The *portières* were in charge of the integrity of the enclosure, traditionally ensured by the large doors which separated the community from the outside world: whereas convents usually had two doors, Ursuline houses, in order to serve their educational vocation, had three. As in any religious community, the ceremonial door allowed priests to bring communion to the sick sisters who could not come to receive it in the chapel; moreover, it was through this grand entrance that postulants were received for their trial period. The second door acted as the main gateway in and out of the convent: linking the building directly with the street, it allowed the normal process of daily business, such as deliveries or building repairs. The third door, however, was an innovation since it was created specifically to facilitate the entrance of the day students. It played a crucial part in the life of the houses and, to a degree, was the distinguishing mark of the Order of teaching nuns. The keys opening its two locks were kept separately by the two *portières* who

---

[28] *Règlements des religieuses de la congrégation de Paris,* part 1, p. 4: 'il est nécessaire, [...] pour éviter le désordre et la confusion, que la multitude de personnes et d'occupations a coutume d'apporter, que toutes choses soient bien ordonnées, et que les offices de celles qui y sont employées soient réglés'.

metaphorically supervised and monitored the permeation of the conventual bubble. Although the seal surrounding the religious house was no longer hermetic, these women ensured that no irregular exchanges occurred between the convent and the world outside. The cloister's integrity and, by extension, its reputation depended on their guardianship and their sense of duty.[29]

Thus, the Ursuline formula epitomized a new type of religion for French women, one where teaching modified monastic claustration. This new degree of interaction with the world, through the intermediary of the day pupils, could not fail to bring a new constituency within the convent and to enable these girls to benefit, to a degree, from the spiritual charge conferred by enclosure. Without being members of the cloister themselves, they soaked up its pious atmosphere, experienced its regular routine and learned in its classrooms. While the day students brought part of the world into the convent, they also enabled some of the convent's essence to seep out into the world. In this way, enclosure had become active, embodying the 'fluidity' that Linda Lierheimer described as 'a continuum from the convent to the world beyond'.[30] To use her wording, the Ursuline day classes functioned as a 'bridge', or a 'no-man's land' between the spheres of the public and the private, between the world outside and the conventual space inside of enclosure.[31] The Ursuline sisters had indeed 'expanded the convent into the world'.[32]

The day schools were operated with great caution: every morning, the students gathered outside the exterior door, which was opened for them at eight o'clock and immediately locked again behind them; only then did the teachers enter the classroom by an interior door, itself guarded on the inside by another *sœur portière*. The classrooms, therefore, could be compared to a sort of airlock between the inside and the outside, secured at either end by heavy, double-locked doors: they enabled the day students to enter the convent whilst allowing only minimal contact with the outside world.

In the day classes, the timetable and the curriculum were both simplified versions of those provided for the boarders and this simplification was the logical and pragmatic result of a difference in circumstances. Whereas boarders had lessons all day, day girls came to school, on average, for one and a half hours in the morning and two and a half hours in the afternoon, fitting these sessions around the rest of their working day.[33] Therefore, interns and externs could not cover the same material at the same speed and their programmes were designed accordingly. Once more, the Ursulines showed a capacity of adaptation suited to the particular circumstances of their pupils. For instance, the doors to the classrooms opened at 8.00 a.m. to let in the first group of girls, but they re-opened at 9.00, in order to

---

[29] *Ibid*, f. 18.
[30] Linda Lierheimer, 'Redefining Convent Space', p. 218.
[31] *Ibid.*, p. 217.
[32] *Ibid.*, p. 212.
[33] *Règlements des religieuses de la congrégation de Paris*, part 2, p. 143.

enable those who could not arrive earlier to benefit from the rest of the morning teaching. Similarly, the timetable varied according to the seasons or weather conditions. On days of severe weather, classes started later to ensure that a maximum of students had extra time to travel to school; in winter, lessons finished earlier to enable students to return home safely during the daytime.[34] So, for all its insistence upon order and routine, the Ursuline system was always sufficiently flexible to serve its ultimate purpose.

The distribution of specific times for specific lessons was not a standardized practice rigidly applied throughout France regardless of local particularities. Various Ursuline houses organized themselves in slightly different ways so as to suit their own specific circumstances; their *modus operandi* shared the same essentials but remained eminently adaptable according to the pragmatic laws of supply and demand. For instance, the Parisian convent in the Faubourg Saint Jacques adapted its school day in a slightly different way from that of Toulouse,[35] and the houses of Provence or the Comtat-Venaissin, though following quite an analogous routine, also differed very slightly in points of detail.[36]

However, although their communities undeniably displayed elements of fluidity, this crossing of traditional boundaries did not by any means imply that the sisters abandoned traditional categorization. Thus, although the innovations of the Ursuline day schools allowed groups of diverse backgrounds to meet, co-existence usually prevailed over real interaction and genuine exchange. The daily breach of enclosure by representatives of the outside world symbolized, to some extent, the end of the division which kept the convent and the city absolutely separate. With the day girls, a degree of inclusion replaced separation, since local girls were able to benefit from education that, thus far, had belonged inside the sphere of enclosure only. However, the teaching of the *externes* was never allowed to jeopardize the nuns' stability or to disturb the cloister's order. As was the case with the boarders, interaction between nuns and externs was kept to a minimum:

> The day pupils are kept separately, under the responsibility
> of the *principale des pensionnaires*; their exercises are the
> same as those of the boarders. If the day pupils are
> numerous and the structure of the house permits it, they will
> have a classroom of they own and a special mistress will
> look after them.[37]

---

[34] *Ibid.*, pp. 149-150.

[35] M. A. Jégou, *Les Ursulines du Faubourg Saint-Jacques à Paris (1607-1662). Origine d'un monastère apostolique* (Paris, 1981), pp. 148-49

[36] C A. Sarre, *Vivre sa soumission*, pp. 560-61.

[37] ADHG, 221H-28 bis, 5, f. 12: 'Les demi-pensionnaires sont à part, et c'est la principale des pensionnaires qui en est responsable; les exercices sont les mêmes que ceux des pensionnaires. Si les demi-pensionnaires sont en grand nombre et que la maison le permet, elles auront une pièce à part et une maîtresse particulière qui s'occupera d'elles.'

Whereas the teaching of boarders entailed only limited disruption to the regular regime of a cloister, the daily entrance of pupils necessitated major changes in the *modus operandi* of the entire house. Therefore, the amenities of the convents were assigned for specific purposes, the very architecture of the building echoing the extreme categorization which defined early modern mentalities in general and the Ursuline lifestyle in particular.

. In 1615 in Toulouse, for instance, when the *congrégées'* house was in the process of becoming a religious establishment, the vicar general Jean de Rudelle had evaluated its suitability for this new purpose. He described finding four classrooms near the sacristy and, on the other side of the nearby *parloir*, a large room, which he then allocated to make two extra classrooms. He noted that, for the purpose of teaching day girls, these last two classrooms would be better situated than the older four, because they were further from the heart of the convent itself and nearer the exterior side of the building.[38]

The 1616 papal brief gave specific directives regarding the organization of the school for the day pupils: despite letting the Ursulines pursue their teaching vocations, the pope expressed reservations regarding the nuns' mingling with their students:

> It is neither good nor proper for the said nuns that the said young women from the outside world should live or be instructed amongst them. Thus, on another side of the church (and yet within the enclosure of the convent), a large building will be erected, around which a grill or bars will be fitted.[39]

This injunction was present in all the Bulls granted to Ursuline houses during the seventeenth century. Indeed, letting 'the world' into the convent was a significant change in the conception of Tridentine monastic life for women. Contact with day students was potentially the most threatening aspect of Ursuline teaching: the physical presence of lively creatures, unaccustomed to the dignified demeanour required from those who dwelt in the cloister, was a potentially disruptive element and was therefore checked by close supervision:

In this respect as in many, the Ursulines across France developed a standardized *modus operandi* designed to be pragmatic and unobtrusive to conventual routine. Once the day students entered the walls, they were to go straight to the place dedicated to their teaching. They were in no circumstance to smuggle in any writings or other items to anybody in the convent, either nun or boarder. Any girl found doing so would be punished the first time, and if she

---

[38] ADHG, 221H-4.

[39] ADHG, 221H-25, f. 26: 'il ne nous a pas [...] semblé bon ni bienséant pour les dites religieuses que les dites jeunes filles du monde vivent et soient instruites parmi elles; on bâtira d'un autre côté de l'église, (dans la clôture toutefois du monastère), un grand corps de logis, autour duquel on mettra une grille ou des barreaux.'

relapsed into the same offence, she would be punished and excluded from the day school.[40]

Although no evidence survives of such offences having actually occurred (in Toulouse at least), the disruptions which might have arisen from the smuggling of written material into the house would have been immense. Inside the walls, the only authorized readings consisted exclusively of devotional works, which were envisaged as means of deepening one's relationship with God. Thus, reading was meant to help nuns and boarders in their meditations and to elevate their minds towards the divine. However, any writings smuggled in by day girls would have been likely to have been of a different nature altogether. Romances and novels, pamphlets, comedies or satires were all deemed unsuited to the spiritual propriety of the cloister, since they aimed to entertain and amuse, thereby debasing their readers with worldly frivolities. Even personal correspondence in the form of letters or notes, if exchanged between inmates and day students, might trap the sisters and boarders in mundane concerns and, perhaps more dangerously, risked sowing the seeds of discontent in the cloister by awakening feelings of longing, homesickness, curiosity or envy. Compared with the nuns, the novices or even with the boarders, the day pupils were the representatives of 'the world', the only ones to have contact with outside affairs.

This severity was a symptom of fear towards girls who came directly from a world which lay just outside the convent's impassable doors. Indeed, the presence of the day students greatly increased the possibilities of the sisters' straying from their austere path. This danger was anticipated not merely for the sisters themselves but also for their boarders, upon whom enclosure was also enforced although many of them might not have any particular propensity towards religious life. Kept at a suitable distance from the routine of the religious house, the day girls would in this way benefit from all the opportunities offered by Ursuline education - dispensed by enclosed virgins - without yet running the risk of endangering the order of the institution.

Such a tendency to categorize people according to the groups to which they belong and to enforce their physical segregation was also carried through into the school itself, where interaction between the pupils (boarders and *externes*) was restricted in various ways. First, physical separation was ensured by allocating specific rooms in which the pupils would live and learn. Then, it was only the teachers who came in contact with the students, and not all Ursulines were required to teach at all times. Parayre explained that in the Toulousain establishment, each classroom was served by a teaching sister.[41] When a class became too large for

---

[40] ADHG, 221H-28 bis, 5, f. 12: 'Les filles en demi-pension étant entrées dans le monastère iront droit au lieu qui leur sera destiné, avec défense de porter en façon quelconque aucun écrit ou autre chose à personne du monastère, soit religieuse soit pensionnaire, et celle qui sera convaincue de l'avoir fait sera châtiée pour la première fois, et si elle retombe dans la même faute, elle sera châtiée et mise hors le monastère.'

[41] R. P. Parayre, *Chronique*, part 1, p. 142.

one teacher to manage on her own, a second one of her *consœurs* was designated to help. Generally, a tutor would be expected to cope with as many as 40 pupils single-handedly before requesting the help of another.

In this way, not all the members of the Ursuline congregation worked as teachers. In fact, some sisters specialized in religious offices (such as the *sacristaine* or the *maîtresse de chœur*) while those with a keen educational vocation were encouraged to focus upon the classroom as much as they possibly could. The obituaries of France's Ursulines specifically mention the ardour of some sisters who remained involved with the classroom either as teachers or supervisors for several decades and until prevented by old age, infirmity or death. However, although specialization allowed the sisters to dedicate themselves to responsibilities for which they were particularly gifted, even the important duty of teaching, which lay at the heart of the Ursuline vocation, was considered as no different from any other office. It was therefore to be discharged for a period of time but could be changed for other functions, on a rotation system. Thus, with the consent of the *prieure*, even an acclaimed pedagogue could take time out of the classroom and offer to carry out other duties. The number of mistresses varied according to the number of pupils. This rotation system, which ensured that each Ursuline was allowed to serve Mary and Martha in turn without sacrificing either one for the sake of the other, was at the core of the Ursuline *raison d'être*.

Unfortunately, documents relating to this aspect of the school's life are no longer extant; it is therefore impossible to know how many of the Ursuline sisters would have been acting as teachers at any one time. Ursuline historian C.A. Sarre also came across a similar gap in the records where, for the 40 convents he analyzed in Provence and the Comtat Venaissin, there were no documents indicating the exact numbers of those involved in the classrooms.[42] However, his suggestion that each house may have included around six teachers seems very convincing; for instance, the visitation report for Toulouse mentions six classrooms and the documents for Bordeaux indicate the same.[43]

Daily routine was extremely demanding on the mistresses, who combined the observance of as many features of conventual life as they could with their school duties. Between 4.30 when they awoke and 8.00 when they entered the classrooms, their time was spent in the same way as their *consœurs'*. At 8.00, they taught reading, writing (for more advanced pupils) and sewing, before accompanying the girls to Mass at 9.00. At 1.00 in the afternoon, they would proceed as they did in the morning with lessons in reading, writing and sewing, which were then followed by recitation. The last lesson of the day was between 3.00 and 4.00, when they taught Christian doctrine. After 4.00, the tutors were allowed a half hour's recreation before going back to the choir or to their cells to

---

[42] Claude Alain Sarre, *Vivre sa soumission,* p. 312.

[43] *Ibid.,* p. 324.

pray, meditate, read or sew.[44] The remainder of the day was spent in the same manner as the rest of the community, in religious occupations.

The Ursuline experiment, despite often limiting its innovations by traditional restraints, represented a promising advance in the field of Catholic female education. An element of modernity - the controlled relaxation of enclosure in a female religious community - helped to perpetuate the Catholic tradition which so often proved wary of novel initiatives. Since they took their daily learning back home with them (possibly discussing it later with their mothers and friends as they went about their chores), the day girls acted as intermediaries between the cultural, educational and religious influence of the convent and the wider society of Toulouse. In other words if, on entering, they brought something of the secular world into the convent, on going out, they took something of the convent into the world.

Thus, in many respects, Ursuline institutions presented the same profile as any traditional convent following the religious life as described in the twenty-fifth session of the Council of Trent, with a variety of offices allied to a clear distribution of both space and time for particular purpose.[45] Yet, their educational vocation implied that, if they preserved elements of traditional religious life, convents could not remain entirely faithful to the totality of the monastic model. The new paradigm of the teaching nun, combining two functions which had so far appeared irreconcilable, seemed to capture the spirit of the seventeenth-century wave of devotion. However, the practicalities of combining classroom and cloister entailed a number of adjustments to traditional monastic life: in order to achieve equilibrium between the active and contemplative lives, the usual *modus vivendi* of religious women had to be carefully reassessed and reorganized.[46]

We have seen that in terms of the institutional organization of her religious project, Mary Ward had chosen to preserve a profile which respected the usual hierarchical repartition of roles and duties in orthodox convents. Yet although the English Ladies' way of life was in fact comparable to that of the Ursulines, in their case this choice was pragmatic rather than ideological. These patterns were adopted because they made good sense and because they offered a practical method to manage an institution efficiently. However, the Institute's Ignatian vocation meant that a complete endorsement of the Ursuline *via media* was not practical since it would imply the sacrifice of some crucial aspects of the Ladies' mission, which could find its purest expression only in the imitation of the Jesuit way of life.[47] The major concrete difference between both Orders was of course the fact that one observed enclosure whilst the other did not. As a

---

[44] ADHG, 221H-28 bis, 5, f. 16.

[45] Session 25, 3-4 December 1563, Decree on regulars and nuns, chapter 5, in Norman Tanner (ed.), *Decrees of the Ecumenical Councils* (London, 1990), vol. 2, pp. 777-78.

[46] Linda Lierheimer, 'Female Eloquence and Maternal Ministry', p. 92.

[47] M.C.E. Chambers, *Life*, vol. 1, pp. 22-34.

consequence, many of the preoccupations with categorization and separation which were essential to Ursuline life became entirely redundant for the English Ladies; this was visible in the religious organization of the communities and was also sharply felt in the Institute's schools.

The Ursulines, in order to anchor the Catholic faith in local girls, had opted for a compromise which allowed the co-existence of teaching and contemplation. This represented a noticeable advancement in the role of women in the Catholic effort of evangelization, although the strictures of religion meant that their formula had to function in terms of controlled fluidity and co-existence rather than true inter-penetration. In contrast, the English Ladies borrowed some elements of conventual heritage, but also rejected others in order to achieve their own Ignatian system: they aspired to be active proselytizers, enjoying freedom of movement and initiative on the same level as the Jesuits. On the Continent, their houses functioned in a manner comparable to that of Jesuit colleges, welcoming and training new members as well as pupils, interns and externs. Moreover, their unenclosed lay status allowed them to explore avenues which were never open to nuns, and, by implication, gave them more room to innovate: thus, the divide between lay and religious which kept French religious teachers separate from their pupils did not apply to the Institute's schools. Mary Ward envisaged full interaction between her followers and their pupils, away from the divisive structures at work in the ensemble of the Ursuline establishments in France.

This difference was embodied in the architectural structure of the Institute houses, in which there was no equivalent to the physical separation which was imposed on and accepted by the Ursulines. The divide between members and pupils was in no way as marked in the Institute as it was in the standard Ursuline house: since Mary Ward's foundations had resisted transformation into traditional convents, such segregation was unnecessary. The members generally lived together, in a community without rigid partitions amongst themselves; this same spirit applied to their boarders and was reflected in the very layout of the establishments, which facilitated inclusion rather than isolation. The boarders shared their teachers' dormitories and refectories, in constant interaction with one another. They could be on friendly terms, speak even outside the classrooms and have free access to one another at all times; more importantly, everybody shared the same experience of the divine in common daily devotions which gathered pupils, novices and lay and professed members.

This interaction between teachers, Mothers and pupils provided a sense of equality and flow which could not have been provided by the Ursuline model which, as we have seen, the English Ladies were recurrently encouraged to adopt. Their system was altogether better suited to the nature of an Ignatian project than the rigidity of Ursuline demarcations would have been; this flexibility allowed real interaction between the Ladies and the girls they catechized. The Institute's boarding schools were first designed on the model of their first house in St Omer's Rue Grosse. They were meant to accommodate English Catholic girls and provide them with sound religious and secular education before sending them back to their home country. Conversely, the day classes catered mostly for local pupils, whose typical morning would start at 7.00 with Mass in the local church, followed by lessons from 8.00 to 10.00 and morning prayers. The afternoon sessions resumed at 12.30 with prayers, lessons from 2.00 to 4.00 and evening prayers and the recitation of the rosary at 4.00.[48]

The precautions designed to allow the teaching of day girls without jeopardizing the integrity of the establishment's enclosure, the segregation and compartmentalization which were so essential in Ursuline schools were, of course, not necessary in the schools of the English Institute, since there was no religious enclosure to protect. The Ladies were at liberty to go out whenever they required, which in turn implied that the daily entrance of students into their classrooms was in no way perceived as a perilous exercise in which the day school acted as a sort of airlock between the world of perdition outside and the spiritual sacred space inside. The flow of day pupils was a non-threatening event which did not involve a well-rehearsed routine requiring doors to be opened and locked according to a precise timing. As a direct consequence of this, the very relationships between the tutors and their tutees were of an altogether different nature, favouring contact, interaction and fluidity.

Yet lack of religious status and enclosure, although liberating for the teaching Ladies and their pupils, went hand in hand with some practical difficulties. The Ladies' teaching role was crucial and the reputation of the Institute largely rested on their shoulders. Indeed, amidst the controversy generated by the Institute's unorthodox nature, the flawlessness of its members' lifestyle was a precondition of their acceptance and only the most stringent standards could keep at bay public attacks on their moral character; in addition, the professionalism of their pedagogy must be without reproach if it was successfully to ward off all potential calumny. Thus, the teachers were entrusted with a highly important mission, and Mary Ward was careful in selecting those in whom she would entrust the reputation of her schools.

All these factors became all the more enhanced in England; there, the Ladies must not only be sure never to cause public outrage, they were working under cover in all discretion and exercised the utmost caution in their demeanour, for their appearance could, if found suspicious, precipitate the exposure of the whole school. They therefore dressed normally, wore no habit and gave every outward appearance of total normality. Their neighbours might suspect the house to be a Catholic house, but they certainly were not able to confirm their suspicions on the basis of the English Ladies' dress. In most cases, they also concealed their identity by assuming false names and using lay titles such as 'Mrs'.

Considering the responsibilities involved in the post of Mistress or teacher in the English Institute, it is hardly surprising that it implied a very specific and

---

[48] BCA, B33, Mary Roswitha Etscheit, 'The Place of Mary Ward in the Education of Catholic Girls during Penal Times', chapter V, p. 20.

arduous period of training which was perhaps not necessary for the French Ursulines. When a young woman decided to enter the Institute, she first went through two years of probation, as explained in the Institute's Plans; during that novitiate, if she intended to be a teacher (as opposed to a Mother or an Associate), time was set aside for her vocational training as a future teacher. This could take around six months, if the situation permitted. Considering the crucial importance of the teachers for the future success of the Institute, educational training was a most important part of preparation for the apostolate. For example, it was reported that Helena Catesby (novice mistress in Munich before she became Superior in Augsburg in 1682) 'devoted very great care and hard work to instructing her novices not only in the mysteries of our religion but also in the methods to be employed when teaching children catechism in school'.[49] Indeed, the Institute of Mary gained an outstanding reputation for excellence in the domain of teacher training, and its success was attributed to its ability to use the novitiate as a training ground; in this way, it had inaugurated a new way of life for women, one which was shaped on the model of the male clerks regulars and which adapted the Jesuit organization as faithfully as possible.

The lifestyles adopted by the English Ladies and the French Ursulines were bound to become very different once the Frenchwomen embarked upon their gradual process of conventualization; however, they retained a common core based upon their adoption of the mixed life. As each Order engineered a way of life capturing the complexity of its organization (one allowing for an Ignatian model, the other for enclosure), this dual essence belonging both to action and contemplation remained their essential defining trait. In the houses of the English Institute and in the convents of the French Ursulines, hierarchy as well as time and space were organized so as to serve both the educational vocation of the women and their religious nature. Individuals were defined by their religious positions and the offices of which they were in charge, but they were also identified with respect to their engagement in the classroom. The Institute's less formalized *modus operandi* did not signify a lesser commitment to a religious type of vocation, and the English Ladies never envisaged their Institute merely as a lay sorority, the contemplative practice of which would be entirely replaced by the apostolate. Divorcing themselves from the usual polarization which conceived of action and contemplation in terms of *exclusion*, they strove towards the *inclusion* of both ideals concurrently, thereby escaping any sterile duality and embracing a functional alternative, a third way. Through this inclusive ideal, Mary Ward's Institute would transcend the traditional dichotomy between lay apostolate and religious contemplation, and reconcile the two functions in the 'mixed' life it chose in imitation of Christ himself.

---

[49] BCA, B33, Mary Roswitha Etscheit, 'The Place of Mary Ward in the Education of Catholic Girls during Penal Times', chapter V, p. 12.

   This was an ideal which the Ursulines embraced ardently, but which they were prevented from putting into such vivid practice by their vow of perpetual enclosure. In the Ursuline formula, monastic observance was modified but by no means abandoned in order to cater for the demanding, tiring and time-consuming duties of the teachers. The *modus operandi* adopted by these pioneering women testified to their dedication to both the active and the contemplative life and demonstrated that, far from rejecting all elements of conventual observance, they were seeking to include these at the very heart of their organization. The new model of the teaching religious woman was nothing if not a continuity, an extension of the traditional model of the enclosed nun.

Chapter 7

Modernity and Tradition:
Imitating the Cloister

Love not the world, neither the things that are in the world.
If any man love the world, the love of the Father is not in
him. I John 2, 15.

As Elizabeth Rapley has noted, 'the Catholic Reformation has been portrayed as a watershed in religious life, the turning away from the old medieval monastic ideal of flight from the world to a new ideal of involvement and service in the world.'[1] Yet this chapter will contend that the active vocations of both the French Ursulines and the English Ladies, representatives of this 'Catholic Reformation spirit', did not function to the exclusion of contemplative features of spirituality: quite the contrary, their model of educational and missionary life was enriched by a deep trend of introspective and quasi-monastic piety.[2] The English Ladies and the French Ursulines were but two expressions of a wide-ranging female movement which voiced the desire of the seventeenth-century laity not only to become involved in the Catholic Reformation's evangelical mission but to see their efforts officially recognized as part of the very fabric of the Church. As such, both communities strove to organize their institutional structures and their daily routines in a manner which would allow them to be true to their dual essence and to honour both Martha and Mary, allocating equal importance to action and to contemplation, embracing the model of the cloister while celebrating the duties and the richness of the 'mixed' life in imitation of Christ.

In order better to understand the complexities of the early modern dialectic of action and contemplation, one must take great care to avoid the trappings of historical foreshortening and resist the temptation to oversimplify the reality of conventual piety as a passive life of prayer which was altogether cut-off from the world and involved neither physical mobility nor interaction with others. The eighteenth-century anti-clerical writer Denis Diderot gave a literary voice to this point of view via the intermediary of his heroine, who feared a cloistered life more

---

[1] Elizabeth Rapley, 'Her Body the Enemy: Self-Mortification in Seventeenth-Century Convents', *Proceedings of the Annual Meeting of the Western Society for French History* 21 (1994) 26.

[2] Colleen Marie Seguin, '"Addicted Unto Piety": Catholic Women in England, 1590-1690' (unpublished PhD dissertation, Duke University, 1997), p. 291.

than she feared death: 'My body is here [in the convent] but my heart is not; it is outside: and if I had to chose between death or perpetual enclosure, I would not hesitate to die.'[3] According to such an interpretation of contemplation, it seemed that since the Council of Trent had reinforced the rules on female enclosure, any woman who wished to enter a religious type of life was in fact forcefully coerced into cloistered passivity and into complete subjection to male episcopal authorities, in a life which would carry few rewards for her.[4] Consequently, when Catholic women manifested the desire to pursue active vocations or to undertake evangelical work, their endeavours could at first glance be interpreted as manifestations of their rejection of the traditional conventual model and as expressions of a strong will to reclaim their lives. The apostolate, as the opposite of claustration, would therefore come to be valued as empowering and liberating, whereas its counterpart would be reduced to passivity and constraint. Yet, judgements such as these have now been exposed as simplistic and far from sound; in the complexity of seventeenth-century inter-relationships between religious and secular concerns, how did women who chose an apostolic life feel about the traditional cloister? How did they envisage the dynamic between action and contemplation?

Apostolate and prayer went hand in hand for the new 'teaching nuns' and 'Jesuitesses'; far from being mutually exclusive, they enriched each other and even found their *raison d'être* together. Documents analyzed in this chapter will demonstrate that the general position of the French Ursulines *vis-à-vis* the devotional practices of monasticism was not unlike the English Ladies': for both groups, a teaching and catechizing vocation did not, *ipso facto*, imply hostility towards the more established forms of female religious life. If their own calling was of an active kind, they nevertheless regarded the traditional elements of female religious observance as ultimately desirable and holy. We will see that, even in the earliest stages of their lay congregations, long before they sought papal approval, these proselytizers often chose to observe a regularity which was very much in keeping with medieval traditions; they also held chastity, poverty and obedience as the pillars of spiritual perfection and wrote at length on the merits of such monastic virtues.

Perhaps more surprisingly, mortification was also one of the highly esteemed traditions of the cloister adopted by the new congregations. This chapter

---

[3] Denis Diderot, La Religieuse, p.287: 'Mon corps est ici mais mon cœur n'y est pas; il est au dehors: et s'il fallait opter entre la mort et la clôture perpétuelle, je ne balancerais pas à mourir.'

[4] See Carol Christ and Judith Palskow, *WomanSpirit Rising: A Feminist Reader in Religion* (San Francisco, Cal., 1979); Rita Gross (ed.), *Beyond Androcentrism: New Essays on Women and Religion* (Missoula, Mt., 1977); Ursula King (ed.), *Religion and Gender* (Oxford, 1995); Julian O'Faolain and Lauro Martines, *Not in God's Image* (London, 1979) and Judith Plaskow and Carol P. Christ (eds.), *Weaving the Visions: New Patterns in Feminist Spirituality* (San Francisco, Cal., 1989).

will show how, although extreme asceticism was apparently contrary to teachings of Ignatius Loyola or François de Sales, a spirit of austerity survived right at the core of the female congregations which embraced their evangelizing ethos with the most passionate dedication. In fact, the teaching nuns, far from detaching themselves from the spirituality of the cloister, aimed at placing the essence of conventual piety at the heart of their mission. Thus, although attachment to the extreme austerities typical of medieval mysticism was not the norm, it was more common than might have been anticipated in active communities which embodied the apostolic spirit of the age.

Earthly angels: monastic virtues in the world

The French Ursulines and the English Ladies were filled with the religious sentiment which characterized seventeenth-century Catholicism; whilst partaking of the evangelical impulse of the Catholic mission of recovery, by nature active in the field, they nevertheless coveted elements of the 'perfect' life of spiritual isolation in the convent. In France as in England, the seventeenth century witnessed a wave of popular devotion which transformed the public face of Catholicism; although early modern piety opened up avenues for an apostolate rooted in the world, particularly for women, it remained imbued with the values of mystical piety. In both realms, secular women increasingly wished to base their lives upon the virtues traditionally associated with the cloister, striving to become earthly angels, the embodiment of monastic perfection amidst the chaos of secular society.

The French *flambée de dévotion* rooted spirituality firmly into the world: women freely chose to remain secular and to cultivate piety even amongst the daily distractions of secular life. Yet, their choice by no means signified a degradation in the perceived value of the cloister: it merely represented a shift in the definition of religious perfection, which had begun when François de Sales, in his *Introduction à la vie dévote*, extolled the virtues of a pious outlook applied to an otherwise 'normal' life. Accordingly, lay *dévotes* strove to remain as pure and as fervent as would be expected of them if they entered a convent. This choice demanded courage and spiritual fortitude, since it was perceived as a difficult challenge. Outside the safety of enclosure, without the support of regular monastic observance, these zealous Catholics tried to achieve a state of constant communion with God by bringing the spirit of the cloister into their everyday lives. Therefore, although devout women opted to remain in the world more than ever before, there was no global rejection of the values of the cloister but, on the contrary, an effort to adopt them from within society.

The famous Madame Acarie (1566-1618), for instance, has become the epitome of this salon piety which, in turn, embraced the ideals of religious houses. This pious *engouement* was far from being the preserve of the Parisian circles: the ladies of the provincial urban social elites, in keeping with this movement, turned to philanthropy as their ultimate moral concern. The *dévotes* formed spontaneous sororities, such as the congregation of the Visitation, striving mostly towards the education of girls, or the Sisters of Charity working for the poor in the city's general hospital, as their complement to support regular convents. Others, such as the *Madeleines repenties* and the *Dames de la Miséricorde* cared for prostitutes or helped prisoners. Dedicated to the well-being of their Catholic neighbours and applying themselves to pastoral work, forsaking the vanities of society and shunning ephemeral fashions, women everywhere adopted sobriety as the guiding virtue regulating their behaviour, their interests, their dress and every aspect of their daily lives.

This deep respect for the religious life was also all-pervasive within the microcosm of the French Ursulines, whose attraction for the religious ideal of the 'perfect' life led to a somewhat ambivalent relationship with claustration and monastic virtues. Thus, after starting their work in a congregated form they had believed most suited to their vocation, they gradually submitted to claustration in the first half of the century, a change which, for the majority, was effected without resistance and which has been the object of much debate amongst historians of the Order. Yet, one would logically have expected the early *congrégées* to have been fiercely attached to the freedom of movement which went hand in hand with their apostolate; these women had, after all, forsaken the prestige of established convents in order to join lay, uncloistered communities.

Indeed, the movement of claustration of independent Ursuline settlements across France did not altogether proceed without difficulties and the fact that a number of communities felt strongly opposed to the change has not escaped the attention of modern historians, some of whom have concluded that the movement towards formal enclosure was generally the outcome of autocratic decisions taken by bishops and imposed upon Ursuline communities without their consent. C.A. Sarre, for his part, wrote that 'enclosure imposed itself, or to be more precise, it was imposed upon the Ursulines by the ecclesiastical hierarchy'.[5] This argument seems to be supported by examples of such Provençal houses as Carpentras, Brignoles and Riez, and of other southern establishments such as Narbonne, where the *congrégées* petitioned against their elevation into a religious Order, claiming that their educational vocation could not possibly be fulfilled in a cloistered house. Despite vociferous protestations, this lay congregation had no choice but to be transformed into an enclosed convent in 1658, thereby bringing to an end the experiment of the *congrégées* in France.[6]

There was, however, one exception. Anne de Xainctonge, the foundress of the Dole community, refused enclosure throughout her life and although she and

---

[5] C. A. Sarre, *Vivre sa soumission*, p. 83: 'La clôture s'est imposée, ou plus précisément, elle a été imposée aux Ursulines par la hiérarchie ecclésiastique.'

[6] Elizabeth Rapley, *The Dévotes*, p. 57.

her followers answered to the name of the Company of St Ursula, their version of Ursuline life was much more akin to the first followers of Angela Merici than to their French equivalent. In order to preserve the quintessential spirit of the Merician enterprise, Xainctonge, when prompted to choose a religious rule, was careful not to adopt the rule of St Augustine, as the newly cloistered Ursulines had done. Instead, she chose the Rule of the Company of St Ursula, also known as the *Règle de Tournon*, which had been granted to the Italian *congrégées* in 1597 by Clement VIII. This little-known text, as Marie-Amélie Le Bourgeois has pointed out, was the only Ursuline document in which a canonical loophole allowed religious female groups to avoid submitting fully to enclosure.

This meant that, although the women of Dole renounced the official title of *religieuses* and remained a lay community, they were granted social and legal recognition through this official document which approved the Company's congregated way of life, with its commerce with the outside. In this way, while all the French congregations were gradually shutting their doors to the secular world, Anne de Xainctonge was able to salvage her company's geographical mobility; with time, as the divide between their very different lifestyles increased, the Dole establishment retained 'nothing of the Ursulines, but their name'.[7] As they drifted away from their conventual *consœurs*, they applied themselves increasingly to the imitation of the Jesuit model, in a manner reminiscent of Mary Ward and her English Ladies. Hence, Xainctonge's determination to avoid enclosure, combined with the high-profile cases of houses such as those of Narbonne or Aix en Provence for instance, seem to indicate that the transformation from lay congregations with an apostolic brief into a religious Order did not correspond to the women's own wishes.

Yet, with the exception of Dole, all of the Ursuline houses in France were transformed into cloisters during the course of the seventeenth century, a relatively short time considering their numbers. Such a rapid metamorphosis leads to the inference that the early Ursulines' attachment to their evangelical brief did not imply their rejection of the religious state and raises a fundamental question: was the movement towards claustration really imposed from above upon reluctant women, or was it partly the result of the Ursulines' own evolution towards a philosophy which inscribed monasticism into the very definition of the apostolate and the 'mixed' life?

In order to explore this intriguing question, an analysis of the early history of the Toulouse congregation is much needed. As the founders of the first establishment of Ursulines to become functional in France outside the Comtat Venaissin and its Provençal branches, Marguerite de Vigier and her followers were

---

[7] Marie-Amélie Le Bourgeois, 'Les Ursulines d'Anne de Xainctonge (1606). Contribution à l'histoire des communautés religieuses féminines sans clôture'. Thèse de doctorat, Faculté de théologie et de sciences religieuses, Institut Catholique de Paris, 1995, p. 148.

the first pioneers of the formula of the *congrégées;* as such, their decisions during the first few years of their work would be of momentous relevance for the entirety of the Ursuline family which subsequently developed throughout France. It is a fact well documented that, after receiving a papal Bull elevating their establishment into religion in 1614, the *congrégées* had refused to take the habit unless an official mention of their day classes was included in the document. In their dealings with Rome, they were determined to preserve what they considered their primary *raison d'être*, the teaching of day pupils, which could not be continued under the prescriptions of the traditional cloister described in the 1614 Bull. It was only in 1616 that the Toulousaines finally became nuns, having obtained a Brief which defined their vocation as a pedagogical one and ordered them to teach 'externs' as well as boarders. This surprising reaction could be construed as an indication that the Ursulines of Toulouse were as attached to their non-enclosure as Mary Ward's English Ladies were to theirs and resented their freedom of movement being curtailed by conventualization.

But one must not take this episode out of its wider context; a closer look at the community's documents has highlighted the little-known fact that Marguerite de Vigier and her sisters had lodged a request for their house to be elevated into religion as early as 1609 and that their desire to become recognized nuns had been frustrated by years of delay before their renewed appeal to Rome eventually produced the Bull authorizing them to enter religion. Seen from this perspective, it appears that enclosure was very much the *congrégées'* wish - a decision which was delayed in order to find a formula which would be true to their catechetic vocation, but certainly not because the women rejected the monastic world. Thus, the pioneers of the Ursuline work in France not only accepted the cloister, they embraced it and actively sought its life of spiritual perfection.

This interpretation is further supported by the fact that the Toulousaines had begun to operate some degree of separation from the world from a very early stage. In 1607, Marguerite de Vigier had agreed with her *consœurs* that they should remain inside their house on the Rue des Trois Rois Vieux and leave the pastoral work in the city to the good care of the lay sorority affiliated to the congregation, the *Dames de Sainte Ursule.* The fact that Marguerite de Vigier's followers had decided to seclude themselves in their house of their own accord, without any evidence of official ecclesiastical or municipal pressure at this early stage, indicates that they were not adverse to the values of monastic life but on the contrary were seeking to imitate them. Quite simply, their initial formation as *congrégées* had been the most pragmatic to begin their work in the city.

One could argue that the congregation resorted to this self-imposed claustration in response to public reserve towards a spatially mobile gathering of young women. Indeed, the Ursulines were finely attuned to the social perceptions of their close neighbours and probably sensed that this novel way of life, in a community but without enclosure, was highly likely to provoke public disapproval. Therefore, it is quite possible that their decision to remain in their quarters was, to a degree, a response to exterior pressure: although they could not embrace full claustration, which precluded all contact with the world, the teachers nonetheless endeavoured to respect as many of its defining features as they could, mainly by not exhibiting themselves travelling about the city streets.   The Ursulines of Toulouse therefore re-defined their formula: they were to stay in their house and undertake the teaching and catechizing of the youth, while their lay associates, the *Dames de Sainte Ursule*, undertook apostolic work in the world.[8]

However, this self-censorship was highly unlikely to derive purely from such considerations, and there is evidence to show that although adopting partial seclusion had practical benefits, it also sprang from the Ursulines' own wishes, from their own yearning for what they still regarded as an ideal. This explains both why the Toulouse congregation petitioned for enclosure in 1609 and why there was, across France, very little resistance to this shift towards claustration: it was a step which many *congrégées* were quite happy to take. As Elizabeth Rapley has argued: 'It would be a great mistake to imagine that the imposition of *clausura* was a hardship to all Ursulines. For many of them it was, rather, a progression to a more perfect form of life, one fully in tune with the spirit of the Counter-Reformation.'[9]

Toulousain documents corroborate this argument and show that the sisters held contemplation and monasticism in high regard. Though a fully hermetic type of enclosure would have negated the Ursuline vocation, the monastic ideal still commanded much respect and remained, to many sisters, the privileged channel towards the 'perfect' life of contemplation and heightened spirituality. In fact, even as they were refusing the uncompromising terms of the 1614 Bull of monastic enclosure and petitioning for the brief allowing them to interact with day girls, the *congrégées* showed how highly they valued the efficacy of orison by embarking upon a 40-hour long communal prayer.[10]

Far from rejecting traditional values through their new model of the teaching nuns, the Ursulines advocated all the virtues thought befitting religion, professing above all a particular affection for chastity, the epitome of perfection in a woman and, according to Parayre, the principal virtue of the Order, second only to the love of God. In the opening of his work, the chronicler praised their schools as 'seminaries of chastity', the pupils of which often went on to make a private vow to remain pure before joining a community.[11]   According to him, the congregation was sent by God in order to 'enhance the brightness of virtue in Christianity in the more dangerous and weaker sex', a clear testimony to his own

---

[8] The idea of the lay *Dames de Sainte Ursule* was adopted by establishments throughout the country after the process of conventualization, as an efficient way to preserve the evangelical brief of the Ursulines' initial 'mixed' life.

[9] Elizabeth Rapley, *The Dévotes*, p. 57.

[10] ADHG 221H-37, *Mémoires*, f. 46 and R. P. Parayre, *Chronique*, part 1, p. 111.

[11] R. P. Parayre, *Chronique*, part 1, p. 25.

views on female constancy.[12] Because of their dealings with the day pupils, these agents of the outside world, the Ursulines' morality could not be achieved merely through keeping temptations at bay within the safety of cloister but resided in the impregnable tower of the self. Even if their physical enclosure was not intact, that of their moral values was tightly sealed against sin.

The ambiguous relationship between apostolic women and the ideal of the cloistered religious life was not exclusive to the Ursulines. In fact, it was present in England amongst recusant women and, perhaps more surprisingly, amongst the English Ladies of Mary Ward's Institute as well. In fact, a look at the context in which Mary Ward's spirituality developed, as well as a consideration of the early stages of her vocation will illustrate how the vocation which is today known as innovative and daringly *avant-garde* found its genesis in less well publicized, yet equally significant orthodoxy.

During the times of the penal laws, Catholic piety was undergoing a phase of intense revival which, to avoid persecution, was either interiorized and limited to the sphere of the household or publicly expressed by travelling to religious houses across the Channel. Many of the recusants who chose to stay in their native land rather than enter religion strove to replicate some of the conventual patterns in their own homes, producing an essential feature of recusant piety: the concept of the quasi-cloister, where lay Catholics sought to model their household routines on the regularity of a religious Order. For instance, in 1591, the Jesuit Henry Garnet (1555-1606) praised Eleanor and Anne Vaux's house in Warwickshire as the refuge of 'many holy women consecrated to God'. Anstruther suggested that a female community might have operated there, following what he called 'the regular observance of a religious house'. He added that Anne Vaux had taken private vows of religion and was 'to all intents and purposes a nun'. Under Henry Garnet's direction, she had surrendered her property to support a 'motley community' formed by herself and her sister Eleanor, as well as Eleanor's two children and her adoptive daughter Frances Burroughs, a young woman renowned in posterity for rebuking the pursuivants who frightened her mother with their uncivil manners at night. They also shared their house with some of the Jesuit Robert Parsons's relatives (including his mother and one of his nephews), as well as with Henry Garnet's servant, Nicholas Owen, later to become a Jesuit lay brother.[13] When in June 1592 Garnet moved with the Vaux sisters out of Warwickshire and into London, their lives were described as 'as near conventual as the troubled times would allow'.[14]

When John Gerard (1564-1637) became chaplain to Elizabeth Vaux (Eleanor's and Ann's sister-in-law), his first endeavour was to organize the

---

[12] *Ibid.*, p. 58.

[13] Godfrey Anstruther, *Vaux,* p. 191.

[14] *Ibid.*, p. 195

household's life on a near-monastic model. His advice to the recently widowed Elizabeth Vaux was unequivocal: she ought 'to set cares of the next world before those of this'. In a manner typical of English recusant spirituality, he directed her to shape her life and that of her household on the model of conventual perfection:

> As [Elizabeth Vaux] could not give God her virginity, she
> would offer Him a chaste life. She would practise poverty,
> in the sense that she would put all she possessed or came to
> possess in the service of God and His servants; and she
> herself would be a kind of handmaid to them to wait on their
> wants. Lastly, and before all else, she would be obedient.
> She would carry out what she was told to do as perfectly as
> if she had made a vow.[15]

Gerard was exhorting Elizabeth Vaux to follow a regime which was as close to consecrated life as the situation in an English household allowed: she would strive for chastity, poverty and obedience as wholeheartedly as if she had taken religious vows. This was not out of the ordinary. The imitation of the cloister was a widespread practice amongst recusants; it was, in fact, one of the main features of the spiritual revival of the clandestine Catholic community of the time and characterized the atmosphere of the Babthorpe household, in which Mary Ward herself grew up. In her autobiographical notes, Ward recorded how, as a young recusant in England, she had felt deeply impressed by her family's fortitude; her grandmother, Ursula Wright, was a Yorkshire recusant who had spent no fewer than fourteen years in prison for refusing to renounce her faith. She noted that, during her stay with her at Ploughland, near Holderness (East Yorkshire), she had been edified by the way in which the old lady wove acts of asceticism into the fabric of her life, constantly alternating monastic observances with her quotidian chores.[16]

A little later, between 1600 and 1606, at Osgodby, the seat of Lady Grace and Sir Ralph Babthorpe, she was introduced to the quasi-religious lifestyle observed by the family and its servants.[17] The Jesuit priest James Sharpe (alias Pollard, 1577-1630), who ministered to the family, recounted how the household lived according to a monastic model and described its daily practices at length.[18] In a conscious attempt to imitate the regularity of conventual offices, the Babthorpes observed a daily *horarium*. On working days, the priest said two morning Masses, one for the servants at six o'clock and the other at eight o'clock for those who did not attend the first. Every afternoon, at four o'clock, he said Vespers and Compline for the gentry members of the household. On Sundays and

---

[15] Philip Caraman, *John Gerard,* p. 147

[16] BCA, B4, autobiographical notes, ff. 2-3.

[17] Henriette Peters, *Mary Ward*, pp. 44-54.

[18] Adam Hamilton, *The Chronicle of the English Augustinian Canonesses*, p. 180. See also Roland Connelly, *Women of the Catholic Resistance*, pp. 191-93.

holy days, the doors were locked while the members of the household heard Mass and sermons and the children were later taught catechism. The locking of the doors before Mass, although primarily a practical precaution, symbolized on a metaphorical level the mental shutting out of the world during times devoted to contemplation. Moreover, most members of the Babthorpe family meditated and prayed daily, following the *Spiritual Exercises* and retiring to bed at nine o'clock after their evening Litanies; the family's spirituality was further enhanced by fortnightly confession and communion.

During her stay at the Babthorpes as a recusant girl, Mary Ward herself had found personal ways of bringing the ethos of the cloister into her secular time and space; she assigned a cardinal virtue to each day of the week and dedicated each room of the building to a particular saint. Her desire, in those early years, was to enter a religious house on the Continent, where she could take the habit and become a nun, dedicating her every waking moment to contemplation, prayer and meditation. In fact, she had begun her religious journey by stressing introspection and the traditional virtues of cloistered nuns and it was only in later stages that it gradually evolved towards involvement in the world.[19]

It could be argued that English recusant women, far from seeking to innovate and escape the strict regime of the cloister were, on the contrary, attempting to follow Catholic tradition with renewed devotion. Since they had been deprived of their freedom of worship, recusant households had turned inwards in order to foster traditional contemplation and imitate the religious model of the 'perfect' life as faithfully as their daily occupations in England allowed. The spirituality exemplified in the household practices of prominent recusant figures could also be cultivated in prison. Indeed, many recusants' desire to leave the world to devote themselves freely to contemplation was nowhere more evident than when they were held captive: far from pining away, they often thrived in prison, if not physically, at least spiritually.

In some gaols, such as the London Fleet, prisoners were allowed servants to attend upon them; they could see their friends or even procure books and writing material. Although locked up in their individual cells at night, they were allowed to meet other prisoners during the day. It is, therefore, not surprising that Catholics who were detained under these conditions should pray together and form themselves into small, closely-knit units where spatial confinement lent a semblance of monastic enclosure to a detainee's life. Within the walls of a prison-convent, Catholics could spend their days quite abstracted from the outside world and dedicate their time to contemplation.

In the 1590s, Lady Grace Babthorpe (1563-1635) made use of captivity in this way, to further the perfection of her devotional life, when she and five other

---

[19] See Jeanne Cover, *Love, the Driving Force*; Margaret Littlehales, Mary *Ward (1585-1645)*. Note also articles such as Lavinia Byrne, 'Mary Ward's Vision of the Apostolic Religious Life', 73-84; Joseph Grisar, 'Mary Ward, 1585-1645, *The Month* 12.22 (1954) 69-81; and Immolata Wetter, 'Mary Ward's Apostolic Vocation'.

ladies were incarcerated in Sheriff Hutton Castle on the orders of the Earl of Huntingdon, President of the Council of the North.[20] Although these ladies were supposed to be kept in solitary confinement, their resourcefulness enabled them to make the most of their stay in the gaol. Lady Babthorpe managed to procure a priest who heard her confession and even brought Holy Communion to her, standing outside the bars of her windows at night. Emboldened by this first success, she used a hammer and a chisel to cut out the stone around her window, thereby allowing the priest to come inside her cell and say Mass during the night, before escaping, unnoticed, before daybreak. Every night, Lady Babthorpe let him in and then replaced the grate when he was gone.[21] She tried to ensure that her fellow-prisoners shared her privilege and helped them to see the priest.

For the rest of their two-year imprisonment, this subterfuge enabled the women to enjoy a degree of spiritual freedom which counterbalanced their physical confinement. Interestingly, they made no attempt to use the enlarged window to make good their escape. In fact, they had very little to gain from regaining their liberty: their religious life would not have been improved by physical freedom but would, if anything, have been burdened with the chores of the supervision of gentry households. In prison, recusants of both sexes enjoyed the possibility of re-creating the contemplative regime of the monastery: thus, confinement behind walls, whether in gaol or in a cloister, served to focus the Catholic mind upon devotion.

Eventually, after years of persecution in England, Sir Ralph and Lady Grace Babthorpe decided to leave their estate in Osgodby and retire to relative anonymity in London. However, their reputation as recusants preceded them and their house was raided. Unable to obtain the quiet religious observance they sought, they retreated to Louvain, where Sir Ralph died in 1617. Lady Grace Babthorpe resolved on remaining a widow and dedicated her life entirely to God; not surprisingly, her religious ideal was a contemplative life. Therefore, despite friends' and priests' exhortations to remain in England, where they believed she could be more useful to God through her involvement in the recusant network, she chose to retire to a convent. In 1621, she became a Canoness of St Augustine in St Monica's Convent in Louvain, where she was professed at the same time as one of her grand-daughters, Grace Constable.[22] In time, Lady Babthorpe's vocation for the contemplative life was shared by many of her descendants and several of her grandchildren entered religious orders; one of her daughters, Barbara, who had been Mary Ward's childhood companion during her six-year stay at Osgodby, had

---

[20] John Morris, *The Troubles of Our Catholic Forefathers*, p. 228. Among those imprisoned there with her were Lady Constable of Holderness, Mrs Ingleby of Ripley, Mrs Metham of Metham, and Mrs Lawson of Brough.

[21] *Ibid.*, p. 231

[22] *Ibid.*, pp. 233-236 and Adam Hamilton, *The Chronicle of the English Augustinian Canonesses*, pp. 180-182 and pp. 202-213.

joined the Institute at its very inception and later became Superioress of its Roman branch for over nine years.

Lady Babthorpe was not alone in her choice of Continental exile: religious vocations were rife and Hugh Aveling estimated that up to 5,000 English Catholics travelled to the Continent to enter the religious life between the years 1598 and 1642.[23] While men mostly flocked to the newly established English College in Douai, women found refuge in a variety of pre-Reformation monasteries. This is what Mary Ward herself did when in 1606, at the age of 21, she finally persuaded her father to allow her to leave for Flanders and become a member of the local Poor Clares. Although her father believed she would have achieved more for the Catholic cause by making a good marriage and becoming an active recusant, she had persevered in her desire for religious life on the Continent. In fact, it was only after she had stubbornly turned down four suitors that she was finally granted her wish.

To the young Mary Ward, the monastic lifestyle seemed best suited to the pursuit of spiritual perfection and the salvation of the soul, since it offered the closest relationship possible on earth with the divine. This belief lay behind the early organization of the houses of the Institute which, from the very beginning, had adopted a semi-monastic lifestyle which, in many respects, bore the hallmark of religious observance, with each time of the day corresponding to a duty and each place being allocated a function.

Further proof of Mary Ward's spiritual orthodoxy can be found in her own papers and correspondence, where she extolled traditional monastic virtues as ideals towards which one ought to strive. Ward identified chastity as the most desirable of all virtues, particularly in women: 'Of all virtues to which I was drawn with greatest affection was chastity.'[24] This dedication to religious values continued into her later life and the 1616 *Ratio Instituti* specified that the members of the Institute should take a private vow of chastity, the transgression of which would incur irrevocable expulsion, regardless of circumstances: Ward was determined that her followers would be of perfect virginal countenance and 'altogether angelical'.[25]

Such attachment to monastic values, and in particular to chastity, had its roots in her six-year stay with the Babthorpes, which engendered the awakening of her personal religious vocation. In that Catholic household, the women gathered together whilst sewing or embroidering; it was on such an occasion (as the pictorial biography known as the *Painted Life* chose to recall) that the young and impressionable Mary Ward was told the story of a nun who, after breaking her vow of chastity and giving birth to a child, had been allowed to re-enter her

---

[23] Hugh Aveling, *The Handle and the Axe*, p. 98.

[24] BCA, B4, autobiographical notes (transcribed in Emmanuel Orchard (ed.) *Till God Will*, p. 10.)

[25] BCA, B18, *Ratio Instituti*, f. 16.

community.[26] Thereafter, the offender was constantly reminded of the seriousness of her sin: as a penalty, she was made to lie before the chapel door so that all the other nuns had to step over her on their way to the choir. On hearing the story, Mary Ward was reportedly not shocked by the severity of the punishment but edified by its example, from which she conceived a greater respect for virginal purity and the rigour of religious austerity.

Therefore, when the young woman finally entered religion in 1606, it is significant that she chose the Poor Clares at St Omer, since this decision expressed a spirituality centred on inner reflection: as she later confessed in her 1620 letter to the Nuncio Albergati, she could not as yet envisage a religious purpose outside the cloister. She explained that, initially, she had felt attracted to the traditional religious lifestyle and anticipated 'content in solitude and abstraction from the world':

> I had no particular vocation to one Order more than another, only it seemed to me most perfect to take the most austere that a soul might give herself to God, not in part but altogether since *I saw not how a religious woman could do good to more than herself alone. To teach children seemed then too much distraction ... as therefore to hinder that quiet and continual communication with God which strict enclosure afforded.* [...] I found a far more sensible content in solitude and abstraction from the world.[27]

Thus, the foundress of the Institute which was deemed so unacceptable that it had to be suppressed by Urban VIII in 1631, began her religious journey in a remarkably unthreatening way, holding medieval religious values as paragons of perfection.

When she left the Poor Clares of St Omer, Ward could have chosen to enter any one of the many religious and lay communities which were thriving in that town. The community of the Daughters of St Agnes had been established there around this time: following an Augustinian rule similar to that of the Ursuline *congrégées*, their vocation was educational and they devoted themselves to the basic lay education and the Catholic instruction of local girls, regardless of their social backgrounds. It is, therefore, a testimony to Mary Ward's dedication to traditional monastic life that she did not show any interest in this pious community of *dévotes*, but chose to remain linked with the Poor Clares.[28]

One of the most telling attestations of Ward's faithfulness to the conventual model was her early affinity with clausura and the contemplative channels it offered; paradoxically, the innovator whose steadfast refusal of enclosure led to the suppression of her Institute, started her project with some type

---

[26] *Painted Life*, panel 9.
[27] BCA, B5, letter 4 to Nuncio Albergati, 1620 (italics mine).
[28] Henriette Peters, *Mary Ward*, p. 73.

of semi-cloistered *modus vivendi*, which she described in her 1612 *Schola Beatae Mariae* as follows:

> And although this Institute of its nature does not allow of the strict cloister in the present condition of England, still, far from having the house open to all, we desire rather to have cloister so strictly observed that no access is to be allowed to any extern whatsoever in the Chapel and [boarding] schools [...]. But necessary and serious conversations will be referred to the grill destined for that purpose, and no one shall go without permission of the Superior who shall be present at the conversation so that, should the Superior later require it, she may be able to recount what she has heard.[29]

This passage plainly indicated that in 1612 the foundress expected her Institute to compensate for its lack of strict enclosure by implementing some safeguards to guarantee the integrity of the religious house and of its boarding school. The model of enclosure and grills is entirely similar to the system of parloirs we have seen adopted by the cloistered Ursulines, and indeed by all other monasteries. Clearly, what was to become a ground-breaking vocation had in fact originated from unassuming and traditional beginnings, endorsing most of the received conceptions of female religious perfection. Thus, in order to understand the nature of Mary Ward's work, it is essential to remember that the Institute's opposition to enclosure did not spring from the personal abhorrence that its foundress may have felt, but from her dedication to her vocation to 'Take the Same of the Society', a calling which did not allow for any separation from the world.

Hence the Institute's archives contradict the stereotype of a rogue community of women intent on divorcing themselves from centuries of tradition. Rebellious natures do not emphasise obedience as one their chief spiritual aims; yet, as Mary Ward took the Spiritual Exercises around 1612-1614, she promised to subject her own will to that of her director. In her 35 resolutions, obedience was a prominent feature, in a gesture of self-denial which confirmed her attempts to bridle her own desires.[30] In resolution 10, she declared: 'I will never contradict in desire, word, nor action the will of my superior'. This determination to be impeccably obedient was reiterated several times throughout the text, in declarations such as: 'I will embrace all his [her director's] words and commands with great conformity of will and judgement and will execute all that he commands or desires with great devotion, reverence and promptitude.'[31] Later still, her resolve verged on the ascetic when she stated:

---

[29] BCA, B18, *Schola Beatae Mariae*, item 14, italics mine.

[30] BCA, B9, notes written during the Spiritual Exercises, 1612-14.

[31] *Ibid.*, resolution 11.

I will not permit in myself the least repugnance to whatsoever obedience shall ordain, nor nourish in myself a contrary opinion. My will with obedience shall be always one and the same in every occasion, whether the thing be great or small, prosperous or adverse, easy or hard.[32]

It is edifying that the woman who has been portrayed by some of her contemporaries as a troublesome innovator, if not an out-and-out rebel, should choose to apply herself to the pursuit of spiritual perfection through the channels of such monastic values as chastity, separation from the world and obedience. Moreover, she indicated that this was to be the path of her followers and described the office of the mistress of the novices as one essential to ensure that the prospective nuns were 'exercised in solid virtues, and rightly instructed in the practice of prayer, that they become active lovers of solid mortification and true enemies of self-will and self-love'.[33] The English Ladies were therefore far from rejecting the established paradigm of religious excellence; on the contrary, they strove towards its complete assimilation and regarded it as the only sound basis for their novel foray into the female apostolate.

Thus, during her formative years, Ward's devotion had taken the form of the utmost introspection in her daily prayers, fasts and various acts of austerity and humility. As Jeanne Cover remarks, Ward appeared to be influenced by devotional literature rather than by the mass of controversial writings which fed the religious debate in the seventeenth century; she was guided in her spiritual search by influential works such as Robert Southwell's *A Short Rule of Good Life* and Theatine Lorenzo Scupoli's *The Spiritual Conflict* (1589).[34] The former, dedicated to lay women, especially in England, was meant to guide them in their daily examination of conscience and help them to avoid sins. The latter was not directed to a lay female readership but to those who had entered the religious life; its aim was similar to that of Southwell's treatise, and Mary Ward seems to have been greatly affected by both. Moreover, her desire for an enclosed religious life was encouraged by her reading of Ignatius Loyola's *Spiritual Exercises*, which she used for the guidance of her soul during her stay with the Babthorpes. Although Loyola's work was not specifically designed for women, many female recusants followed them through a desire to retire from the chaos of the world and lead the ascetic life of the cloistered religious. The English Ladies were far from rejecting the traditional ideal of religious perfection; on the contrary, they regarded it as the only sound foundation on which to base their novel foray into the female apostolate.

---

[32] *Ibid.*, resolution 27.

[33] BCA, B18, *Ratio Instituti.*

[34] Jeanne Cover, *Love, the Driving Force*, p. 33.

"The soul is in the body as in a tomb"

Mary Ward shared a common spiritual heritage with her closest followers, who also experienced intense inner spirituality through their devotional practices. The necrology of Barbara Babthorpe (1591-1654) maintained that 'her spiritual gifts far surpassed her natural talents, though these were of a very high order', which suggests that Barbara Babthorpe may not have felt talented or even drawn to a teaching apostolate, and may have preferred more traditional avenues of communication with the divine through contemplation and prayer. She certainly practised austerities and self-denial and was reputedly 'severe and hard, unmerciful even to herself', a rigid discipline of the self which was counterbalanced in her kindness to others and impartial government.[35]

Another of Mary Ward's closest collaborators was Winifred Wigmore (1594-1656). This young woman worked with the foundress throughout her life and her sweet character had, according to her necrology, earned her the title of 'the little Saint'; her life was characterized by her meekness and her extreme personal poverty, and by the self-effacing dedication of her time and possessions to the well-being of others. Her eulogist equally praised her high degree of piety.[36] Through the example of these sisters, who shared Mary Ward's inclination towards contemplation and her respect for recognized monastic values, it becomes clear that the Institute, despite its active nature, aspired to some of the more traditionally monastic ideals. In fact, the English Ladies combined their new way of life with the observance of many traits of medieval religious practice.

For instance, they resorted to the discipline much more frequently than might have been anticipated in an apostolic congregation, the rules of which clearly stated: 'as regards external mortifications, our manner of life may appear only ordinary, since no one is, by the Institute, obliged [...] to perform external penances and austerities'.[37] As early as 1612, one of their supporters, bishop Blaes of St Omer himself, described the English Ladies - Mothers, associates and teachers - in laudatory terms, describing their lives as monastic, austere and ascetic. It was surprising that, although the rules of the Institute freed its members from physical chastisement which, by weakening the body, would prove counter to the active mission of the 'soldiers of God', some members of the Institute demonstrated their attachment to the heroic virtues of medieval monasticism in penitential practices.

Mary Ward herself castigated her body regularly. When she first worked in London in the year 1609, she underwent a long period of penance which she later described as continual and so harsh that her health was left diminished.[38] Since she was forced to abandon her austere black dress in order to work in

---

[35] BCA, box 4, B, f. 4.
[36] *Ibid.*, f. 15.
[37] BCA, B18, *Ratio Instituti*, f. 5.
[38] BCA, B4, Autobiographical notes.

England incognito, she resolved to wear a hair shirt underneath her garments, thereby honouring traditional monastic asceticism even in the midst of English gentle society. This was a subversive gesture in which Ward introduced the asceticism of the Catholic monastery into the circles of fashionable Protestant society. ' [She] went clothed as became her birth for matter and manner and wore underneath a most sharp hair cloth which by continuance did eat into her flesh, nor did she omit her daily disciplines, oft fasting and much watching.'[39] In this very act, Mary Ward operated an inversion of values, transforming polite society into the new forum for her monastic discipline. Even as she pursued an active vocation in the world, she practised constant self-denial, eating but one meal a day for the first seven years after setting up her foundation, sleeping exclusively on straw beds and undertaking many other forms of penance.[40] Such resolve to punish the senses was apparent in the resolutions Mary Ward took during the Spiritual Exercises:

> Seeing that my loathness to suffer has been the cause of so
> many evils, I propose henceforward to embrace all contrary
> things as due for my sins, and the part and portion which for
> myself I have chosen.[41]

In these ways, Mary Ward did not shrink from punishing herself for all but the smaller defects, and her spirituality was imbued with a trend of asceticism worthy of the most austere regular Order.

Some years later, in 1618, the foundress wrote down a few brief notes during a spiritual retreat she undertook when spending some time working on English soil; her desire to punish herself for her perceived shortcomings remained as present as ever and found their expression in statements such as 'I wanted a sorrow', '[I] had some desire and resolution to begin a course of mortification'.[42] Such forms of penance were not a requirement but rather the expression of her personal asceticism: her understanding of religious perfection implied the observance of strict religious rules. Mary Ward's ascetic penchant was also shared by some other members of the Institute such as Frances Bedingfield, whose necrology recorded that :

> she learnt to despise the world and its vanities before ever
> having tasted of them for, from her fourteenth year, she had
> renounced all for God. Far from flattering her body, she
> brought it to subjection by fasting, chains, discipline often
> and many other like painful things.[43]

---

[39] BCA, A12, *Briefe Relation*, f. 15.

[40] *Ibid.*, f. 16

[41] BCA, B9, notes written during the Spiritual Exercises, 1612-14, resolution 5.

[42] BCA, B9, retreat notes, April 1618.

[43] BCA, box 4, necrologies, f. 17.

Nor was Bedingfield alone in this austere outlook: it is interesting to notice that, when Mary Ward was in prison in Munich in 1630 during the months leading to the Institute's suppression, she repeatedly urged her followers not to undertake overzealous acts of penance which could cost them their health. She wrote to Elizabeth Cotton about her close friend Mary Poyntz, who were then responsible for the Munich community of around 40 members: 'Mother Rectress, with respect, shall do no corporal penances but what I first know - nor you neither.' Four days later, she insisted: 'For penances, twice a week you both take the discipline for the space of a *De Profundis* and no more; and once, and once only, James may wear a haircloth and Peter a bracelet. I say again, I would have neither of you pray after ten nor before six, seven hours a bed.'[44] Her worry is constant and palpable about her *consœurs* and the lengths to which they might go in her absence, perhaps even in an effort to secure God's intercession for her release. Through these letters, mortification and penance appear to be common practices in the Institute.

Such indications of a propensity towards monastic catharsis, although they are the exception rather than the norm, nevertheless appear in the Institute's documents with more regularity than might have been anticipated considering the novel, Ignatian nature of the Ladies' vocation. It is, therefore, clear that the English Ladies' spirituality derived directly from that to which they had been habituated in English recusant circles. As members of one of the most pioneering female religious enterprises in early modern Europe, they nevertheless held monasticism and contemplation in high regard and did not envisage their Institute as a way of freeing themselves from the constraints of the cloister. Thus, the image of Mary Ward as a feminist adventurer who purposefully set out to destroy centuries of tradition in the Catholic Church is an anachronistic misinterpretation of the genesis of an Institute whose active vocation did not imply a rejection of the traditional features of monastic piety but, on the contrary, found spiritual nourishment in contemplation and respected the cloister as a path to perfection.[45]

The same generalization holds good for the Ursuline communities throughout the period: contemplation, the ability to pray for extended periods of time, abstraction from the senses, all these characteristics of piety feature frequently in the list of virtues recurring throughout the hundreds of death notices collated by the Paris community. One of the factors which sometimes led researchers to infer that the Ursulines valued action over contemplation was the sisters' choice of the Rule under which they would operate when they became religious. All communities elected the Rule of St Augustine as best suited to their vocation being, as it was, adapted to a lifestyle which observed the traditional monastic regime, whilst at the same time allowing enough flexibility to enable the nuns to pursue an active apostolate.

---

[44] BCA, B5, lemon juice letters dated 14 February and 18 February 1631.

[45] Patrick Collinson, ' "Not Sexual in the Ordinary Sense"', pp. 127-8.

Yet, the Rule of St Augustine, flexible though it was, did not represent a dispensation from all penitential rigour altogether. Indeed, the documents of the Toulouse community point to the contrary. In her seminal study of the French Ursulines, Gueudré explained this seeming anomaly by surmising that Marguerite de Vigier had taken the Rule of St Augustine to the extreme, imitating the ascetic practices of the convent of the *Chanoinesses de Saint-Augustin* which was reputed through the city for its stringent discipline and its regular recourse to mortification.[46] She then went on to conjecture that the severity of the asceticism in Toulouse was the result of the misunderstanding of its over-zealous foundress. Yet, this does not seem to have been the case. The *congrégées* had embraced penitential practices out of choice, many of them years before they became nuns, and not as a result of the mistaken judgement of Marguerite de Vigier. We saw how in 1607 they had locked themselves away inside their house on the Rue des Trois Rois Vieux. Later, in 1612 (four years before their elevation into religion) they had adopted a quasi-monastic lifestyle, taking up the customs of the most rigorous convents:

> [the congrégées] applied themselves more particularly to the practice of religious virtues [...] and even to the austerities prescribed by the Order [of St Augustine]. They wore the hair shirt for several years, slept fully clothed and observed many fasts and days of abstinence; this went on for several years until their superior commanded them to stop and to write more moderate constitutions, since he feared [such asceticism] would render them less fit to the exercise of the Institute of the Christian Doctrine.[47]

In this instance, the sisters' early zeal for penance was checked by the supervision of male authorities; yet, the same episode recurred in 1619, when Jean de Rudelle's visitation report on the convent expressed his concern at finding several iron belts and thin straw mats in the sisters' cells. The former he confiscated, putting them into the care of the superior; as for the latter, he required the superior to take care that they should not prove adverse to the women's health.[48]

---

[46] M. C. Gueudré, *Histoire de l'ordre des Ursulines*, vol. 1, pp. 118-19. Gueudré referred to the same congregation's fasts, wakes, night prayers, wearing of hair shirts and sleeping on straw which Parayre exposed episodically in the *Chronique*, part 2.

[47] ADHG, 221H-37, *Mémoires,* f. 98: '[les congrégées] s'exercèrent plus particulièrement à la pratique des vertus religieuses [...] et même aux austérités de l'ordre. Elles portèrent plusieurs années chemises de laine, couchèrent vêtues et firent plusieurs jeûnes et abstinences et continuèrent plusieurs années jusqu'à ce que le supérieur leur commanda de le laisser et de dresser des constitutions plus douces parce qu'il craignait que cela les rendît moins propres à l'exercice de l'Institut de la Doctrine Chrétienne.'

[48] ADHG, G- 663, item 23, f. 16, *Visite de l'église du collège et monastère de Ste Ursule de l'ordre de Saint Augustin de Toulouse*, 24 July 1619.

It is true that in Toulouse, exceptional penitential practices feature in many of the members' biographies. Catherine de Pins (1585-1664), in religion *sœur* de saint Bonaventure, wore the hair shirt, chastised her flesh with a metal chain and slept on a thin straw mattress on the bare floor. Parayre declared that she treated her body 'like her worst enemy' and knew no mercy for herself.[49] Yet, Toulouse was no more atypical in its penitential practices than it was with its teaching customs. Thus, Ursuline asceticism expressed itself in various ways all across France and the death notices of some sisters testify to the extremities they were willing to go to; the most widespread forms of penance were prolonged fasting, flagellation, the wearing of a hair shirt and sleeping on straw beds, or even on the floor, denying the body any basic comfort.

The numerous death notices kept in Paris prove that extreme forms of penitential practices were not confined to any one community in France; many of them make uneasy reading, as the deceased sisters' biographer recalled self-inflicted punishments with often undisguised admiration. Although necrologies were evidently written to portray the departed in the most edifying light possible, their testimonies are valid indicators of Ursuline practices. They indicate that extreme self-mortification was not the lot of the majority and was exceptional enough to be dealt with as an oddity. In some cases, it was to be admired, whilst in others it was to be feared. However, though such notices are the exception rather than the norm, they recur much more often than might be anticipated in an Order whose vocation has been taken to embody the apostolic, moderate spirit of the seventeenth-century Catholic revival.

To mention but a few, Barbe de la Motte, in religion *sœur* de la Présentation, edified the community of Elbeuf by fasting constantly and sleeping in what was described as 'a kind of coffin, with a nasty pillow made of straw, without mat or mattress'; she wove death into the very fabric of her daily life, thereby expressing her detachment from this world.[50] Marguerite Loyauté, of the community of Meaux, 'treated her body like a slave and a mortal enemy', taking the discipline with an iron chain and refusing to eat her own food, feeding only on her sisters' leftovers.[51] She denied herself any warmth in the winter months, regardless of the outside temperatures; such gestures were meant to suppress all love for this material world and signify, through the channels of physical suffering, that her mortal coil was of little value to her.[52] In the Havre de Grace, Adrienne Theterel went one step further and willingly immersed herself in extremely cold water until she reached a state of hypothermia.[53] Marie Heyles, of Bayeux,

---

[49] R. P. Parayre, *Chronique*, part 2, p. 30.

[50] BA, ms 4991-19, Elbeuf, January 1694: 'Son lit n'était qu'une espèce de bière, avec un méchant oreiller de paille, sans paillasse ni matelas'.

[51] BA, ms 4992-64, Meaux, October 1691: 'Elle traitait son corps comme son esclave et son ennemi mortel.'

[52] BA, ms 4991-19, Elbeuf, 30 January 1694.

[53] BA, ms 4992-1, Havre de Grâce, 12 September 1690.

considered her body as no more than a 'carcass', to which she bore 'implacable hatred': she flagellated herself up to nine times a day. When, after a particularly vigorous session, she was found vomiting blood, her superior felt compelled to put an end to her self-punishment.[54]

Penance did not always take the form of self-denial: sometimes, sisters would, on the contrary, force themselves to eat or drink vile substances, usually the blood or pus from the wounds and sores of the sick, which they would kiss as metaphorical representations of the wounds of Christ.[55] Among many such examples, some stand out by the extent of mortification involved. The trope of the body as the enemy is picked up repeatedly, as in the notice on Geneviève Cousteughol, of Montferrand, whose necrology declared that: 'she would gladly have torn her body to pieces, treating it like a deadly enemy', before describing scenes of ferocious self-flagellation, in which she splattered her blood over the walls of her cell and soiled her stockings in blood stains.

Cousteughol's cathartic craze did not stop at the usual practices of penance but sought yet further forms of self-abasement which were probably shocking even to her *consœurs*. Her necrology related that she vowed not only to smell but also to eat what is prudishly described as 'a foul and stinking thing'.[56] Cousteughol repeated her gestures of self-humiliation when, in keeping with the gestures of medieval saints, she kissed and licked the face of one of her day pupils who suffered from a condition which affected her skin with open sores and wounds. This might have been one step too far even for her *consœurs*, who recorded that, unsurprisingly, the girl never came back to school after this episode. A lay sister in Moulins, Marie Gasparde de Sainte Catherine de Sienne also combined privation of comfort with self-imposed ordeal: not only did she endure the bitterest cold without ever warming herself by the fire, she also ate 'nasty leftover bits of rotten and corrupt meat', to which she added ashes and absinthe. On occasion, she sucked the ulcers and wounds of the sick and swallowed their pus.[57]

Such abhorrent acts of penance were also recorded in Toulouse with the young Marie de Liberos, whom we met as the girl who escaped marriage in 1606 to find refuge with the Ursulines against her parents' will; we saw how her utter dedication to her teaching duties had rendered her one of the most successful catechizers of the congregation and how she took her vision of the lighted torch to rural areas where she re-Catholicized entire neighbourhoods. Here we meet her

---

[54] BA, ms 4990-211, Bayeux, December 1643: 'Son corps était aussi peu considéré d'elle qu'une carcasse [...] elle lui portait une haine implacable.'

[55] See Caroline Bynum Walker, *Holy Feast and Holy Fast: The Religious Significance of Food to Medieval Women*, (Berkeley, Los Angeles, Cal. and London, 1987).

[56] BA, ms 4992-175, Montferrand, 4 January 1692: 'Elle aurait mis son corps en pièces, le traitant comme son ennemi capital', 'une chose fort sale et puante'.

[57] BA, ms 4991-205, Moulins, 29 October 1692: 'des méchants restes de viande gâtée et corrompue'.

again, but this time as one consumed by self-debasing urges. For Liberos, who successfully contrived to combine proselytizing with self-mortification, a teaching vocation in no way implied a lessened fervour for the religious strife towards perfection. Not satisfied with the usual practices of fasting and penance, she used her term of office as the community's nurse to abase herself still further. When one of her patients suffered from a severe pulmonary infection, its pectoral excreta so vile 'as to bring her heart into her mouth', the penitent nevertheless resolved to conquer her disgust and forced herself to kneel on the floor in order to kiss, then to lick the sick sister's sputum off the tiles. On another occasion, she forced herself to kiss the instrument with which she had just given her *consœur* an enema.[58] In these ways, Marie de Liberos combined, in her person, the religious observance and apostolic zeal which formed the dual essence of the Ursuline ethos.

Besides penitential practices, the Ursuline attachment to the traditional features of monasticism can also be illustrated in the sisters' experiences of mystical enlightenment. Once more, the death notices demonstrate that, throughout the country, many of the teaching nuns displayed a marked propensity for intense prayer, abstraction from their senses and divine revelations. The Ursulines of Montferrand described one of their members, Marie de Joüane (in religion *sœur* de la Présentation) as a pure mystic. Such were her gifts of contemplation that her biographer recorded:

> a mayfly or the leaf of a tree provided her with ample
> subjects of contemplation. God intoxicated her with his
> sacred wine, which causes all creatures to lose all memory;
> he put her in a state which was more passive than active [...]
> through these prayers during which she would spend ten or
> twelve hours, holily alienated from her senses, in ecstatic
> transports.[59]

Even in the very description of her raptures, the passive voice was employed to mirror the scene: God was the active subject, whilst Joüane was the object of the verbs. Here, she became passive, a mere recipient for the divine inspiration to which she abandoned herself, body and soul, with a regularity which suggested a true mystic, in constant communication with God. This is not a feature one might have expected from a woman who deliberately chose to enter a religious Order with an active pedagogical brief. Yet, her case was far from being an abnormality and most communities had their mystics: the dual essence of the Ursuline vocation

---

[58] R. P. Parayre, *Chronique*, part 2, p. 347.

[59] BA, ms 4991-162, Montferrand, 19 August 1693: 'un petit moucheron, une feuille d'arbre, lui fournissait un ample sujet de contemplation. [Dieu] l'enivrait de ce vin sacré, qui fait perdre le souvenir à toutes les créatures, et la mettait dans un état plus passif qu'actif, [...] dans ses oraisons où elle a passé les dix et douze heures dans un saint aliénement de ses sens, et transport extatique.'

was therefore embodied in the individual gifts of its representatives, some of whom felt in communion with God whilst they were teaching, whilst others were more inclined to feel his presence through the medium of contemplation.

Such inclination to mysticism can be further illustrated by the example of Anne Dubois, in religion *sœur* de la Visitation (1604-1670), who joined the Toulouse community in 1622 only to refuse the habit after her year of novitiate, arguing that she had become too lax in her devotional practices in the course of that year. Feeling guilty about her own indolence, she asked permission to undertake a second novitiate, during which her piety became of a more strongly contemplative nature, with particular devotion for the Eucharist and mental prayer.[60] Her visions and revelations portrayed God as a lover and her description of her ecstasies was filled with intense eroticism:

> What sweetness does God bestow upon my soul! What bonding kisses! What loving caresses! He holds her in His arms and uncovers His divinity to her; He shows her His divine perfection, He speaks to her as to a friend, assuring her He delights in her love, in her simplicity ... He caresses me like a small child, embracing me with such softness, to make me all His.[61]

In this short extract, the vocabulary used expressed a type of union with God which was far from purely spiritual. Though the author began to describe the delights of her soul, she soon abandoned this dichotomy separating body and mind, to become inclusive of her entire self. She did not desire union with God solely through her soul ('her') but through her whole being ('me'), to achieve perfect unison: 'to make me all His.' Embracing the bodily senses through which she received his divine love, she arrayed her vision of God with all the attributes of a heavenly lover and found a sense of intense well-being in his embrace. *Sœur* de la Visitation practised daily fasts, vigils and mortification to fight her bodily needs and cravings. Ultimately, her sensuality found its expression in the heightened communication with God which she transcribed in her poetry. As she succumbed to various illnesses, her cathartic inclinations drove her to chastise her body all the more and, through corporal suffering, she abandoned herself to the delights of her visions.

Thus, the very women who braved both popular opinion and canonical law in order to follow their pioneering evangelical vocations were also embracing the most elevated aspects of spiritual life. Abstracted from their physical beings, they elevated their souls towards the heavens and nurtured an intimate, mystical

---

[60] R. P. Parayre, *Chronique*, part 3, pp. 79-165.

[61] *Ibid.*, p. 109. 'Que de douceurs Dieu communique à mon âme! Que de baisers d'union! Que de caresses amoureuses! La tenant entre ses bras, lui découvrant sa divinité, lui faisant voir ses perfections divines, lui parlant familièrement, l'assurant qu'il se plaisait dans son amour, dans sa simplicité [...] me caressant comme un petit enfant, me pressant avec tant de douceur pour me faire toute sienne.'

relationship with the divine. The practical, catechizing essence of the teaching nuns did not preclude their quest for spiritual perfection through the channels of contemplation. One of the earliest members of the Toulouse community, Bertrande Sanchez, in religion *sœur* de Saint Augustin (1585-1648), had been received in the convent despite her feeble physical constitution. Although it was clear from the start that she would not be fit to undertake the hardships of classroom teaching, her contribution to the Ursuline spirit of her community was nevertheless treasured by all: mystically inclined and uncommonly erudite, she excelled at reading devotional treatises and particularly favoured the works of St Augustine in their Latin original. She would read his sermons to the whole congregation, nurturing its religious spirit and counselling her *consœurs* in matters of piety.[62] Since Parayre does not mention her teaching, it seems likely that she specialized in this area and did not take part in the classrooms activities of the school.

Amongst the teaching nuns, the divine light was extended to those with an active vocation. Jaquete de Maynie (*sœur* Saint Jean l'Évangéliste), who earlier illustrated the activist educational zeal of the early Ursulines of Toulouse, was so dedicated to teaching day pupils that she acted as the leader of the small group of *congrégées* who refused to enter religion on obtaining the papal Bull which initially made no mention of their open school. Maynie was, therefore, the archetype of the young Toulousaine with an active vocation which led her to insist on being employed in the classrooms even when she became ill and to continue teaching after suffering what was probably a stroke which left her paralysed in one arm.[63]

Yet, her proselytizing zeal never functioned to the exclusion of more mystical spiritual traits. As well as edifying her *consœurs* by undertaking the toils of the classroom despite her debilitating disease, she was renowned for her deep inner piety and for the time she spent in isolation, praying and abandoning herself to contemplation. The intensity of her devotion to Christ shines out from the numerous poems and canticles she composed, some of which Parayre transcribed in his *Chronique*. Like Anne Dubois, she also developed a heightened spirituality which allowed her to describe her relationship with Christ in exalted, sensual style:

> Ha, I pine / And am / Continually / Consumed / With love /
> Like a burning furnace. / If, by chance, you meet him, / Alas,
> tell him I cannot last; / Indeed, His love has set my heart
> ablaze / So much that it is nearly all consumed. / Support me,
> / Poor me,/ My sisters / I die / Of love / I am burning night
> and day.[64]

---

[62] *Ibid.*, pp. 265-79.

[63] *Ibid.*, pp. 71-73.

[64] *Ibid.*, part 1, p. 80. In French: 'Ha je languis / Et suis / Toujours / D'amour / Brûlant / Comme un fourneau ardent / Si le bonheur le vous fait rencontrer / Las dites lui que je ne

This passage is but one example amongst many which showed all the characteristics of intense mysticism and would not be out of keeping in the context of a strictly monastic cloister. In fact, the high incidence of similar mystical experiences seems to indicate that Ursuline spirituality had dismissed the usual binarity which traditionally opposed action and contemplation. On the contrary, their educational vocation, though focused on an active brief, praised contemplation as a special path towards perfection and union with God: transcending any simple dichotomy, the spirituality of the teaching nuns functioned more subtly, combining an acute awareness of its educational vocation with a profound reverence for the traditional model of the monastic lifestyle.

It may be that, far from divorcing themselves from traditional religious values, English Ladies and French Ursulines sought to use them as the very foundation stones of their innovative movements. They were, in fact, the condition *sine qua non* of the success of their enterprises. Since they proposed to work outside the usual sanctuary of the enclosure, the teaching nuns believed that they ought also to possess every religious virtue combined with unwavering constancy and unshakeable fortitude. The moral rigour of the cloister, for these educators, was to be found in the fortress of their own hearts. Thus, even in such active and pioneering congregations, Catholic women manifested a strong attachment to the established values which equated 'perfect' spiritual life with contemplation, monastic observance and penance. Although extreme ascetic practices were the exception rather than the rule, they were more common than might be anticipated from apostolic women whose catechetic vocation involved their voluntary abandonment of the cloister. This, however, presents a problem. If the English Ladies and the French Ursulines held the monastic ideal in such high esteem, then why did they initially choose a path so dramatically different from that of the monastery?

---

peux durer / Tant son amour a mon cœur embrasé / Qu' il est déjà presque tout consommé / Soutenez-moi / Las moi / Mes sœurs / Je meurs / D'amour / Je brûle nuit et jour.'

For both Us + ELs, apostolate was a gesture of self - abnegation. Nevertheless, they expected sanctification of souls in exchange

Chapter 8

To Leave God for God's sake: The Apostolate as Self-Abnegation

> The Spirit itself bears witness with our spirit, that we are the children of God: And if children, then heirs; heirs of God, and joint-heirs with Christ; if so be that we suffer with him, that we may be also glorified together. For I reckon that the sufferings of this present time are not worthy to be compared with the glory which shall be revealed in us. Romans 8:12.

There can be no doubt that the French Ursulines and the English Ladies embraced many characteristics of monasticism, despite their complete commitment to their active pedagogical vocations. Though they refused traditional enclosure for themselves, they often reiterated their admiration for claustration as a protector of virtue and a safeguard of spiritual serenity and order. Even as they opted for an active apostolate, they revered contemplation as a perfect path towards the divine and an efficient way to advance Catholic progress in Europe. In this respect, our modern understanding of the relationship between action and contemplation contributes to the usual puzzlement over active communities' esteem for monastic values, which we often see as paradoxical.

Since cloistered piety has all but disappeared from modern life, physical isolation and immobility have, on the whole, come to represent passivity and inactivity, notions the twenty-first century is quick to dismiss as useless. Subconsciously shaped by today's values which equate action with empowerment and contemplation with subjection, we often misunderstand the French Ursulines or the English Ladies, those appealing, determined women who braved public opinion and ecclesiastical censure in order to join unrecognized teaching communities instead of more prestigious (and, just as importantly, less controversial) convents. We expect them to provide examples of strong characters refusing to limit themselves to the gender-defined boundaries of the religious life. Their resolve, we assume, must indicate a degree of ambition combined with a strong desire to chose a different option: their choice, therefore, must be the manifestation of their self-will, refusing to limit themselves to the gender-defined boundaries of religious life.

However, the modern dichotomy between action and contemplation can be misleading. It is arguable that these early modern pioneers did not envisage action as a means of liberation from the Church, but rather as a gesture of ultimate sacrifice to it. Rather than a liberating movement of feminist empowerment, claiming new rights for religious women, could the catechizing mission of these apostolic women be seen as an act of self-denial?[1] This chapter will argue that these new congregations embraced the Counter-Reformation accent on teaching and catechizing not as a route to self-empowerment but, quite the contrary, as a gesture of self-abnegation; in a subtle trans-valuation of the medieval ideal of sublimation of the self through acts of mortification, the educational apostolate came to replace the more ostentatious practices of monastic asceticism as a means of abasement and a proof of devotion to God.

The apostolate, an act of self-abnegation

Exceptional vocations rarely reveal themselves with immediate clarity and, as Mary Ward exemplifies, they sometimes take several years to come to maturation. Ward's calling to the apostolate came to her as an unexpected blow. We have seen that, a young woman, she had felt particularly drawn to the austerity of strict traditional convents and she had envisaged piety only in the context of an orthodox Order. She confessed to a spirituality which had been centred upon the self, looking inwards rather than outwards; we can recall her own words:

> I saw not how a religious woman could do good to more than
> herself alone. To teach children seemed then too much
> distraction ... as therefore to hinder that quiet and continual
> communication with God which strict enclosure afforded.
> [...] I found a far more sensible content in solitude and
> abstraction from the world.[2]

The foundress of the Institute retained a personal affinity with orison and solitude, she felt bound to the monastic ideals of chastity, poverty and obedience as strongly as by a solemn vow and sought solace in the isolation of the religious life.

Such personal disposition led her to spend much of her time in silent prayer, absorbed in contemplation of the divine and seeking guidance from the Holy Spirit, hoping to be told how she, as an individual, could serve God and his Church. The simple yet essential key to understanding Mary Ward's extraordinary vocation, its seemingly boundless ambition and its non-negotiable terms derives

---

[1] See, Roberta Gilchrist, *Contemplation and Action: The Other Monasticism* (London, 1995); Thomas Merton, *Contemplation in a World of Action* (Notre Dame, Ind., 1999); Barbara Newman, *From Virile Woman to WomanChrist*; and Elizabeth Petroff, *Body and Soul: Essays on Medieval Women Mysticism* (New York, 1994).

[2] BCA, B5, letter 4 to Nuncio Albergati, 1620.

from this passive, receptive stance: through the channel of contemplation, Ward recorded being led to experience visions or revelations which, she believed, allowed her to be in communication with God. She received her pedagogical and Jesuistic vocation directly as a result of these enlightenments. According to her, the Institute of the English Ladies was entirely of God's making; she was but the mere recipient of his will, the empty vessel which he filled with his holy purpose and sent on his mission. But how did a young woman with a traditional monastic vocation come to change direction so dramatically as to become an intrepid 'Jesuitess' leading a new movement denounced as heretical by some and distrusted by most? What was the sequence of events which led to the transformation of Mary Ward's piety?

In the awakening years of her vocation, Mary Ward experienced a series of mystical episodes. We have seen that, despite the happiness she had anticipated in the regularity of a monastic house, her life with the St Omer Poor Clares left her dissatisfied and inaugurated an era of what she described as spiritual turmoil.[3] Having been accepted in the convent as a lay sister only, a non-enclosed status which implied daily begging in the city streets in order to provide for the Choir nuns, the young Yorkshire recusant could not envisage fulfilment in a lifestyle for which she had not been prepared. Yet, from the beginning, her desire to embrace whatever path she believed to be most pleasing to God was emphasized, as she noted:

> I stood silent for a while, feeling an extreme repugnance to
> their offer, but reasoning within myself that the Rules being
> the same and the place offered me only more abject and
> contemptible, this disinclination and repugnance could only
> come from pride.

Crucially, Ward recounted in the same document that George Keynes SJ had urged her to accept this place in the St Omer Poor Clares, saying that is was the will of God, a declaration which made such a deep impression upon her that she was able to reflect years later: 'These words "the will of God" so pierced my heart that I had no inclination to say or think anything else.' [4] Thus, resolved to conquer her 'pride' and to put the service of God before her own comfort, she accepted the position from a spirit of humility which, as we will see, encompassed her relationship with the divine and defined her personal rapport with her own vocation.

However, her fears about the suitability of this arrangement were confirmed: the butt of the antipathy of Mary Stephen Goudge, the community's

---

[3] See Anthony Clarkes (ed.), *The Heart and Mind of Mary Ward* (Wheathampstead, 1985); Emmanuel Orchard (ed.), *Till God Will*; M.P. Parker, *The Spirit of Mary Ward* (London, 1963); and Immolata Wetter, 'Mary Ward's Apostolic Vocation', *The Way*, supplement 17 (1972) 69-91.

[4] BCA, B4, autobiographical notes.

abbess, and deprived of the guidance of the novice mistress who, because of an illness, had to remain within the enclosure from which she was excluded, Mary Ward found her only solace in prayer. It was in such a context that, on St Gregory's Day in 1607, she went through the first of a series of divine inspirations: she recorded becoming inwardly convinced that her mission was to found a separate congregation for the English sisters of the Order, regrouping in one community all English-speaking Poor Clares and thereby creating a more homogenous entity sharing not only the same language but also the same recusant background, the same culture and a similar religious outlook, shaped by their English experience.[5] She later reminisced:

> Deprived of all human aid, I turned to God, my only help, who without delay and as if he had awaited a similar privation, favoured me with frequent and clear lights, accompanied with peace and strength of soul far more than I had ever before experienced. He showed me that this was not to be my vocation, and that I could without scruple depart.[6]

This revelation was the first step in the direction which her whole life was to assume; from this day on, her mind turned away from desires of solitary prayer and became occupied with the spiritual help she wished to procure her English fellow Catholics. This momentous change was incurred through visionary channels and through what Mary Ward herself described as divine inspiration.

After some deliberations with the ecclesiastical authorities of St Omer, she was allowed to initiate a separate establishment for the English Poor Clares; in 1608 she left the old house and its abbess, for a new house in Gravelines, within the same diocese. The Gravelines community - placed under Bishop Blaes's jurisdiction - began with only five of the members of the St Omer convent, who were transferred to their new home in a closed carriage, but soon welcomed four English new postulants; it represented a harbour where those who had fled repressive England could live together and share their spiritual freedom in the same religious house.

Yet even after such an important shift in her spirituality, Mary Ward still found no rest. A year later, in 1609, she was visited by another vision through which she became convinced that her vocation was not to be a member of any enclosed order at all: the contemplative life towards which she felt drawn was not to be her destiny.[7] When, in 1620, she wrote to Mgr Albergati to explain how this vision had caused her to abandon the austerity of the Poor Clares in order to adopt a missionary ideal filled with uncertainties, she described an epiphany in which joy and hope were intertwined with anxiety and foreboding:

---

[5] See M.C. Chambers, *Life of Mary Ward*. vol. 1, pp. 138-140.
[6] BCA, B4, autobiographical notes.
[7] Henriette Peters, *Mary Ward*, p. 106 and M.C.E. Chambers, *Life*, vol. 1, p. 227.

> There came suddenly on me such alteration that the
> operation of an inexpressible power could only cause, with a
> sight and certainty that there I was not to remain, that some
> other thing was to be done by me, but what in particular was
> not shown. [...] To leave what I loved so much, [...] to
> expose myself to new labours, which then I saw to be very
> many; to incur the several censures of men, and the great
> oppositions which on all sides would happen [...] afflicted
> me exceedingly.

The revelation had caused her intense turmoil since it had implied that, despite her
yearning for contemplation, she was not meant to be an enclosed nun. This
episode, known as the vision of St Athanasius's day, commanded her to inaugurate
an active life for female religious based on the model of the Society of Jesus.

Mary Ward had no doubt that her vocation was the fruit of God's
summons which had compelled her, almost against her will, to leave behind her
ideal of the 'perfect' life of monastic solitude and contemplation. It was with great
apprehension that she had received her calling to found an active Order, foreseeing
the difficulties this would entail and the opposition she would encounter.
Moreover, such a course of action meant that she was obliged to leave her
community of Poor Clares, the spiritual ardour of which she respected deeply even
if it was not, in the end, the life best suited to her. However, as she confessed to
Mgr Albergati, she realized that her personal inclinations had to be forsaken in
order to obey God's commands and she explained: '[I had] no power to will or
wish any other than to expose myself to all these inconveniences, and put myself
into God's hands with these uncertainties.'[8] Once more, the path indicated to her
was not one which she would have spontaneously thought of, not even one towards
which she felt attracted, but one which she embraced nonetheless because she
believed it was her godly duty.

In the aftermath of this episode, Ward became prey to many doubts; she
knew she had to leave her Poor Clares convent, but she was not sure what else she
was meant to do. When reflecting upon what might be required of her, she could
only envisage entering another convent of a different Order: she even debated with
her confessor whether she should enter the Teresians, so convinced was she that
her calling was to be monastic. Still in a state of discontent regarding her vocation,
she took private vows in 1609, promising obedience to her confessor and spiritual
director, the Jesuit Fr Lee, and pledging to spend some months in England helping
her oppressed Catholic compatriots. As she worked in England, groups of women
gathered around her and a female network of social welfare and spiritual guidance
was brought into life.

At this stage, Mary Ward still wavered between her desire for
contemplative life and her calling for the apostolate in the world. Her work in

---

[8] BCA, B5, letter 4 to Mgr Albergati, 1620.

England was perhaps the trigger of another divine revelation which enlightened her as to her God-given purpose. The 'Glory' vision showed her that her vocation was not to be a member of any enclosed order but rather to find a new way of making herself and her companions agreeable to God:

> I was abstracted from out of my whole being, and it was shown to me with clearness and inexpressible certainty that I was not to be of the Order of St Teresa [as Fr. Lee had suggested], but that some other thing was determined for me, without all comparison more to the glory of God than my entrance into that holy religion would be. I did not see what that assured good thing would be.[9]

So far, the young woman had come to realize and to accept that she was not to become a traditional nun, but on the contrary that she would be an apostolic woman, a pioneer of some new way, with all the uncertainties and all the hardships that his would involve. Yet she remained entirely in the dark about the precise nature of her mission, and this vagueness was another burden which weighed heavily upon her tormented mind. In her letter to the Nuncio Albergati, she recalled abandoning herself to the guidance of the spirit - as she had already done twice before - despite her deep feelings of apprehension:

> [...] though in that instant of time my understanding was clearly convinced that the thing then put before me was truly good [...] and my will so possessed as left without power, then or ever after, to love or elect any contrary thing, yet to have still all denied me, and nothing proposed in particular seemed somewhat hard.[10]

Thus, Mary Ward the Yorkshire recusant had longed for the ideal of monastic perfection in contemplation and isolation, but it was as if her God had other plans for her: in this conflict of interest, the young woman decided to embrace not what *she* would personally prefer, but what came to her from Him, through her visions. Eventually, the way in which she was to fulfil her divine purpose was unveiled in 1611, when God commanded her to 'Take the same of the Society'. Some years later, in a letter she wrote to the Nuncio Albergati in Cologne, the foundress described what she presented as the most powerful episode in a series of divine inspirations:

---

[9] BCA, B4, autobiographical notes.
[10] BCA, B5, letter 4 to Mgr Albergati, 1620.

> I heard distinctly, not by sound of voice, but intellectually
> understood, these words, "Take the Same of the Society", so
> understood, as that we were to take the same, both in the
> matter and the manner, that only excepted which God by
> diversity of sex has prohibited.[11]

This final command came to her as a relief, a 'comfort and strength' which changed her entire soul. Thereafter, her design for a community of English women took a new form: after years of indecision and a personal inclination for the contemplative life, she took a decisive turn towards the apostolate. Through this ultimate epiphany, she understood that she was to found a Society of Jesus for women. In this way, the Ignatian Institute came into being when its foundress surrendered her own will to obey that of God. Far from being an expression of assertive rebellion, her action was one of self-denying trust.

In order to understand the nature of Mary Ward's Institute, the mystical elements of its genesis cannot be underestimated. Indeed, Ward founded a radical female Order which not only pointed out the inadequacies of post-Tridentine religious life but also presumed to bridge the divide between the sexes in the Church. Such a militant challenge seems revolutionary, intent on the demise of the old order and driven by the wilful ambition of a determined, charismatic leader. Yet, one must avoid the pitfalls of textual blindness and consider the creation of the Institute in context: Mary Ward never claimed that her own will or charism were at the source of her Ignatian project; as a mystic, she was simply obeying the divine commandment to found a Society of Jesus for women. She was a deeply religious woman who felt drawn to the cloister and respected the Catholic tradition. We have seen how her writings insisted upon the importance of established monastic virtues even for her 'soldiers of God'. Chastity, poverty, humility, obedience, regularity, the canons of female religious perfection were so many ideals to which the English Ladies aspired. When they embarked upon their mission, Mary Ward and her followers were not indulging their own inclinations but rather sacrificing themselves to fulfil the will of God.

This interpretation of the Institute's nature is supported by Mary Ward's documents, which show that the apostolate was to be considered as an act of abnegation in itself. The 1616 *Ratio Instituti* showed how the English Ladies' missionary way of life, with all its uncertainties and its adversities, had come to replace the hardships of penitential practice of the cloister. The sisters made their teaching and catechizing their personal gift to God, an offering which could not be made by enclosed communities:

---

[11] BCA, B5, letter 4 to Mgr Albergati, 1620.

As regards external mortifications our manner of life may appear only ordinary, since no one is, by the Institute, obliged to observe strict enclosure, or to wear a determined religious habit, or to perform external penances and austerities; [the English Ladies] are not called to a life in which they can devote themselves only to themselves; but that, having Divine Love alone in view, they are to prepare themselves to undertake any labour whatsoever in the education of instruction of virgins and young girls.[12]

In this passage, the foundress was urging her followers to refrain from penitential practices which could hinder them from fulfilling their apostolic duties. Indeed, Mary Ward herself knew the pressure of excessive penance: during the months she had spent in London in 1609, she had undertaken to push her endurance to the limit and her asceticism her taken its toll on her body. She reported: 'I continued in corporal penances during the months that I remained in England, and did no little injury to my health, especially being occupied at that time with some fervour in winning and aiding others.'[13] Of her own confession, the young woman had taken her austerity too far, allowing it to put her own health, and by extension her apostolate, into jeopardy. This attitude was, by 1616, expressly to be foregone: the Ladies' educational vocation was to be understood by all as their primordial *raison d'être* and as such it was to take precedence over everything else, even the established practices of the 'perfect' life. In fact, teaching became a replacement for asceticism, a hardship undertaken for the love of God and to prove one's entire devotion to him by leaving aside one's own comforts: it was an act of self-denial *per se*.

In that sense, the rebel 'Jesuitesses' were not entering their high-profile mission out of a desire for exposure or for increased female power not only in the Church but in society at large: although they realized that their vocation could not fail but to cause the former and might, if successful, achieve the latter, the Ladies were acting out of abnegation, renouncing the rewards of contemplative piety and undertaking works for the Christian education of girls. Their educational brief was a hardship, an act of self-sacrifice to God and to the furtherance of the faith. Thus, the English Ladies operated a transvaluation, they re-interpreted the ideal of medieval asceticism and inscribed it firmly within the active spirit of the Catholic mission of recovery. By putting the spiritual welfare of others before their own and choosing what they believed to be the more arduous path, they were able to reconcile the principles of monastic asceticism with their novel Ignatian vocation.

Indeed, some members were said to have taken up their teaching mission despite a natural, even physical, inclination to the contrary; in her death notice, Mary Clifton was praised for her constant teaching efforts 'notwithstanding her

---

[12] BCA, B18, *Ratio Instituti*, f. 5.

[13] BCA, B4, autobiographical notes.

delicacy'.[14] Like many others, Clifton's initial intention was to enter a traditional convent; only later did she come to embrace the Jesuit-like ideal of the Institute as a more perfect way to give herself entirely to what the foundress referred to as 'the greater glory of God and the common good'.[15] Active teaching represented a means towards sanctification, an act of self-denial undertaken as the ultimate gift to God. The educational mission of Mary Ward's followers can therefore be construed as an act of selflessness undertaken as the ultimate sacrifice to God; it was, as the *Institutum* put it, 'a pathway to God'.[16]

Most revealingly, Ward's spirituality, like that of so many of those working selflessly in the English mission to ensure the survival of Catholicism, abounded not only with notions of asceticism but with the ideal of martyrdom as means to achieve perfection. The *Painted Life*, her posthumous pictorial biography, provided a vivid illustration of her early piety, highlighting her assimilation of established ideals of religious excellence. It insisted particularly on martyrdom, the most glorious way in which English recusants could offer their lives entirely to God. The tenth painting (which is reproduced in the appendices of this book) related how as a Catholic girl of sixteen in Yorkshire, Mary Ward had read the lives of the holy martyrs and had felt strongly drawn to their fate herself, yet she was led to understand that this was not the fate most agreeable to God.

The main subject of the picture, she stands at its centre with, at her feet, traditional symbols of martyrdom and death such as knives, axes, spears and various instruments of torture. To the left is a gruesome scene in which Catholics are put to death, their executions shown at the various stages of hanging, burning, disembowelling and quartering. As Ward literally embraces the gallows with both arms, she looks upon the scene with visible longing, her ecstatic expression belying the horror of the tableau. From a young age, Mary Ward had grown accustomed to the violence of religious persecution and viewed self-sacrifice as an efficient means for the attainment of sanctity. In an England where Catholics regularly were victims of searches, fines, trials, imprisonment and even execution, Tudor and early Stuart English recusancy was inextricably intertwined with martyrdom. In her formative years, the young recusant considered dying for her faith to be one of the most perfect ways - if not *the* most perfect - to achieve sanctification in the eyes of God.

Yet, a small panel on the top right-hand corner of the picture, directly opposite the scene of the executions, reveals Mary Ward's divinely-inspired understanding that martyrdom, the gift of one's physical life, was not as pleasing to God as the gift of one's spiritual being. The scene offers a sharp contrast to the horror facing it: there, Ward appears alone, facing a single majestic candle, absorbed in prayer; her serenity is almost palpable and is meant to convey her

---

[14] BCA, box 4, necrologies, f. 15.
[15] BCA, B18, *Memorial to Gregory XV*, 1622.
[16] BCA, B18, *Institutum*, f. 20.

acceptance of the insight which indicated to her that God required spiritual rather than bodily sacrifice.[17] At that juncture, her spirituality became one in which ideals of martyrdom or of extreme asceticism, which centred on the self, were replaced by a deep concern for the spiritual welfare of others. The hardship to be endured would derive from her vocation to serve her neighbour through education, catechesis and apostolic works.

Mary Ward always anticipated considerable obstacles. Her reflections inspired by the *Spiritual Exercises* concluded: 'It is necessary that we arm ourselves with a great desire to suffer much and many crosses.'[18] Yet these difficulties did not so much deter as galvanize the English Ladies in their zeal for an apostolate which they embraced as the most arduous path and a mirror image of the life of Christ himself. In her later notes of 1618, Ward explained her embracing of suffering as her willingness to sacrifice her whole being in the pursuit of her divine vocation:

> I then offered myself to suffer with love and gladness whatsoever trouble and contrariety should happen in my doing of his will [...] presented that perchance there was some great trouble to happen about the Confirmation of our course, and with this I found a great and new love to this Institute and a near embracing or union of affection with it; I offered myself willingly to this difficulty, and besought our Lord with tears that he would give me grace to bear it.[19]

Thus, at the age of 33, Mary Ward was prepared to follow her imitation of Christ to its ultimate conclusion: she was ready to die, not for the salvation of her own soul only, but for that of her fellow Catholics. This desire was still present some years later; in 1621, on her way to Rome in order to present the pope with the *Institutum*, she stopped at Loreto, where her English biography related she 'took for her part and portion to labour and suffer for Christ, having lively represented [sic] to her the much she was to suffer'.[20]

Ward was indeed to pay a high price for her vocations, since she was imprisoned and declared a heretic; after her arrest in 1631, the Curia entrusted her guard to a convent of the Order of St Clare (Angers), where the mother superior Catherine Bernardin hoped Mary Ward might remember the early vows she had taken in St Omer and become an enclosed nun. During her detention, the prisoner's health declined abruptly, yet when she wrote to her sisters, her tone was one of fortitude and resignation, taking some kind of pleasure in her forced isolation. She wrote: 'I think I am in a cloister, and shut in. [...] Here we sometimes fry and sometimes we freeze, and that's all there is to do. Three little

---

[17] *The Painted Life*, panel 10.
[18] BCA, B9, notes written during the Spiritual Exercises, 1612-14, resolution 35.
[19] BCA, B9, *Various Papers*, 'The Loneliness', f. 34.
[20] BCA, B12, *Briefe Relation*.

windows closely walled up, our door chained and double-locked, and never opened.'[21] The chamber in which she was held captive was, fittingly, an isolation room for the sick who were feared to be contagious. The symbolism is striking, for Mary Ward did indeed represent a sickness in the Church, one who had become corrupted and who threatened to infect others if she was not cut out altogether. Yet she urged her companions not to worry for her and reassured them that she found enough comfort in the knowledge that she was imprisoned for following God's will to feel as content in her cell as in a palace.

This fortitude in the face of peril was an experience shared by several members of the Institute, such as Winifred Wigmore (who was held in Liège in the convent of the *sœurs Grises*), Frances Bedingfield in England or Susanna Rookwood, who died in 1624 and whose necrology reported that:

> she was extraordinary zealous for the glory of God. Many times she suffered for the Roman Catholic faith, being often in danger of imprisonment and death. She concerted many and strengthened and consoled others. [...] She was Superior in England for three years and three times was imprisoned for her faith, when she greatly helped her fellow sufferers by her example and encouragement.[22]

The thirtieth panel of the *Painted Life* illustrates Mary Ward's complex spirituality most explicitly, capturing her re-interpretation of the medieval notions of martyrdom and cloistered contemplative devotion and her understanding of the active apostolate as a better, more complete way to please God. It shows Mary Ward in 1619, when she understood that saving the souls of others would be a greater gift to God than offering him her own soul in a convent or on the gallows.[23] Kneeling to the right of the scene, she is looking upon three different types of protagonists. In the top left-hand corner, martyrs, in their death agonies, are sacrificing their lives for their faith. In striking contrast to the violence of such a scene, the right-hand corner of the painting depicts a group of male and female figures from various older established Orders, all deeply absorbed in prayer in the company of illustrious saints.[24] However, it is the third party upon which Mary Ward is smiling, a motley gathering of pilgrims and simple people representing the masses she evangelized and converted by her teaching.

The caption to this panel explained: 'In 1619 at St Omer, when Mary was fervently thanking God for the grace of her vocation, He revealed to her that to help to save souls is a far greater gift than the religious life or even than martyrdom itself.' It is clear that Mary Ward saw the ideal of the 'perfect' life embodied by

---

[21] BCA, B5, letter dated February 1631.

[22] BCA, box 4, necrologies, f. 20.

[23] *The Painted Life*, panel 30.

[24] The Saints represented are Benedict, Pachomius, Francis of Assisi, Dominic, Clare, Bridget, Scholastica and Teresa of Àvila.

the old Orders as essentially centred on the self and focused upon individual personal salvation; the paradigm of martyrdom with which she grew up emphasized the sanctification of the martyrs themselves. Conversely, the Institute's vocation was to be a selfless one, a calling whose altruistic nature would use the channel of education and catechesis in order to secure the salvation of many souls: the workers in such a noble enterprise could not fail to be favoured by God.

Despite their contravention of the decrees of the Council of Trent, the English Ladies were not rebelling against the established order of their Church. On the contrary, when they abandoned the ideal of monastic life and the serenity of private devotion in order to labour as evangelists in the world, their vocation became their cross. Their mixed life was their ultimate sacrifice, one in which the active apostolate which spearheaded the Counter-Reformation was combined with elements of traditional spirituality, in a subtle adaptation of the medieval values of self-abnegation to the new conditions of the seventeenth-century apostolic drive.

This transvaluation, in which the apostolate itself became an instrument of penance, is also at the core of the redefinition of religious life undertaken by the French Ursulines. In fact, nothing illustrates the closeness of the French teaching nuns and the English Institute better than their emphasis upon their catechetic vocation as an act of self-denial and religious altruism. Just as the purely contemplative life was not to be the Institute's particular vocation, neither was it that of the Ursulines who, although they revered monastic values, did not consider them to be their ultimate goal. To them, sacrifice in the service of God lay not in solitary introspection but in active, socially-inclusive teaching. The text of the Toulouse constitutions echoed that of other French houses in declaring that '[the sisters] should not be content to be simple religious, but also transmitters of Christian doctrine'.[25] The desirable and holy state of cloistered contemplation was to be relinquished and surpassed by the Ursulines who, in their classroom duties, opted for a more arduous vocation.

The way in which the Ursulines linked the values of the cloister with their decidedly evangelical calling was entirely akin to the Institute's combination of tradition and innovation: they envisaged their educational vocation as a kind of ascetic practice in itself. The primary aim of the Order was to train as many pupils as possible in the Catholic faith and to this end, the sisters, putting others before themselves, forsook strict contemplation (with its emphasis upon the self) in order to focus upon their teaching. As Rapley explained, their educational vocation led them 'to leave God for God's sake', encapsulating in this phrase the tension between classroom duties and monastic practice, the former requiring some degree

---

[25] ADHG, 221H-28 bis, 5, f. 44: 'elles ne se doivent pas contenter d'être simples religieuses mais aussi régentes de la doctrine chrétienne [...] on tâchera de leur faire bien reconnaître l'excellence de cette vocation, et celles qui n'auront pas inclination ou disposition à ce dessein ne seront reçues en façon quelconque'.

of relaxation of the latter, and yet being meant to serve the Church faithfully.[26]　In this way, teaching represented the ultimate sacrifice to God, since it required the willing abandonment of the joys of contemplation for the toils of the school.

We have seen how Mary Ward believed that the 'mixed' life of the teaching nun was what God required of her; her visions had convinced her that this educational vocation was the most perfect way to please her divine spouse.　The same mystical motivation is also found at the very heart of many Ursuline endeavours such as that of Marie Guyart, in religion *sœur* de l'Incarnation.　This pioneer of the Canadian mission, perhaps the most famous of all seventeenth-century Ursulines, explained how her proselytizing zeal was nothing but the result of God's inspiration through the mystical channels of divine revelations.　The conviction that God was working through her strengthened her readiness to suffer many hardships for her mission; like Christ, she was willing to abandon herself to the will of her Father and give up her life for the salvation of others.[27]　Antoinette Micolon was also comforted in her times of despondency when she received a divine vision through which God exhorted her not to despair in the face of adversity and assured her that she was indeed doing his will.[28]

Many Ursulines who felt personally inclined towards a life of prayer as a more direct way to communicate with the divine, deliberately chose to teach in order to offer the fruits of their labour to God.　Hélène de Boutet, in religion *sœur* de Saint François (1598-1636), who became professed in Toulouse in 1622, did not opt for a teaching Order in order to indulge her personal preference, but because she understood such a decision as a sacrifice to God.　This was a way of life which she envisaged as more demanding and yet ultimately more rewarding than the solitude of contemplation because it implied transcending the sphere of the self in order to help her many pupils, thereby saving their souls - and hopefully those of the countless friends and relatives they might influence - as well as her own.[29]　However, despite the constant state of extreme weakness brought upon her by chronic illness, she refused to be dispensed from her pedagogical duties, insisting that her work in the classroom helped her to forget herself and her infirmities and to focus her mind on offering her best endeavours to God.　Teaching, for her, was the best remedy.　Absenting herself from her classes caused her great mental unrest since she appeared to consider bodily respite and the opportunity to delight in quiet prayer as an act of self-indulgence.　She viewed her work as a kind of mortification (since it took such a toll on her health), which she dedicated to the glory of God. In Parayre's words:

---

[26] Elizabeth Rapley, *The Dévotes*, p. 145.
[27] Leslie Choquette, ' "Ces Amazones du grand Dieu": Women and Mission in Seventeenth-Century Canada', *French Historical Studies* 17: 3 (1992) 627-55.
[28] Henri Pourrat, *Mémoires de la mère Micolon*, p. 150.
[29] R. P. Parayre, *Chronique*, Part 3, pp. 219-229.

she was moved [to teach] by a pure zeal for the salvation of souls rather than by any pleasure it may have procured her. Indeed, the duties of the classroom have no great intrinsic attraction and, of their nature, are more repulsive than they are attractive.[30]

Of course, one should keep in mind Parayre's own prejudices as an Augustinian more inclined towards devotional and contemplative pursuits than the practicalities of school teaching. However, Hélène de Boutet undoubtedly envisaged her active vocation as a way of sacrificing her life to God in a more selfless manner than through the observance of traditional monastic contemplation.

A similar attitude to teaching was displayed by another sister, Marguerite Boyer, in religion *sœur* de Saint Benoît (died 1652). Affected by an infirmity which caused her hands and feet to ossify into the shape of a claw, she resembled 'a skeleton', 'of only skin and bones. Unable even to dress or feed herself without assistance, she nevertheless insisted on 'dragging herself' to the classrooms to give her lessons. Since she was physically unable to superintend the teaching of any practical skills such as sewing or embroidering, and even less of writing, she specialized in teaching the basics of reading to the youngest students, taking particular interest in the local girls who lived in the city, sometimes in very deprived conditions. Her dedication to her educational vocation found daily proof in her insistence on teaching the *externes* despite her own physical disabilities.[31]

Marguerite Boyer's propensity towards self-abnegation may have been the reason for the choice of her name in religion, *sœur* de Saint Benoît, a clear sign of her endorsement of Benedictine values. Anecdotes like hers appear in the manuscripts of many of the French houses in the seventeenth century, and the link between monastic self-abnegation and apostolic teaching was frequently stressed in the obituaries which found their way from various French establishments to the Faubourg Saint Jacques in Paris.

The necrology of Marguerite de Moï-Richebourg (*sœur* Marie de Jésus), of the congregation of Magny, for instance, emphasized both her tendency towards asceticism and her zeal for teaching, highlighting the relationship between both aspects of the Ursuline vocation. After describing her regular self-chastisements, the text concluded that the very zeal which moved her to such penitential practices also made her the perfect candidate for the educational vocation of her Order:

---

[30] *Ibid.*, p. 225: '[elle était mue plus] par un pur zèle du salut des âmes que par quelque complaisance qu'elle y eût, car ces emplois n'ont pas de soi de grands attraits, et rebutent d'eux-mêmes plus qu'ils n'attirent'.

[31] *Ibid.*, pp. 308-316: 'un vrai squelette [...] n'ayant plus que la peau et les os'; 'ce qui était encore plus surprenant en cette patiente sœur, était de la voir se traîner aux classes pour y instruire les filles'.

[she used] hair shirts, penitential belts, daily discipline, frequent fasts [...] This great inner disposition and the love she had for God rendered her a most proper subject for our holy institute, where she was employed for nearly as long as she stayed in this her house of profession, so fruitfully and usefully that it was visible to all, training the children to piety and the Christian virtues in an efficient manner.[32]

The reasoning was simple: since both her asceticism and her teaching vocation sprang from her desire to please God, the very fact that she chastised her senses with alarming regularity showed an inclination towards penance which predisposed her to become an inspired teacher, one who would recoil neither in front of the coarseness of her pupils' minds nor be put off by the labours implied. This implicit link between classroom duties and penance is found in many other obituaries, such as those of Joséphine Arson of Saint Malo, Suzanne Syette of Angers or Marie Heyles of Bayeux.[33]

These instances illustrate the way in which even the sisters who were most dedicated to their novel educational calling actually transvalued elements of medieval observance in their individual briefs, through the channels of asceticism and abnegation. Despite the heterogeneity of their Order, where each house remained independent from the other, there is enough evidence across France to infer that the Ursulines did not envisage teaching as a mode of empowerment (in the modern sense), replacing the model of prayer, silence and subjection of the cloister with an active manner of life meant purposefully to free women of the restrictions imposed upon them by the patriarchal hierarchy of the Church. Their pedagogical vocation was not so much a vindication of their rights as an offer of service in which they put others before themselves, thereby becoming the very incarnation of religious self-sacrifice.

The French Ursulines or the English Ladies, when they initiated religious movements which transcended the established patterns prescribed by the Council of Trent, acted neither out of a desire to reject a conventual model they found obsolete or restrictive nor in a bid to ensure more power for women within the Church and within society at large. These pioneers of a new female religious life often expressed their understanding of their vocations in terms which remained very much in keeping with the medieval trope of self-sacrifice, and the persistence

---

[32] BA, ms 4990-177, Magny, 4 November 1681: ' [elle pratiquait] les haires, les ceintures de rosettes, les disciplines journalières, les jeûnes fréquents [...] Ces grandes dispositions intérieures et l'amour qu'elle avait pour Dieu la rendirent un sujet très propre pour notre saint Institut, où elle a été employée presque tout le temps qu'elle a demeuré dans sa maison de profession, avec tant de fruit et d'utilité que cela se voyait à l'œil, formant les enfants à la piété et aux vertus chrétiennes de façon efficace'.

[33] BA, ms 4990-148, Saint Malo, 5 September 1686; BA, ms 4990-167, Angers, 6 October 1680 and BA, ms 4990-211, Bayeux, December 1643.

of such a traditional figurative representation indicated that they had accepted and indeed appropriated the normative scale of religious values which they had inherited. Therefore, the richness of their spirituality derived from this marriage of monastic convention and Counter-Reformation evangelic drive: they reconciled the moral ideals which symbolized centuries of religious life with the new pragmatic and active mission of the Catholic Church. French Ursulines and English Ladies constructed their religious identity in imitation of Christ, sacrificing themselves for the salvation of the multitude. Foregoing the 'perfect' life of the cell and the spiritual comforts of the contemplative life, opening themselves to public criticism and scandal by initiating movements which seemed unorthodox, risking their lives in dangerous times of persecution, they suffered, like their Lord had suffered before them, for the greater good. Although they both refused the strict model of the monastic life, they should not be regarded as feminist 'loose cannons' within the Catholic Church but rather as women whose seventeenth-century vocation operated a rich trans-valuation of medieval asceticism and inscribed a teaching apostolate within a traditional religious and penitential context.

'A pathway to god': action as the new way towards perfection

The Ursuline educational vocation was elevated far above the simple functions of pedagogy: it represented the gift of women whose desire to serve the Church had steered them away from the privileges of a contemplative lifestyle towards the rigours of a teaching apostolate. Since they were undertaken for the glory of God and the advancement of the Church, and since their fruits were all presented to God, the duties of the teaching apostolate became elements of religious observance in themselves. Parayre wrote unequivocally about his perception of the Toulouse Ursulines' choice of life:

> This female Order is preferable to all others, as the most
> excellent and the most useful to the Church, since its goal is
> nobler and its occupations involve mixing the active with the
> contemplative life, prayer with action and exercises of love
> of God with charity to one's neighbour.[34]

Here, Parayre insisted that the Ursuline lifestyle was more valuable to the Church than the way of life defined by the Tridentine Decrees of 1563. To him, the combination of action and contemplation bestowed exceptional cachet upon the congregation and he rated the Ursulines' mixed life as superior to the purely

---

[34] *Chronique*, part 1, p. 21: 'Cet ordre de filles est préférable à tous les autres, comme plus excellent et plus utile à l'Église, à cause de sa fin plus noble et de ses emplois, qui mêlent la vie active avec la contemplative, l'oraison avec l'action, et les exercices de charité envers Dieu et ceux du prochain.'

contemplative life of the traditional nunneries. The Toulousain congregation itself reasserted the intrinsic value of its dual vocation:

> The life of the Ursulines is none other than that led by the
> Son of God in this world, and that of his Holy Mother and
> the apostles after he rose to heaven. [...] it is the mixed life
> of contemplation and action [...] the most assured way [...]
> and the most profitable to the glory of God, to the good of
> His Church and to the salvation of souls.[35]

The Ursulines' formula did not constitute a one-dimensional rejection of the model provided by the canons of Trent. On the contrary, contemplation and the active apostolate were mutually beneficial and worked in symbiosis. Thus, their evangelical outreach depended on the spiritual work undertaken inside the cloister; their ability to proselytize efficiently was the fruit of the meditation and teaching in the convent. Indeed, in order to catechize others, the sisters required a profound knowledge of the faith themselves. But evangelization demanded much more than factual expertise about holy Scriptures and the Catholic creed: it called for personal conviction, for a mature and well-rounded piety, a self-assured devotion which the nuns developed and cultivated in their monastic practices and their daily prayers. In this way, the Ursulines' classroom performance benefited from their incessant spiritual training in the cloister.

There is no doubt that the Ursulines believed their vocation to be a significant step towards their own spiritual salvation; as they denied themselves the raptures of the mystical channels of communication with the divine, they committed entirely to the furtherance of the faith and the succour of their neighbours in need. Yet, their choice was not entirely selfless, since they saw, in their evangelical undertakings, the means to secure their own sanctification. This inference is strengthened by the community's constitutions, in which the superiority of the active life was once again reiterated in a text which exhorted the sisters to refrain from any penitential practices which would impede their daily teaching. The Ursulines, pedagogues and catechizers *par excellence*, were reminded never to give priority to asceticism over evangelization, however fervently they wished to give themselves entirely to God through such demonstrations. Their vocational calling was, in itself, as pleasing to him as any act of mortification; their educational duties were a holy sacrifice, one for which the sisters would gain their place in heaven. The Ursuline *via media* was therefore a guaranteed way to the divine: '[it is] most certain that the works and the labours they undertake to achieve the aims of their vocation [...] are the mortifications the

---

[35] ADHG, 221H-37, *Mémoires*, f. 2: 'La vie des Ursulines n'est autre que celle que le fils de dieu a mené en ce monde, et sa sainte mère avec les apôtres après sa montée au ciel. [...] c'est la vie mixte mêlée de la contemplation et de l'action [...] la voie la plus assurée [...] et la plus profitable à la gloire de Dieu, au bien de son Église et au salut des âmes.'

most agreeable to God'.[36] In their choice of an educational vocation, the teaching nuns sought to save others but also to save themselves. Their self-sacrifice, their opting for the hardships of the apostolate, all combined to secure their everlasting crown. The 'mixed' life in imitation of Christ was a direct path toward sanctification.

As we have seen, the choice of a teaching vocation was often a painful one for some of the early Ursulines; it involved poverty, material discomfort and, more importantly, social opprobrium. Yet, the French proselytizers embraced their ordeal wholeheartedly, for they believed it was their own cross, their passion, a suffering which would, in time, grant them grace and salvation. Marie Hoc-Quinquan (*sœur* de l'Incarnation), for instance, was a devout young woman whose desire was to begin a congregation of Ursulines in Saint Denis, near Paris.[37] Since her requests to the Parisian house in the Faubourg Saint Jacques had remained unanswered, she took action into her own hands and, with one of her friends, started a small school for girls in Saint Denis. Although their school soon became a success, both women were scorned and ostracized by former acquaintances. Yet, this loss of social status gave pleasure to Marie Hoc-Quinquan, who was strengthened in her resolve to live her life in imitation of Christ. Suffering in the service of others was an honour to her: like Christ, she would gladly endure public opprobrium in the knowledge that her teaching saved souls, both her pupils' and her own. Finally, when the Ursulines of Paris sent some of their sisters to found a convent in Saint Denis, Marie Hoc-Quinquan became *sœur* de l'Incarnation and rejoiced in having been instrumental to a project which could not fail to ensure her own spiritual elevation. On a similar note, in 1620 in the town of Tulle, Antoinette Micolon was experiencing difficulties which led her to doubt the value of her pastoral work; yet, in typical Ursuline manner, she was soon reassured by the inner conviction that she was obeying the will of God and would, therefore, be rewarded.[38]

Such desire to suffer in the service of the Catholic faith sometimes took on more extreme forms and verged upon aspirations for martyrdom. Marie Guyart, the famous *sœur* de l'Incarnation who began the Ursuline movement in the Canadian wilderness, found great stimulation in the hardships and the horrors which faced her in the colonies. Even as she was contemplating her vocation to go to Canada, her confessor's opposition served only to motivate her to gather more information about the mission with a number of Jesuits. When she arrived in Quebec in 1609, she found the wild weather and daily privations a fitting context for her enterprise. But shortages and climatic harshness were the least of the missionaries' worries: their settlements repeatedly came under attack from the Iroquois tribe, their resources were sacked, their houses set on fire, their people

---

[36] ADHG, 221H-28 bis, ' [il est] très certain que les peines et travaux employés pour les fins de leur vocation [...] sont les mortifications les plus agréables à Dieu'.

[37] BA, ms 4992-2, Saint Denis, 23 October 1690.

[38] Henri Pourrat (ed.), *Mémoires de la mère Micolon*, p. 183.

abducted, beaten or killed. This was a situation in which enclosure could not be practically implemented and therefore could not offer the Ursulines any protection. Yet, when she wrote back to France in order to inform her Order of her progress and to exhort her *consœurs* to join the mission, she deliberately chose not to keep these hardships secret but on the contrary to recount them in detail. Her biographer believed that this seemingly paradoxical choice was in fact perfectly adapted to the Ursuline spirit: 'She knew from experience that a religious soul is tempted above all else by the promise of a cross, of peril and of suffering. Therefore, this was the bait she used to lure them to Canada.'[39]

These anecdotes are but a few amongst many. In fact, the importance of the imitation of Christ was emphasized in many Ursuline constitutions. Paris, for instance, exhorted its sisters to delight in the difficulty of their vocation, since it brought them closer to their divine spouse:

> The sisters who are destined for the instruction of schoolgirls
> must consider their duties with the utmost affection. Indeed,
> it is through this occupation that they imitate most closely
> the Son of God, who principally dedicated his own lifetime
> to teaching the poor and the uneducated.[40]

In this way, the women's altruistic vocations, their efforts to overcome social boundaries in order to reach out to the most disadvantaged strata of society were the expression of the Ursuline transvaluation of spiritual perfection. The teaching nuns embraced the traditional values of the medieval cloister only to transcend them and apply them to their apostolic brief. In a subtle reinterpretation of monastic principles, the Ursuline teaching mission and the salvation of souls replaced the isolation of the cell as a new path towards sanctification.

Physical and moral suffering, material and emotional deprivation, personal and public humiliation were also the bitter portion of the English Ladies. The 1620s saw a rising tide of opposition to the Institute, even in the smallest establishments. Later, the proclamation of the 1631 Bull of suppression and Mary Ward's subsequent imprisonment in Munich, placed her followers in even greater turmoil. In a letter to the pope in that year, Ward described these dark times in a poignant passage which brings to life the very wretchedness of her 'Soldiers of God':

---

[39] Charles Sainte-Foi, *Vies des premières Ursulines de France tirées des chroniques de l'ordre* (Paris, 1856), p. 208: 'Elle savait par sa propre expérience que ce qui tente une âme religieuse, c'est surtout les croix, les périls et la souffrance. C'était là aussi l'appât qu'elle leur offrait pour les attirer au Canada.'

[40] *Règlements des religieuses de la congrégation de Paris*, part 2, p. 158: 'Les religieuses qui sont destinées à l'instruction des écolières externes, s'y doivent porter avec d'autant plus d'affection, qu'en cette occupation elles imitent de plus près le Fils de Dieu: lequel pendant sa vie a voulu principalement instruire les pauvres et les ignorants.'

> I have been publicly accused and declared a heretic, schismatic, obstinate and rebellious by the Holy Church. I have been arrested as such and incarcerated and driven to the point of death by the ailments that the nine weeks of imprisonment to which I have already been subject have already caused me.[41]

Her condemnation also affected her disciples most cruelly: the stain on her good character, by association, marred the reputations of her followers and her fall was shared by all. Bitterly, she complained of the unfair treatment that had befallen her sisters:

> The infamy of [my] being marked out in every place as guilty of such wickedness, and of being thrown into the jaws of death by order of the Holy Church for having supposedly committed such atrocities, has resulted in great suffering being inflicted upon all the members of our company. Our Ladies have been mocked by the heretics for having abandoned their fatherland and families; they have been despised by their closest relations; their annual income has been unjustly seized so that in four of our colleges it has been necessary to ask for alms.[42]

She bemoaned the injustice of popular and ecclesiastical censure, especially since she envisaged the apostolate as a pathway to the divine. Yet it is apparent from her correspondence with other members of the Institute that Ward considered their teaching vocation as the manifestation of their absolute and complete abandonment to the will of God, and as a direct conduit towards the salvation of their souls. She believed that the difficulties hindering her Institute's progress, the recurrent attacks against the Ladies' integrity and the general suffering they endured, were as nothing compared to the reward God had in store for them. In October 1627 she wrote to one of her companions, Mother C. Morgan:

> It is a singular comfort to me to understand that those under your care proceed so well both in virtue and learning; continue your fidelity, and zeal in advancing those young ones, whose good going forward will be here to your comfort and increase your lasting crown.[43]

She evidently believed that dedication to the education of young girls would reap a double harvest. It would bear immediate and visible fruit in the mission for Catholic recovery, improving their pupils' knowledge of God and enabling them to

---

[41] BCA, B5, letter 86, f. 93 d.

[42] *Ibid.*

[43] BCA, B5, letter 44, f. 71.

read devotional works. Thus, women who had been educated by the English Ladies were fully armed to face the hardships that awaited them in this life, particularly if they returned to live under the repressive English penal laws. By the regular practice of the Ignatian *Spiritual Exercises,* mental prayer and sound doctrinal foundations, their training would enable them to remain steadfast in the faith. But there was another kind of harvest to be reaped from this educational mission, and one which would benefit the members of the Institute directly. Ward firmly believed that her followers were efficiently working for the salvation of their own souls by giving away their lives in the service of others.

In light of these reflections, it is necessary to return to Ward's perceived assertiveness, the particular brand of asperity in defending women's abilities which leads many of the modern readers who encounter her for the first time to think of her as a feminist. Her claim that women, as well as men, could be perfect (a claim likely to shock, if not to alienate her contemporaneous critics altogether), has been seen as her chief characteristic. Yet, there may be a different interpretation to Ward's famous words: 'I would to God that all men would understand this verity: that women, if they will, may be perfect, and if they would not make us believe we can do nothing, and that we are but women, we might do great matters.'[44]

In the second address to her followers, she phrased this somewhat differently, in a manner which indicated that her vindication of female worth sprang not from feminist self-assertion but rather from her conviction that the Institute's apostolate and its evangelical lifestyle were sure to bring perfection to those who undertook it, since they not only emulated the life of Christ, but also represented the divine will as it manifested itself to her on the occasions of her many mystical revelations. According to Mary Ward, 'women may be perfect as well as men, *if they love verity and seek true knowledge*'.[45] By 'knowledge', she did not mean the erudition which derives from scholarly learning, since this had no intrinsic value without what Ward referred to as the true knowledge of the divine spirit. This proviso was essential; perfection, she believed, was not within the reach of any woman by her own efforts, but only attainable by those who followed the will of God as, she trusted, her English Ladies did by embracing the Institute.

This reassessment of Ward's meaning is confirmed in the third of her addresses to her spiritual sisters, in which she told her audience:

---

[44] BCA, B17, f. 3.
[45] *Ibid.*, f. 5, my italics

You are spectacles unto God, angels and men; it is certain
that God has looked upon you, as he never looked upon any.
[...] Men you know look diversely upon you as new
beginners of a course never thought of before, marvelling
what you intend and what will be the end of you.[46]

It is clear that she believed that she and her followers, by starting a Society of Jesus
for women, were performing God's will. The self-denial involved in their
renunciation of the cloister in order to undertake base work among the people and
face all the hardships of a pioneering congregation would soon reap a harvest
greater than any other, since they were fulfilling God's command. By sacrificing
their lives to this struggle in the world, they were gaining their place in heaven,
alongside the martyrs of the faith and the missionary priests with whom they
worked in recusant England.

For both the English Ladies and the French Ursulines, the apostolate was
a gesture of self-abnegation, a choice to help others before themselves. This
religious altruism emerged from the very redefinition of spiritual perfection which
was emerging in seventeenth-century Europe, a rich conceptual construction which
embraced the medieval normative scale of moral values - idealizing chastity,
obedience to God's will and self-denial - whilst adapting it to the early-modern
evangelical drive of the Counter-Reformation. The 'mixed' life and its mingling
with the world therefore became more than mere necessities if the Church was to
strengthen its links with its people: enhanced by such religious transvaluation, they
were enjoying new cachet and became considered as an efficient way towards
spiritual perfection. Action was then portrayed as more pleasing to God than pure
contemplation, since education and catechism classes were instrumental to the
salvation of countless souls in a manner which would have been impossible to
traditionally cloistered nuns. Therefore, in imitation of Christ, the teaching nuns
suffered adversity gladly; the stumbling blocks in their path were so many trials of
their fortitude, but the French Ursulines and the English Ladies always continued
to hope. They had a conviction: like Christ, they were sacrificing themselves to the
active life for the glory of God. Like him, they would be rewarded a thousandfold
and gain, through this new form of martyrdom, the sanctification of their souls.

---

[46] *Ibid.*, f. 6.

Conclusion

For daring to break traditional gendered role definitions and breaching the Decrees of the Council of Trent, women like the Toulouse Ursuline Françoise Rabonite and the English recusant Mary Ward were charged with witchcraft and heresy. Yet, although their briefs were innovative, neither the French Ursulines nor the English Ladies were deliberately setting out with the aim to rebel against an established order which they may have deemed obsolete or repressive. Their educational mission emerged from their ambition to serve the Church, and their attachment to their vocations did not imply any kind of contempt towards those of others. In fact, the sisters upheld the traditional notions which equated the contemplative life of the cloister with the more desirable and more rewarding 'perfect' life.

The comparative analysis of female congregations such as the English Institute and the French Ursulines illustrates the gradual changes which affected the place occupied by women in the early modern Catholic Church throughout Europe. We have seen how the proselytizing and educational drive of their initial vocations led both movements to propose a new form of female religious life, one in which women borrowed the model of the male clerks regular in order to integrate female participation fully within the Catholic movement of recovery which characterized the seventeenth-century. They lived in communities which, they hoped, would soon be recognized as part of the fabric of the Church; yet, they insisted on remaining active in the secular world and performing their pastoral and evangelical duties amongst lay women and girls.

However, the women in both movements were mistaken on one count: they believed that the value of the educational and catechizing work they proposed to undertake would be self-evident, particularly in the context of a wide-ranging mission of Catholic recovery which used secular education and religious instruction as its principal tools. Yet, since the Church did not consider the 'mixed' life suitable for women religious, the fate and the acceptability of these female teaching Orders came to rest entirely upon the status that they would adopt. Therefore, in response to varying degrees of opposition and in order to develop formulae which they deemed intrinsically suited to the efficient implementation of their projects *in situ*, both movements adopted different ways of life. Whilst the Ursulines opted for compromise with the established norm and embraced conventual life, the English Ladies, in contrast, wished to remain unenclosed and independent, imitating the Society of Jesus insofar as that was feasible for women. These existential choices would have a direct impact upon the degree of latitude which the congregations enjoyed in the subsequent pursuit of their educational briefs.

In France, when the Ursulines became nuns, they were allowed to teach only on condition that they remained within the walls which symbolized their separation from the world. Therefore, the sisters themselves did not enjoy spatial mobility and were always under the strict control of the local episcopate. Their compromise with Tridentine requirements did, to a degree, limit their range of action and certainly did not permit them to experiment or innovate in the areas of pedagogy or catechesis: clerical supervision and physical enclosure ensured that the acceptable area of female teaching could not encroach upon the male preserve of preaching.

In contrast, the English Institute's imitation of the Society of Jesus implied that the English Ladies were, theoretically at least, free from such episcopal control; they were able to pursue their vocations on an entirely new scale, outside enclosure and interacting with the girls and the women whose re-Catholicization they targeted. Thus, their curriculum was not restricted to the sphere of traditional female schooling; on the contrary, it was shaped on the teaching dispensed in Jesuit schools, and the Ladies' evangelizing took on missionary traits when they set to work alongside the Catholic priests in the English mission. To the contemporaneous onlooker, Mary Ward took female education beyond its customary boundaries by encouraging advanced learning for her pupils and exercising her catechizing apostolate in the world, in a manner reminiscent of male religious preaching.

Nevertheless, although Ward's decisions in the way of life she favoured for her Ladies might seem better suited to an apostolic kind of vocation than that chosen by the Ursulines, the English Institute paid dearly its faithful imitation of its Jesuit exemplars and was eventually suppressed. The French Ursulines, on the contrary, secured their success by embracing a degree of enclosure meant to bring them in line with the Decrees of the Council of Trent. Their constant diplomacy and apparent willingness to compromise placated Church authorities and secular patrons to such an extent that, by the end of the century, there were an estimated 320 communities across the realm of France, all combining a convent and a school for extern pupils.[1] Thus, Ursuline tactics were essential in turning the Order into what Elizabeth Rapley has called 'the feminine teaching congregation par excellence'.[2]

In this respect, the comparison between the English Institute and the French Ursulines may, at times, have conveyed a sense of disparity which partly resulted from the variations between the conditions which affected French and English Catholicism in this troubled period. On the one hand, the French Ursulines spoke the language of the Curia and were able to negotiate with the authorities to find a way which satisfied both their evangelical purpose and the Church's monastic stance for women; on the other hand, there remained an unbridgeable gap

---

[1] M. C. Gueudré, *Histoire de l'ordre des Ursulines*, vol. 2, p. 148.
[2] Elizabeth Rapley, *The Dévotes*, p. 48.

between the militancy of an Ignatian such as Mary Ward (who was raised in the constant danger and urgency which suffused the English recusant mission and therefore knew the value of adaptability in such circumstances), and that of a Roman Curia, prevented by centuries of southern supremacy from ever understanding the full scale of the jeopardy in which English Catholicism found itself.

However, it might be helpful to look beyond national determinism at the larger picture of the global Catholic Church and its relationship with the women in its midst. From this vantage point, it becomes clear that, regardless of circumstantial differences, the English Ladies and the French Ursulines were the pioneers of a new era in female participation in the Catholic Church. As they proposed to contribute to the popular revival of the faith in ways which were inaccessible to established enclosed nuns, both groups were having the same impact on the traditional organization of the Church: they were, in effect, petitioning for the recognition of the ideal of the 'mixed' life for women as well as for men. Thus, these women did, in their own distinctive ways, begin movements which triggered a radical re-thinking of the definition of female Catholic life: in an age of renewal, they implicitly questioned the validity of the 1563 Tridentine Decrees which had reinforced the medieval definition of female religious life as enclosed and under close episcopal control.

As Mary Ward explained in her 1616 *Ratio Instituti*, the definition of women religious as solely cloistered nuns was ill suited to serve the on-going extensive movement of Catholic recovery in Europe. Most eloquently, her Plan argued that 'the female sex also in its own measure, should and can in like manner undertake something more than ordinary in this same common spiritual necessity'.[3] Later, in the 1621 *Institutum,* Ward valued her Institute's educational and catechizing vocation in similar terms, extolling this type of teaching apostolate as 'particularly efficacious for the universal good of the Church'.[4] These were statements that Ursulines founders in France would have endorsed wholeheartedly, as the chronicler of Toulouse indicated when he wrote: 'The religious life which [...] interweaves contemplation and the instruction of the people has a nobler and more excellent goal than that which confines itself to contemplation or to action alone.'[5] Although they did not produce the same kind of openly innovative proposals as the English Ladies, the Ursuline documents extolled the essential value of their teaching duties, commenting that their Order was both necessary and highly effective. Hence, by the end of the seventeenth-century (and although they might not have been fully aware of it at the time) the English Ladies and the

---

[3] BCA, B18, *Ratio Instituti,* f. 1.

[4] BCA, B18, *Institutum,* f. 19.

[5] R. P. Parayre, *Chronique*, part I, p. 21: 'La religion qui [...] rapporte la contemplation à l'instruction du peuple, a une fin plus noble et ensuite plus excellente, que celle qui s'arrête à la seule contemplation, ou à la seule action'.

French Ursulines were the leaders of a conceptual shift which initiated the progressive 'feminization of the Church' itself (with the new teaching congregations in particular) and found its most buoyant expression in its lay corollary, the multiplication of companies of *filles séculières*.[6]

In that sense, the comparison of these two congregations over the long term provides a feeling of underlying unity that is of more consequence than the disparities of their situations in the 1630s. The foundresses of pioneering female congregations were moved by the common will to inscribe feminine participation into the ongoing movement of the Catholic Reformation. They shared a mutual aim, which was to provide a valuable place within the religious fabric of Catholicism where women could serve the Church without being solely devoted to prayer and bound to monastic observance.

The teaching nuns opted for the 'mixed' life in an effort to bridge the traditional dichotomy separating action and contemplation and forge new links between the intense spirituality of the religious house and the activity of the world outside. They did not wish to *choose* between action and contemplation but hoped to *reconcile* them so that both would become interrelated and benefit each other. For both Orders, the arena of the reconciliation of the duties of Martha and the spirit of Mary was the classroom, where the intrinsic essence of their foundations found its concrete expression. It was in their schools that the sisters undertook the secular education of girls and, more importantly, it was there that they catechized generations of future wives and mothers.

The Ursuline formula, although conceding to enclosure, constituted a remarkable departure from the norm of conventual teaching which, thus far, had remained entirely the preserve of boarders who stayed enclosed for the duration of their education. Daily interaction with the day pupils therefore enabled the sisters to take their teaching out of the cloister and into the world. Conversely, Mary Ward's schools were equally effective in allowing Catholic spirituality to flow out into secular society: since they had adopted the Jesuit model, the divide between the tutors and their tutees was dramatically reduced, and the degree of interaction between the English Ladies and those they catechized may account for their schools' popularity. In this way, during the first half of the seventeenth century, congregations such as the French Ursulines or the Institute of English Ladies effected gradual but essential changes within the fabric of the Catholic Church at large. They opened the way for a new kind of religious life for women, one which allowed feminine piety to combine action and contemplation. As they taught thousands of girls, their educational vocations were a precious ally to the mission of Catholic recovery in Europe.

Somewhat paradoxically, it is the success of the Institute's and of the Ursulines' schools which has led to the misinterpretation of their nature and aims. Since the activities of the teaching nuns often went beyond the accepted sphere of

---

[6] See Elizabeth Rapley, *The Dévotes*, pp. 193-96.

the feminine apostolate, the English Ladies and, to a lesser degree, the French Ursulines, were often labelled by their contemporaries as rebels who strove to shake off the shackles of conventional religious life, dissenters whose initiatives aggressively set out to lay tradition to rest. Yet, the sisters' active vocations did not aim to jeopardize or put an end to long-established forms of female religious life; their spirituality was much too rich and complex to be thus simplified as a desire to eradicate the old in order to make way for the new. These pioneers had inherited and embraced the values of monasticism, they respected prayer and contemplation, they acknowledged the sanctity of the cloister and they understood perfectly how one might wish to dedicate her life entirely to God. The difference lay in the fact that the English Ladies and the French Ursulines had found their own way to offer themselves to the divine: when they denied themselves the perfect life of the convent and the spiritual conduit of a constant contemplative life, the teaching nuns embraced action not as a gesture of self-empowerment, but as one of abnegation in the service of the Church.

To these novel Orders, action and contemplation were by no means mutually exclusive, and the tradition of monastic asceticism and self-denial could and indeed should be inscribed at the very heart of their apostolic vocation. Their spirituality yet had much in common with the mysticism of the most devout cloisters, their adherence to their rules betrayed a reformed spirit, and their personal austerity demonstrated their close links with the penitential ideals of the most austere monasteries. Repeatedly, the same women who took such liberties with the rules of enclosure actually expressed their admiration for religious claustration as a safeguard of virtue and a preserver of spiritual serenity and order.

When they abandoned the ideal of monastic life and the serenity of private devotion in order to labour as evangelizers in the world and teachers in the classroom, the English Ladies and the French Ursulines accepted their vocation as their cross. Revealingly, the Ursuline constitutions of Toulouse stated: 'There is no doubt that the labours and works employed to serve [our] vocation and for the charity of one's neighbour are the mortifications most agreeable to God.'[7] This is eloquent proof that, to them, teaching was a form of penitential altruism: their active vocation was to be the sisters' offering to God, in keeping with the ascetic spirituality of the cloister. Far from questioning the medieval definition of female religious life in an effort to liberate women, the French Ursulines and the English Ladies were 'leaving God for God's sake', in the service of the Catholic Church.[8] Their active vocations were a suffering they embraced as a sacrifice in their subtle adaptation of monastic asceticism to the new conditions of the seventeenth-century apostolic drive.

---

[7] ADHG, 221H-28 bis, 5, f. 30: 'étant très certain que les peines et travaux employés pour les fins de [notre] vocation et de la charité du prochain sont les mortifications les plus agréables à Dieu'.

[8] Elizabeth Rapley, *The Dévotes*, p. 145.

Appendices

Appendix 1:
A Toulouse Ursuline in her ordinary habit.
By authorization of the Bibliothèque Nationale de France.

T. IV. p. 165.

Ursuline de la Congrégation de Paris.

Appendix 2:
Ursuline of the congregation of Paris.
By authorization of the Bibliothèque Nationale de France.

Appendix 3:
Portrait of Mary Ward (1585-1645) from the *Painted Life*.
By authorization of the generalate of the IBVM, Munich.

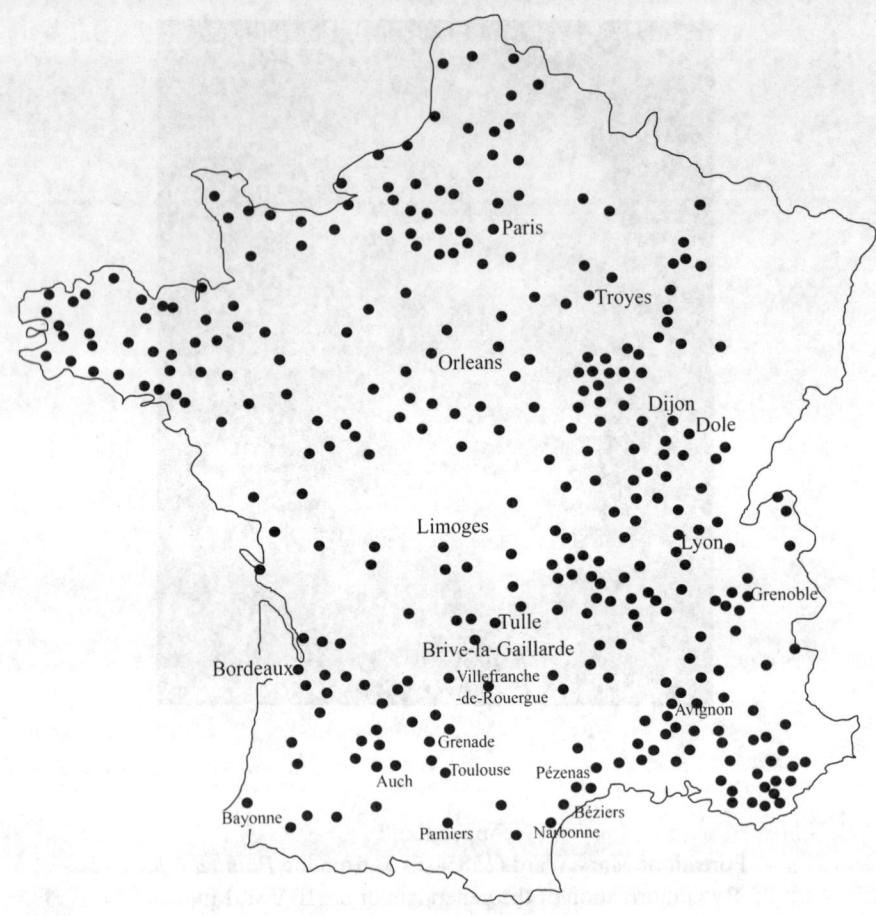

Appendix 4:
Map of Ursuline houses in seventeenth-century France.

Appendix 5:
Map of houses founded by Mary Ward during her lifetime, in England and on the Continent.

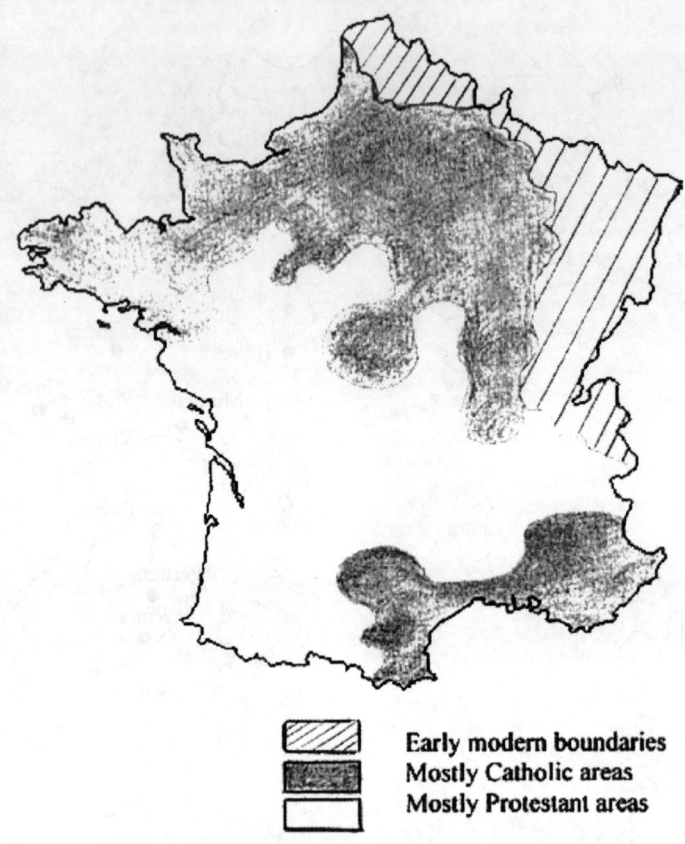

Early modern boundaries
Mostly Catholic areas
Mostly Protestant areas

Appendix 6:
Map of Catholic and Protestant divisions in early modern France.

Appendix 7:
By authorization of the generalate of the IBVM, Munich.

The Painted Life, Panel 9. The English translation of the caption relates an episode of Mary Ward's life at the Babthorpes: 'When Mary was fifteen, she and her aunt, Miss Barbara Babthorpe, were told by a pious woman named Margaret Garrett of the severe punishment inflicted upon a religious, who had acted so as to give scandal. This story made Mary perceive so clearly the excellence of the religious life, that she resolved to adopt it, in order to attain perfection.'

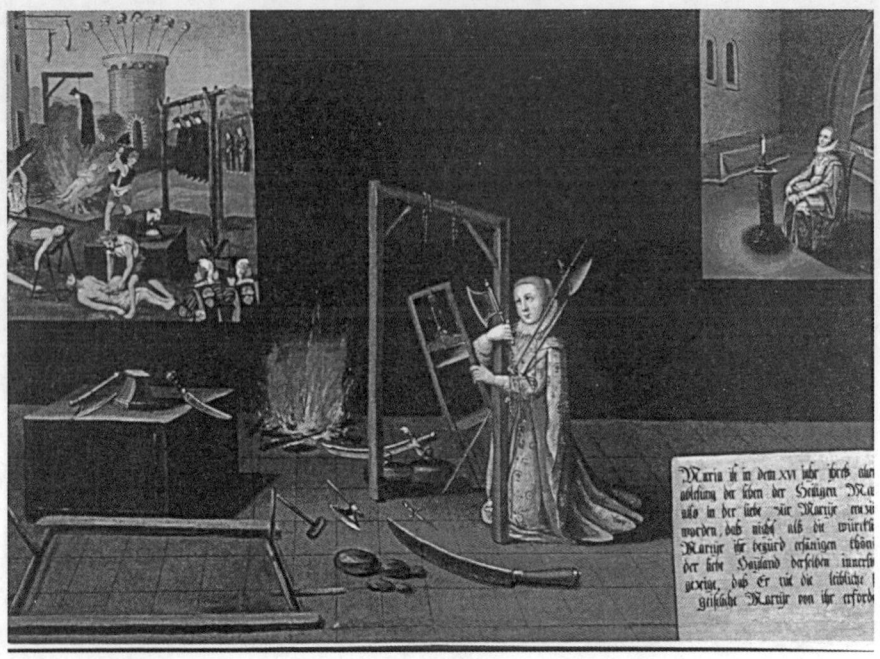

Appendix 8:
By authorization of the generalate of the IBVM, Munich.

The Painted Life, panel 10. The English translation of the caption reads: 'When Mary was sixteen, she read the lives of the holy martyrs, and was inspired with such a desire to follow them, as to long for literal martyrdom, until Our Saviour revealed to her that He required spiritual rather than bodily sufferings of her.'

Appendix 9:
By authorization of the generalate of the IBVM, Munich.

The Painted Life, panel 30. The English translation of the caption explains Mary Ward's vocation as evangelical: 'In 1619 at St. Omer, when Mary was fervently thanking God for the grace of her vocation, He revealed to her that to help to save souls is a far greater gift than the religious life or even than martyrdom itself.'

Bibliography

Primary sources: Manuscript material

Archives Départementales de la Haute-Garonne.

The series marked 221H comprises 43 large bundles of original manuscripts, covering the history of the Ursulines of Toulouse from its inception to its dismantling, 1604-1791. The following bundles were of particular interest:

221H-3: Damaged by fire. The manuscripts it contains have not been numbered, and refer to the houses that were founded by the Toulousain congregation in towns such as Brive-la-Gaillarde, Pamiers or Grenade.

221H-4: Damaged by fire. This holds a manuscript copy of the 1611 royal approval of Vigier's congregation of Ursulines in Toulouse. It also keeps Latin and French copies of the 1614 papal Bull elevating the congregation of Toulouse into a convent of St Augustine, together with Jean de Rudelle's 1615 visitation report assessing the suitability of the buildings on the Rue des Trois Rois Vieux for this purpose.

221H-15: This comprises 233 *professions de foi* of Toulousain Ursulines on individual small squares of parchment, covering the years 1616 to 1773. It also holds licences issued by the archbishop, allowing particular sisters to leave the Toulouse house for a smaller foundation (such as that of Pamiers, for instance).

221H-25: Folio 20 is a French translation of the original 1614 Bull, which mentioned the teaching of enclosed boarders only; this has been used in parallel with folio 26, a French translation of the 1616 papal Brief allowing the Toulousain Ursulines to become enclosed whilst nevertheless undertaking the teaching of externs.

221H-28bis: Amongst a variety of documents, item 5 is the 100-page manuscript book of the *Constitutions du collège et monastère des religieuses de sainte Ursule de Toulouse.*

221H-29: *Livre des prises d'habit*; this register provides entries for each one of the sisters who took the habit in the Toulouse congregation up to 1789. As well as giving dates of entry into the noviciate and dates of profession, this gives an insight into the sisters' social background, citing their fathers' professions and the amount paid for their dowries.

221H-37: *Mémoires du commencement et progrès de l'ordre de sainte Ursule*, 1604-1621. This manuscript book is an early history of the beginnings of the Toulousain congregation, sketching its origins from the original Italian foundation of Angela Merici and the *congrégées* of Avignon.

2221H-41: This is another manuscript copy of the constitutions of the Toulousain house. It has been used in conjunction with the constitutions found in 221H-28bis, item 5.

In addition to the 221H series, some documents are preserved in 1G-663, 1G-664 and 1G-666; of these, bundle 1G-663 is of particular interest, since it gathers 53 copies of the most essential founding documents relating to the history of the Toulouse congregation, such as:

Item 5: *Visite de l'église du collège et monastère de sainte Ursule de l'ordre de saint Augustin de Toulouse*, 24 July 1619.

Item 20: *Donation de ma maison, faite par Arnaud Bourret au couvent de sainte Ursule.*
Item 49: *Mémoire des livres qui sont à l'usage des jeunes pensionnaires.*

Bibliothèque de l'Arsenal, Paris

Four volumes gather hundreds of death notices written, usually, by the superiors of respective convents on the demise of one of their fellow sisters; these necrologies (most of them on printed folios but some of them in manuscript) were later sent to the Parisian house and bound together to serve as a centralized source of information documenting the history of the Order in France.

Ms 4990, 253 folios
Ms 4991, 286 folios
Ms 4992, 196 folios
Ms 4993, 194 folios

Bar Convent, York: archives of the Institute of the Blessed Virgin Mary.

The archives kept in the Bar Convent, in York, contain a wealth of material documenting all aspects of the Institute. Documents cover its early endeavours under the direction of Mary Ward, beyond the 1631 papal suppression up to the foundress's death in 1645. They also cover the entire history of the second Institute, known as the Institute of the Blessed Virgin Mary, up to the present day. The documents kept in this archive are either original manuscripts or certified copies of originals kept elsewhere. Research for this thesis has focused particularly on the following files:

A11: Photographs of the original earliest biography of Mary Ward (known as *The English Life); originally entitled *A Briefe Relation of the Holy Life and Happy Death of our Dearest Mother*, it was written jointly by Mary Poyntz and Winefred Wigmore c. 1650.

A12: A typed copy of *A Briefe Relation.*

B4: Fragments of Mary Ward's autobiographical notes.

B5: Mary Ward's correspondence, 1615-39. This contains copies of 132 of Mary Ward's letters relating to the Institute. It also holds copies of her letters to the Cardinals investigating her Institute in Rome in the 1620s and of her various petitions and Memorials addressed to Pope Urban VIII.

B9: Various papers; a variety of documents relating to the Institute, focusing particularly upon the period around 1619. This gathers a series of notes written during the Spiritual Exercises 1615, 1616, 1619, the *Thirty Five Resolutions Tending to Perfection*, some notes written in 1616 at the Spa, and notes on favours granted in prayer and in a fit of sickness

B17: A copy of the 'Three speeches of our Reverend Mother Chief Superior made at St Omer, having been long absent' in which Mary Ward defends her ideal of a Society of Jesus for women and vindicates the worth of female members in the mission of the Catholic Church.

B18: Under the heading: 'Mary Ward's original idea of the Institute : Original Documents Letters, etc.'. Contains copies of the 1612 *Schola Beatae Mariae*, the 1616 *Ratio Instituti* and the 1621 *Institutum*, together with other documents about the foundress's ideal of her Institute, such as the 1619/20 *Document of Independence*, the 1620/21 *Brevis Declaratio*, the 1622 *Memorial presented to Gregory XV* and the 1623 *Reasons why we may not alter.*

B33, B36 and B39: These files contain a variety of typescripts of modern scholarly works dealing with Mary Ward and education.

C1: Translations of documents regarding the Jesuitesses, documenting the debate that arose mostly in the 1620s and led to the Institute's suppression in 1631. This voluminous file holds papers compiled by Mary Cramlington and gathers a number of translated 'Letters against the Jesuitesses' as well as a translated copy of Urban VIII's Bull of Suppression.

C18: Farm Street documents. This is a bulky register containing copies of documents relating to the Institute, the originals of which are kept in Jesuit archives.

C45: Manuscript register of the members of the house in Hammersmith from 1669 to 1763.

Westminster Diocesan Archives

Series A, *Manuscripta Archivi Westmonasteriensis*:

Vol. 16, 1616-22, containing the Latin *Copia Informationis de Jesuitissis* (Memorial of the English clergy) against Mary Ward's Institute and its counterpart, also in Latin, the *Defensio et Declaratio Instituti Virginum Anglorum*, a report in favour of the English Ladies.

Vol. 17, 1623-24, containing the statement of Mary Alcock, apostate member of the Institute testifying against it in the Godfather's Information about the Jesuitesses.

Vol. 19, 1625-26 and B 25, Roman Letters, 1620 to 1623 also include documents relating to the controversy about the Institute.

Printed material

- Challoner, V.A.L., *Martyrs to the Catholic Faith: Memoirs of Missionary Priests and other Catholics of both sexes that have suffered death in England on religious accounts from the year 1577 to 1684* (1741), Edinburgh: Grange, 1878.
- Foley, Henry, *Records of the English Province*, 7 vols, London: Burns and Oates, 1877-83.
- Gold Thwaites, Reuben (ed.), *The Jesuit Relations and Allied Documents*, 73 vols. (Cleveland, Ohio: Burrows, 1896-1901).
- Hélyot, Pierre, *Histoire des ordres monastiques, religieux et militaires et des congrégations séculières de l'un et de l'autre sexe, qui ont été établies jusqu'à présent*, 8 vols, Paris: N. Gosselin, 1714-1719.
- *Instructions sur les principes de la doctine chrétienne pour l'usage des écoles des religieuses ursulines de Toulouse*, Toulouse: Douladoure, 1695.
- Legué, Gabriel, and Gilles de la Tourette (eds.), *Sœur Jeanne des Anges, supérieure des Ursulines de Loudon (dix-septième siècle): Autobiographie d'une hystérique possédée* [1644], Paris: Millon, 1886.
- Mère de Pommereu, Ursuline, *Les Chroniques de l'ordre des Ursulines recueillies pour l'usage des religieuses du même ordre*, Paris: Eloy Hélie, 1676.
- Morris, John (ed.), *The Troubles of Our Catholic Forefathers related by Themselves*, 3 vols, London: Burns and Oates, 1872-1877.
- Mush, John, *The Life and Death of Margaret Clitherow, the Martyr of York*, ed. G. B. Richardson, London: Richardson, 1849.

- Palmes, William, *Life of Mrs Dorothy Lawson of St Anthony's near Newcastle-upon-Tyne, in Northumberland,* ed. G. B. Richardson, Newcastle-upon-Tyne: Forster, 1855.
- Parayre, R.P., *Chronique des religieuses augustines ursulines de la congrégation de Toulouse,* 3 vols, Toulouse: Guillaume Bosc, 1681.
- Pollen, J.H. (ed.), *Unpublished Documents relating to the English Martyrs, 1584-1603,* Catholic Record Society, vol. 5 (1908).
- Pourrat, Henri (ed.), *Mémoires de la Mère Micolon (1592-1659). Recueil de la vie de la mère ·Antoinette Micolon dite sœur Colombe du saint Esprit, première Ursuline d'Auvergne, fondatrice du couvent d' Ambert, de Clermont, de Tulle, de Beaulieu, d'Espailloux et d'Arlanc où elle est décédée,* Clermont-Ferrand: Française d'édition et d'imprimerie, 1981.
- *Règlements des religieuses ursulines de la congrégation de Paris, divisés en trois livres,* Paris: Louis Josse, 1751.
- *Relation de la conquête du Mogol par Thamas-Koulikan, et de la façon de vivre des dames mahométane; écrite par un missionnaire françois qui est dans le royaume de Bengale, à mad. de S. Hyacinthe, religieuse à Toulouse,* Toulouse: Robert, 1740.
- -Riboti, Augustin, *Examen d'un livre qui a pour titre La Vie du P. Romillon avec plusieurs éclaircissements sur la première institution des congrégations de la Doctrine Chrétienne; et des Ursulines en France,* Toulouse: J. Pech, 1676.
- Sainte-Foi, Charles, *Vies des premières Ursulines de France, tirées des chroniques de l'ordre,* Paris: Poussielgue-Russand, 1856.
- Sales, François de, *Introduction à la vie dévote* in *Oeuvres,* Paris: Gallimard, 1969.
- Smith, Richard, *An Elizabethan Recusant House: comprising the Life of the Lady Magdalen, Viscoutness Montague (1538-1608),* ed. A.C. Southern, London: Sands, 1954.
- Thiers, Jean-Baptiste, *Traité de la clôture des religieuses,* Paris: Dezallier, 1681.
- Wadsworth, James, *English Spanish Pilgrim,* London: Michael Sparke, 1629.

Secondary Sources

- *Books*

- Amussen, Susan, *An Ordered Society: Gender and Class in Early Modern England,* Oxford: Basil Blackwell, 1988.
- Angenot, Marc, *Les Champions des femmes: Examen du discours sur la supériorité des femmes, 1400-1800,* Montréal: Presses de l'Université du Québec, 1977.
- Annaert, Philippe, *Les Collèges au féminin: Les Ursulines; Enseignement et vie consacrée aux dix-septième et dix-huitième siècles,* Namur: Vie Consacrée, 1992.
- Anstruther, Godfrey, *The Seminary Priests: A Dictionary of the Secular Clergy in England and Wales, 1558-1850,* Ware: St Edmund's College, 1975.
- Anstruther, Godfrey, *Vaux of Harrowden, a Recusant Family,* Newport: R.H. Johns, 1953.
- Aron, Marguerite, *Les Ursulines, Les grands ordres monastiques et instituts religieux,* tome 24, Paris: Grasset, 1937.
- Aston, Trevor (ed.), *Crisis in Europe 1560-1660: Essays from Past and Present,* London: Routledge and Kegan Paul, 1975.
- Auguste, Alphonse, *Les Origines du jansénisme dans le diocèse de Toulouse: Notes et documents,* Toulouse: Privat, 1922.
- Aveling J.C.H., *Northern Catholics: the Catholic Recusants of the North Riding of Yorkshire, 1558-1790,* London: Geoffrey Chapman, 1966.

- ------------*The Handle and the Axe: The Catholic Recusants in England from Reformation to Emancipation,* London: Blond and Briggs, 1976.
- Bainton, Roland, *Women of the Reformation, in France and England*, Boston, Mass.; Beacon Press, 1973.
- Bangert, William, *A History of the Society of Jesus,* St Louis, Mis.: Institute of Jesuit Sources, 1986.
- Basset, Bernard, *The English Jesuits,* London: Burns and Oates, 1967.
- Beales, A.C.F. *Education under Penalty: English Catholic Education from the Reformation to the fall of James II, 1547-1689,* London: Athlone Press, 1963.
- Beik, William, *Absolutism and Society in Seventeenth-Century France: State Power and Provincial Aristocracy in Languedoc,* Cambridge: Cambridge University Press, 1985.
- Bell, Rudoph, *Holy Anorexia,* Chicago, Ill.: University of Chicago Press, 1985.
- Bergin Joseph, *Cardinal de La Rochefoucauld: Leadership and Reform in the French Church,* New Haven, Conn. and London: Yale University Press, 1987.
- ------------*The Making of the French Episcopate, 1589-1661,* New Haven, Conn. and London: Yale University Press, 1996.
- Bernoville, Gaétan, *Le Cloître dans le monde: Anne de Xainctonge, fondatrice de la Compagnie de sainte Ursule 1576-1621*, Paris: Grasset, 1956.
- Blet, Pierre, *Le Clergé de France et la monarchie 1615-1666*, 2 vols, Rome: Université Grégorienne, 1959.
- Blumenfeld-Kosinski, Renate and Timea Szell (eds.), *Images of Sainthood in Medieval Europe*, Ithaca, NY: Cornell University Press, 1991.
- Bossy, John, *The English Catholic Community, 1570-1850,* London: Darton, Longman and Todd, 1976.
- Boulding Elise, *The Underside of History: A View of Women through Time*, London: Sage, 1992.
- Bradley, Rose, *The English Housewife in the Seventeenth and Eighteenth Centuries*, London: Edward Arnold, 1912.
- Brémond, Henri, *Histoire littéraire du sentiment religieux en France depuis la fin des guerres de religion jusqu'à nos jours*, 11 vols, Paris: A. Colin, 1971.
- Breslin, Sister Mary, *Anne de Xainctonge: Her Life and Spirituality*, Kingston, N.Y: The Society of Saint Ursula of the Blessed Virgin, 1957.
- Briggs, Robin, *Communities of Belief: Cultural and Social Tensions in Early Modern France*, Oxford: Clarendon Press, 1989.
- Brodrick, James, *Origins of the Jesuits*, London: Longmans, 1949.
- ------------*Saint Ignatius Loyola: the pilgrim years,* London: Burns and Oates, 1956.
- ------------*The Progress of the Jesuits 1556-1579*, London: Longmans, 1946.
- Broutin, Paul, *La Réforme pastorale en France au XVIIe siècle*, 2 vols, Tournai: Desclée, 1956.
- Brown, Joanne Carlson and C. Bohn (eds.) *Christianity, Patriarchy and Abuse: A Feminist Critique*, New York: Pilgrim Press, 1989.
- Bugnion-Secretan, Perle, *Mère Agnès: Abbesse de Port Royal*, Paris: Cerf, 1996.
- Burke, Peter, *Popular Culture in Early Modern Europe*, London: Temple Smith, 1978.
- Bynum, Caroline Walker, *Holy Feast and Holy Fast: The Religious Significance of Food to Medieval Women*, Berkeley, Los Angeles, Cal. and London: University of California Press, 1987.
- ------------*Gender and Religion,* Boston, Mass.: Beacon Press, 1986.
- Caraman, Philip (ed.) *Henry Garnet 1555-1606 and the Gunpowder Plot*, London: Longmans, 1964.
- ------------*John Gerard. The Autobiography of an Elizabethan*, London: Longmans, 1956.

- -------------*William Weston, the Autobiography of an Elizabethan*, London: Longmans and Green, 1955.
- ------------*Saint Angela: The Life of Angela Merici, Foundress of the Ursulines (1474-1540)*, London: Longmans, 1963.
- Carter, Nancy Corson, *Martha, Mary, Jesus: Weaving Action and Contemplation in Daily Life*, Collegeville, Min.: Liturgical Press, 1992
- Certeau, Michel de, *La Possession de Loudun*, Paris: Gallimard, 1970.
- Chalendard, Marie, *La Promotion de la femme à l'apostolat, 1540-1650*, Paris: Alsatia, 1950.
- Chambers, M.C.E. *The Life of Mary Ward (1585-1645)*, 2 vols, London: Burns and Oates, 1882-1885.
- Chapple, Christopher (ed.), *The Jesuit Tradition in Education and Missions: A 450-Year Perspective*, Scranton: University of Scranton Press, 1993.
- Charlton, Kenneth, *Women, Religion and Education in Early Modern England*, London: Routledge, 1999.
- Chartier, Roger, Marie-Madelaine Compère and Dominique Julia, *L'Éducation en France du XVI° au XVIII° siècle*, Paris: SEDES, 1976.
- Châtellier, Louis, *L'Europe des dévôts*, Paris: Flammarion, 1987.
- Chaunu, Pierre, *L'Église, culture et société: Essai sur réforme et contre-réforme*, Paris: SEDES, 1984.
- ------------*Le Temps des réformes*, Paris: Fayard, 1975.
- Cholakian, Patricia Frances, *Women and the Politics of Self-Representation in Seventeenth-Century France*, Newark, Del.: University of Delaware Press, 2000.
- Christ, Carol and Judith Plaskow, *WomanSpirit Rising: A Feminist Reader in Religion*, San Fracisco, Cal.: Harper and Row, 1979.
- Clarck, Elizabeth and Herbert Richardson (eds.), *Women and Religion: A Feminist Sourcebook of Christian Thought*, San Francisco, Cal.: Harper and Row, 1977.
- Clark, Alice, *Working Life of Women in the Seventeenth Century*, London: Routledge, 1992.
- Clarkes, Anthony (ed.), *The Heart and Mind of Mary Ward*, Wheathampstead: Anthony Clarkes, 1985.
- Cognet, Louis, *Post-Reformation Spirituality*, trans. by P. J. Hepburne-Scot, New York: Hawthorn Books, 1959.
- Collinson, Patrick, *Elizabethan Essays*, London: Ambledon Press, 1994.
- ------------*The Religion of Protestants: The Church in English Society 1559-1625*, Oxford: Clarendon Press, 1982.
- Cohn, Norman, *Europe's Inner Demons*, New York: New American Library, 1977.
- Conn, Marie, *Unheralded Women in Western Christianity, Thirteenth to Eighteenth Century*, London: Greenwood Press, 1999.
- Connelly, Roland, *Women of the Catholic Resistance: In England 1540-1680*, Durham: Pentland Press, 1997.
- Coon, Linda L., Katherine J. Haldane and Elizabeth W. Sommer (eds.), *That Gentle Strength. Historical perspectives on Women in Christianity*, Charlottesville and London: University Press of Virginia, 1990.
- Coudenhove, Ida Goerves, *Mary Ward*, trans. by Elsie Codd, London: The Catholic Book Club, 1938.
- Cover, Jeanne, *Love - The Driving Force: Mary Ward's spirituality: Its Significance for Moral Theology*, Milwaukee, Wis.: Marquette University Press, 1997.
- Cressy David and Lori Anne Perrell (eds.), *Religion and Society in Early Modern England: A Sourcebook*, London: Routledge, 1996.

- Cressy, David, *Literacy and the Social Order: Reading and Writing in Tudor and Stuart England,* Cambridge: Cambridge University Press, 1980.
- Cuming, G.J. and Derek Baker (eds.), *Popular Belief and Practice, Studies in Church History* 8, Cambridge: Cambridge University Press, 1972.
- Dagens, Jean, *Bérulle et les origines de la restauration catholique (1575-1611),* Bruges: Descleé de Brouwer, 1952.
- Daichman, Graciela, *Wayward Nuns in Medieval Literature,* Syracuse, NY: Syracuse University Press, 1986.
- Davis, Natalie Zemon, *Society and Culture in Early Modern France. Eight Essays,* Stanford, Cal.: Stanford University Press, 1979.
- De Bruyn, Lucy, *Woman and the Devil in Sixteenth Century Literature,* Tisbury: The Compton Press, 1979.
- Delumeau, Jean (ed.), *La Religion de ma mère: la femme et la transmission de la foi,* Paris: Cerf, 1992.
- ------------*Catholicism between Luther and Voltaire,* trans. by Jeremy Moiser, London: Burns and Oates, 1977.
- Deroy-Pineau, Françoise (ed.), *Marie Guyart de l'Incarnation: un destin transocéanique, Tours 1599- Québec 1672,* Paris: Harmattan, 2000.
- Dhotel, J. C., *Les Origines du catéchisme moderne,* Paris: Aubier, 1967.
- Dickens, A.G., *The English Reformation,* New York: Schoken Books, 1964.
- Diderot, Denis, *La Religieuse* in *Œuvres complètes,* Paris: La Pléiade,1951.
- Du Mege, Alexandre, *Histoire des institutions religieuses, politiques et littéraires de la ville de Toulouse,* 4 vols, Toulouse: L. Chapelle, 1884.
- Duminuco, Vincent J. (ed.), *The Jesuit Ratio Studiorum: 400th Anniversary Perspectives,* New York: Fordham University Press, 2000.
- Dupanloup, Felix Antoine Philibert, *Conférences destinées aux femmes chrétiennes,* Paris: Gervais 1885.
- ------------*Lettres sur l'éducation des filles et sur les études qui conviennent aux femmes dans le monde,* Paris: Jules Gervais, 1879.
- Dures, Alan, *English Catholicism, 1558-1642,* London: Longmans, 1983.
- Eickenstein, Lina, *Woman under Monasticism,* New York: Russell and Russell, 1978.
- Elton, G. R. (ed.), *The Tudor Constitution: Documents and Commentary,* Cambridge: Cambridge University Press, 1982.
- Evennett, H.O., *The Spirit of the Counter Reformation,* Cambridge: Cambridge University Press, 1968.
- Ezell, Margaret, *The Patriarch's Wife: Literary Evidence and the History of the Family,* Chapel Hill, NC.: University of North Carolina Press, 1987.
- Fagniez, Gustave, *La Femme et la société française dans la première moitié du XVII° siècle,* Paris: J. Gamber, 1929.
- Faguet, M. Emile, *Madame de Maintenon Institutrice: Extraits de ses lettres, airs, entretiens, conversations et proverbes sur l'éducation,* Paris: H. Oudin, 1885.
- Fénelon, François de Salignac de la Mothe, *De l'éducation des filles* in *Oeuvres,* vol.4, Paris, 1854.
- Ferguson, Moira, *First Feminists: British Women Writers, 1578-1799,* Bloomington, Ind.: Indiana University Press, 1985.
- Fletcher, Anthony and John Stevenson (eds.), *Order and Disorder in Early Modern England,* Cambridge: Cambridge University Press, 1985.
- Foley, B.C., *Some Other People of the Penal Times,* Lancaster: Cathedral Bookshop, 1991.

- Forster, Robert, *The Nobility of Toulouse in the 18th century*, The Johns Hopkins University Studies in Historical and Political Science 78.1, Baltimore, Mass.: The Johns Hopkins Press, 1960.
- Ganss, George, *Saint Ignatius' Idea of a Jesuit University: A Study in the History of Catholic Education*, Milwaukee, Wis.: Marquette University Press, 1956.
- Gardiner, Dorothy, *English Girlhood at School: A Study of Women's Education through Twelve Centuries*, London: Oxford University Press, 1929.
- Garnier, Samuel, *Barbe Buvée, en religion sœur sainte Colombe, et la prétendue possession des Ursulines d'Auxonne*, Paris: Progrès médical, 1895.
- Garnot, Benoît, *Le Diable au couvent: Les Possédées d'Auxonne (1658-1663)*, Paris: Imago, 1995.
- Gasquet, Francis Aidan, *English Monastic Life*, London: Methuen, 1904.
- ------------ *The Life of Mary Ward, Foundress of the Institute of the Blessed Virgin Mary*, London: Burns and Oates, 1909.
- Gastellier, Fabian, *Angélique Arnauld*, Paris: Fayard, 1998
- Génin, François, *Les Jésuites et l'université*, Paris: Paulin, 1844.
- Gibson, Wendy, *Women in Seventeenth-Century France*, London: Macmillan, 1989.
- Gilbert, Roger Paul, *Marie Guyart, folie de Dieu: récit témoignage*, Montréal: Médiaspaul, 2003.
- Gilchrist, Roberta, *Contemplation and Action: The Other Monasticism*, London: Leicester University Press, 1995.
- Goubert, Pierre, *The Ancien Regime: French Society 1600-1750*, London: Weidenfeld and Nicolson, 1973.
- Graves, Thomas Law, *A Historical Sketch of the Conflicts between Jesuits and Seculars in the Reign of Queen Elizabeth*, London: David Nutt, 1889.
- Greyerz, Kaspar von (ed.), *Religion and Society in Early Modern Europe*, London: George Allen and Unwin, 1984.
- Grisar, Joseph, *Die ersten Anklagen in Rom gegen das Institut Maria Wards 1622*, Facultate Historiae Ecclesiasticae vol. 22, Rome: Pontificia Universita Gregoriana, 1959.
- ------------*Maria Wards Institut vor römischen Kongregationen (1616-1630)*, Facultate Historiae Ecclesiasticae, vol. 27, Rome: Pontificia Universitate Gregoriana, 1966.
- Gross, Rita, M. (ed.), *Beyond Androcentrism: New Essays on Women and Religion*, Missoula, Mt.: Scholars Press, 1977.
- Gueudré, Marie Chantal, *Histoire de l'ordre des Ursulines en France*, 3 vols, Paris: Editions St Paul, 1957-63.
- Guilday, Peter, *The English Catholic Refugees on the Continent, 1558-1795*, London: Longmans and Green, 1914.
- Haigh, Christopher, *English Reformations: Religion, Politics, and Society under the Tudors*, Oxford: Clarendon Press, 1993.
- ------------*Reformation and Resistance in Tudor Lancashire*, Cambridge: Cambridge University Press, 1975.
- Hamilton, Adam, *Mind and Maxims of Mary Ward*, London: Catholic Truth Society, 1959.
- ------------*The Chronicle of the English Augustinian Canonesses of the Lateran, at St Monica's in Louvain, 1548 to 1625*, Edinburgh: Sands, 1904.
- Hanawalt, Barbara A. (ed.), *Women and Work in Preindustrial Europe*, Bloomington, Ind.: Indiana University Press, 1986.
- Hannay, Margaret, *Silent But for the Word: Tudor Women as Patrons, Translators, and Writers of Religious Works*, Kent, Ohio: Kent State University Press, 1985.

- Hardwick, Julie, *The Practice of Patriarchy. Gender and the Politics of Household Authority in Early Modern France*, Philadelphia, Penn.: University of Pennsylvania Press, 1998.
- Harvey, Barbara, *Living and Dying in England, 1100-1540: The Monastic Experience*, Oxford: Clarendon Press, 1993.
- Havran, M.J., *The Catholics in Caroline England*, London: Oxford University Press, 1962.
- Heal, Felicity and Rosemary O'Day (eds.), *Church and Society in England, Henry VIII to James I*, London: Macmillan, 1977.
- Henderson, Katherine Usher and Barbara F. McManus, *Half Humankind: Contexts and Texts on the Controversy about Women in England, 1540-1640*, Urbana and Chicago, Ill.: University of Illinois Press, 1985.
- Hilton, J.A., *Catholic Lancashire. From Reformation to Renewal, 1559-1991*, Chichester: Philimore, 1994.
- Hoffman, Philip, *Church and Community in the Diocese of Lyon, 1500-1789*, New Haven, Conn.: Yale University Press, 1984.
- Hollis, Christopher, *A History of the Jesuits*, London: Weidenfeld and Nicolson, 1968.
- Hooby, Elaine, *Virtue of Necessity: English Women's Writings, 1649-88*, Ann Arbor, Mich.: University of Michigan Press, 1989.
- Hufton, Olwen, *The Prospect Before Her: A History of Women in Western Europe*, London: Fontana Press, 1997.
- Hull, Suzanne, *Chaste, Silent and Obedient: English Books for Women, 1475-1640*, San Marino, Cal.: Huntingdon Library, 1982.
- Huppert, George, *The Public Schools of Renaissance France*, Urbana, Ill.: University of Illinois Press, 1984.
- Janelle, Pierre, *The Catholic Reformation*, Milwaukee, Wis.: The Bruce Publishing Company, 1963.
- Jedin, Hubert, *A History of the Council of Trent,* 2 vols, Edinburgh: Nelson, 1957.
- Jégou, Marie-Andrée, *Les Ursulines du faubourg saint-Jacques à Paris 1607-1662. Origines d'un monastère apostolique*, Paris: PUF, 1981.
- Jewell, Helen, *Education in Early Modern England*, London: Macmillan, 1998.
- Johnson, Penelope, *Equal in Monastic Profession: Religious Women in Medieval France,* Chicago, Ill. and London: University of Chicago Press, 1991.
- Jordan, C., *Renaissance Feminism: Literary Texts and Political Models*, Ithaca, NY.: Cornell University Press, 1990.
- Kamm, Josephine, *Hope Deferred: Girls' Education in English History*, London: Methuen, 1965.
- Karlsen, C. F., *The Devil in the Shape of a Woman,* New York: W. W. Worton, 1987.
- Kelly, Joan, *Women, History and Theory: the Essays of Joan Kelly*, Chicago, Ill.: University of Chicago Press, 1984.
- Kenyon, J. P. (ed.), *The Stuart Constitution: Documents and Commentary*, Cambridge: Cambridge University Press, 1966.
- King, Ursula (ed.), *Religion and Gender*, Oxford, UK and Cambridge, Mass.: Blackwell, 1995.
- Knowles, David, *From Pachomius to Ignatius. A Study in the Constitutional History of the Religious Orders*, Oxford: Clarendon, 1966.
- ------------*The Monastic Orders in England,* Cambridge: Cambridge University Press, 1966.
- Knox, R. Buick (ed.), *Reformation, Conformity and Dissent*, London: Epworth Press, 1977.

- Latreille, A., E. Delaruelle and J.R. Palanque, *Histoire du catholicisme en France sous les rois très chrétiens*, Paris: SPES, 1963.
- Le Brun, François (ed.) *Histoire des catholiques en France du XV° siècle à nos jours*, Toulouse: Privat, 1980.
- Ledochowska, Teresa, *Angèle Merici et la compagnie de sainte Ursule à la lumière des documents*, Rome: Ancora Press, 1967.
- *Les Religieuses dans le cloître et dans le monde des origins à nos jours.* Actes du deuxième colloque international du CERCOR, Saint-Etienne: Publications de l'universitéde Saint-Etienne, 1994.
- Leymont, Hélène de, *Madame de sainte Beuve et les Ursulines de Paris, 1562-1630*, Lyon: Vitte and Perussel, 1890.
- Leys, M.D.R., *Catholics in England, 1559-1829: A Social History,* London: Longmans, 1961.
- Littlehales Margaret, *Mary Ward (1585-1645). A woman for all Seasons: Foundress of the Institute of the Blessed Virgin Mary,* London: Catholic Truth Society, 1974.
- ----------- *Mary Ward, Pilgrim and Mystic*, London: Burns and Oates, 1998.
- Luebke, David (ed.), *The Counter-Reformation: The Essential Readings*, Oxford: Blackwell, 1999.
- Mack, Phyllis, *Visionary Women: Ecstatic Prophecy in Seventeenth-Century England,* Berkeley, Cal.: University of California Press, 1992.
- Maclean, Ian, *The Renaissance Notion Of Woman,* Cambridge: Cambridge University Press, 1980.
- Magee, Brian, *The English Recusants: A study of the Post-Reformation Catholic Survival and the Operation of the Recusancy Laws*, London: Burns and Oates, 1938.
- Makowski, Elizabeth, *Canon Law and Cloistered Women: Periculoso and its commentators, 1298-1545,* Washington, DC.: Catholic University of America Press, 1997.
- Marinella, Lucrezia, *The Nobility and Excellence of Women, and the Defects and Vices of Men*, Chicago, Ill.: University of Chicago Press, 1999.
- Marshall, Sherin (ed.), *Women in Reformation and Counter-Reformation Europe: Private and Public Worlds,* Bloomington and Indianapolis, Ind.: Indiana University Press, 1989.
- Martin, A. Lynn, *The Jesuit Mind: The Mentality of an Elite in Early Modern France*, Ithaca, N.Y: Cornell University Press, 1988.
- Martin, Victor, *Le Gallicanisme et la réforme catholique: Essai historique sur l'introduction des décrets du concile de Trente en France*, Paris: A. Picard, 1929.
- Matchinske, Megan, *Writing, Gender and State in Early Modern England: Identity Formation and the Female Subject*, Cambridge: Cambridge University Press, 1998.
- Mathew, David, *Catholicism in England, The Portrait of a Minority: Its Culture and Tradition,* London: The Catholic Book Club, 1938.
- McGrath, Patrick, *Papists and Puritans under Elizabeth I,* London: Blandford Press, 1967.
- Meek, Christine (ed.), *Women in Renaissance and Early Modern Europe*, Dublin: Four Courts Press, 2000.
- Mendelson, Sara Heller, *The Mental World of Stuart Women,* Amherst, Mass.: The University of Massachusetts Press, 1987.
- Merton, Thomas, *Contemplation in a World of Action*, Notre Dame, Ind.: University of Notre Dame Press, 1999
- Méthivier, Hubert, *Le Siècle de Louis XIII,* Paris: PUF, 1967.
- Mettam, Roger (ed.), *Government and Society in Louis XIV's France,* London: Macmillan, 1977.
- Meyer, A.O., *England and the Catholic Church under Queen Elizabeth*, trans. by J. R. McKee, London: Routledge and Kegan Paul, 1916.

- Migliorino, Miller Monica, *Sexuality and Authority in the Catholic Church*, London: Scraton, 1995.
- Morey, Adrian, *The Catholic Subjects of Elizabeth I,* London: Allen and Unwin, 1978.
- Mullett, Michael, *Catholics in Britain and Ireland, 1558-1829*, London: Macmillan, 1998.
- ------------ *The Catholic Reformation,* London: Routledge, 1999.
- -------------*The Counter-Reformation and the Catholic Reformation in Early Modern Europe,* London and New York: Methuen, 1984.
- Neale, John, *Queen Elizabeth and her Parliaments,* London: Cape, 1957.
- Newman, Barbara, *From Virile Woman to WomanChrist: Studies in Medieval Religion and Literature*, Philadelphia, Penn.: University of Pennsylvania Press, 1995.
- O'Connor, Margarita, Mother, *That Incomparable Woman*, Montreal: Palm, 1962.
- O'Day Rosemary, *Education and Society, 1500-1800: The Social Foundations of Education in Early Modern Britain*, London: Longman, 1982.
- O'Faolain, Julian and Lauro Martines, *Not in God's Image*, London: Virago, 1979.
- O'Malley, John (ed.), *Catholicism in Early Modern History: A Guide to Research*, St Louis, Mis.: Centre for Reformation Research, 1988.
- O'Reilly, Bernard, *St Angela Merici and the Ursulines*, London: Burns and Oates, 1880
- Obelkevich, Jim, Lyndal Roper and Samuel, Raphael (eds.), *Disciplines of Faith: Studies in Religion, Politics and Patriarchy*, London: Routledge and Kegan Paul, 1987.
- Obelkevitch, James (ed.), *Religion and the People 800-1700*, Chapel Hill, NC.: University of North Carolina Press, 1979.
- Olin, John, *The Catholic Reformation: Savonarola to Ignatius Loyola,* New York: Fordham University Press, 1992.
- Oliver, Mary, *Mary Ward 1585-1645. 'That Incomparable Woman'*, London: Sheed and Ward, 1960.
- Orchard, M. Emmanuel (ed.), *Till God Will: Mary Ward through her Writings*, London: Darton, Longman and Todd, 1985.
- Oury, Dom Guy Marie, *Marie de l'Incarnation 1599-1672*, Tours: Abbaye Saint Pierre de Solesmes, 1973.
- Ozment, Steven (ed.), *Reformation Europe: A Guide to Research*, St Louis, Mis.: Centre for Reformation Research, 1982.
- ------------*When Fathers Ruled: Family Life in Reformation Europe*, Cambridge, Mass.: Harvard University Press, 1983.
- Peters, Henriette, *Mary Ward: A World in Contemplation*, trans. by Helen Butterworth, Leominster: Gracewing Books, 1994.
- Petroff, Elizabeth, *Body and Soul: Essays on Medieval Women Mysticism*, Oxford: Oxford University Press, 1994.
- Philip, M. Mary, *Companions of Mary Ward*, London: Burns and Oates, 1939.
- Plaskow, Judith and Carol P. Christ (eds.), *Weaving the Visions: New Patterns in Feminist Spirituality,* San Francisco, Cal.: Harper and Row, 1989.
- Pollen, J.H., *The English Catholics in the Reign of Queen Elizabeth*, London: Longmans and Green, 1920.
- Power, Eileen, *Medieval English Nunneries c. 1275 to 1535,* Cambridge: Cambridge University Press, 1922.
- Prior, Mary (ed.), *Women in English Society 1500-1800*, London: Methuen, 1985.
- Radford, Rosemary Ruether and Eleanor McLaughlin (eds.), *Women of Spirit*, New York: Simon and Schuster, 1979.
- Radford, Rosemary Ruether (ed.), *Religion and Sexism,* New York: Simon and Schuster, 1974.
- ------------*Sexism and God-Talk. Toward a Feminist Theology,* London: SCM Press, 1983

- Raleigh, William Trimble, *The Catholic Laity in Elizabethan England, 1558-1603*, Cambridge, Mass.: Harvard University Press, 1964.
- Ranft, Patricia, *Women and the Religious Life in Premodern Europe*, London: Macmillan, 1998.
- Rapley, Elizabeth, *The Dévotes: Women and Church in Seventeenth-century France*, Kingston, Ont.: McGill, Queen's University Press, 1990.
- ------------*A Social History of the Cloister. Daily Life in the teaching Monasteries of the Old Regime*, Kingston, Ont.: McGill-Queen's University Press, 2001.
- Ravitch, Norman, *The Catholic Church and the French Nation, 1598-1989*, London: Routledge, 1990.
- Reidy, Mary, *The First Ursuline: The Story of St Angela Merici*, London: Burns and Oates, 1962
- Reynes, Geneviève, *Couvents de femmes: La vie des religieuses cloîtrées dans la France des XVII° et XVIII° siècles*, Paris: Fayard, 1987.
- Richard, Michel, *La Vie quotidienne des Protestants sous l'ancien régime*, Paris: Hachette, 1966.
- Rogers, Katharine, *The Troublesome Helpmate: A History of Misogyny in Literature*, Seattle, Wis.: University of Wisconsin Press, 1968.
- Roper, Lyndal, *The Holy Household: Women and Morals in Reformation Augsburg*, Oxford: Clarendon Press, 1989.
- Rowlands, Marie (ed.), *English Catholics of Parish and Town 1558-1778*, London: Catholic Record Society, 1999.
- Rowse, A.L., *The England of Elizabeth: The Structure of Society*, London: Macmillan, 1950.
- Sainte Foi, Charles, *Vies des premières Ursulines de France, tirées des chroniques de l'ordre*, Paris: Poussièlgue Russand, 1856.
- Sales, François de, *Introduction à la vie dévote*, Paris: Gallimard, 1969.
- Salome, Mother M., *Mary Ward: A Foundress of the Seventeenth Century*, London: Burns and Oates, 1901.
- Salvan, Abbé Adrien, *Histoire générale de l'Èglise de Toulouse*, 4 vols, Toulouse: 1856-61.
- Sarre, Claude Alain, *Vivre sa soumission: L'exemple des Ursulines provençales et comtadines (1592-1792)*, Paris: Publisud, 1997.
- Schneider, Robert, *Public Life in Toulouse, 1463-1789: From Municipal Republic to Cosmopolitan City*, Ithaca, NY and London: Cornell University Press, 1989.
- Schochet, Gordon J. (ed.), *The Authoritarian Family and Political Attitudes in Seventeenth Century England: Patriarchalism in Political Thought*, New Brunswick: Rutgers University Press, 1988.
- Schroeder, H. J. (ed.), *Canons and Decrees of the Council of Trent*, Rockford, Ill.: Tan Books, 1978.
- Sheils, W.J. and Diana Woods (eds.), *Women in the Church, Studies in Church History* 27, Oxford: Basil Blackwell, 1990.
- Shepherd, Simon (ed.), *The Women's Sharp Revenge: Five Pamphlets from the Renaissance*, London: Fourth Estate, 1985.
- Sim, Alison, *The Tudor Housewife*, Montreal: McGill-Queen's University Press, 1996.
- Smith, Alan (ed.), *The Reign of James I and VI*, London: Macmillan, 1977.
- Smith, Hilda, *Reason's Disciples: Seventeenth Century English Feminists*, Chicago, Ill.: University of Illinois Press, 1982.
- Smith, Hilda and Linda Cardinale (eds.), *Women and the Literature of the Seventeenth Century*, Westport, Conn.: Greenwood Press, 1990.

- Snyders, Georges, *La Pédagogie en France aux XVII° et XVIII° siècles*, Paris: PUF, 1965.
- Sommerville, Margaret, *Sex and Subjection: Attitudes to Women in Early Modern Society*, London and New York: Arnold, 1995.
- Soulet, Jean François, *Traditions et réformes religieuses dans les Pyrénées centrales au XVII° siècle (le diocèse de Tarbes de 1602 à 1716)*, Pau: Marrimpouey Jeune, 1974.
- Stone, Lawrence, *The Crisis of the Aristocracy 1558-1641*, Oxford: Clarendon Press, 1966.
- Stuart, Susan Mosher, Wiesner, Merry and Bridenthal Renate (eds.), *Becoming Visible: Women in European History*, Boston, Mass.: Houghton Mifflin, 1998.
- Summers, Claude (ed.), *Representing Women in Renaissance England*, Columbia, Mis.: University of Missouri Press, 1997.
- Surin, J. J., *Histoire abrégée de la possession des Ursulines de Loudun et des peines de père Surin*, Paris: Desclée de Brouwer, 1966.
- Tanner, J.R. (ed.), *Constitutional Documents of the Reign of James I*, Cambridge: Cambridge University Press, 1930.
- Tanner, Norman (ed.), *Decrees of the Ecumenical Councils*, 2 vols, London: Sheed and Ward, 1990.
- Tapié, Victor, *France in the Age of Louis XIII and Richelieu*, trans. by D. McN. Lockie, London: Macmillan, 1974.
- Taunton, Ethelred, *The History of the Jesuits in England, 1580-1773*, London: Methuen, 1901.
- Taveneaux, René, *Jansénisme et réforme catholique*, Nancy: Presses Universitaires de Nancy, 1992
- ----------- *Le Catholicisme dans la France classique 1610-1717*, 2 vols, Paris: SDES, 1980.
- Taylor, Larissa, *Soldiers of Christ: Preaching in Late Medieval and Early Modern France*, Oxford; Oxford University Press, 1992.
- Thompson, James, *The Wars of Religion in France, 1559-1576*, New York: Frederick Ungar, 1909.
- Travitsky, Betty, *The Paradise of Women: Writings by Englishwomen of the Renaissance*, Westport, Conn.: Greenwood Press, 1981.
- Trimble W.J.R., *The Catholic Laity in Elizabethan England, 1558-1603*, Cambridge, Mass.: Harvard University Press, 1964.
- Viguerie, Jean de, *Le Catholicisme des Français dans l'ancienne France*, Paris: Nouvelles Editions Latines, 1988.
- Von Greyerz, Kaspar (ed.), *Religion and Society in Early Modern Europe*, London: George Allen and Unwin, 1984.
- Vovelle, Michel, *Piété baroque et déchristianisation en Provence au XVIII° siècle: les attitudes devant la mort d'après les clauses des testaments*, Paris: Plon, 1973.
- Wake, Roy, *Saint Mary's School, Ascot and its antecedents*, London: Haggerston Press, 1994.
- Walsham, Alexandra, *Church Papists. Catholicism, Conformity and Confessional Polemic in Early Modern England*, Woodbridge: Boydell Press, 1993.
- Warnicke, Retha, *Women of the English Renaissance and Reformation*, Westport, Conn.: Greenwood Press, 1983.
- Watson, Foster (ed.), *Vives and the Renascence Education of Women*, London: Edward Arnold, 1912.
- Watt, Diane, *Medieval Women in their Communities*, Cardiff: University of Wales Press, 1997.
- Weber, Alison, *Teresa of Àvila and the Rhetoric of Femininity*, Princeton, NJ: Princeton University Press, 1990.

- Weber, Christin Lore, *WomanChrist: New Vision of Feminist Spirituality,* San Francisco, Cal.: Harper & Row, 1987.
- Wiesner, Merry, *Women and Gender in Early Modern Europe*, New York: Cambridge University Press, 2000.
- Williams, Rowan, *Teresa of Àvila*, London: Geoffrey Chapman, 1991.
- Wolff, Philippe, *Histoire de Toulouse*, Toulouse: Privat, 1974.
- ------------*Histoire du Languedoc*, Toulouse: Privat, 1967.
- ----------- *Toulouse,* Histoire des Diocèses de France, n°15, Paris: Beauchesne, 1983.
- Woodbridge, Linda, *Women and the English Renaissance: Litterature and the Nature of Womanhood, 1540-1620*, Urbana, Ill.: University of Illinois Press, 1984.
- Workman, Herbert, *The Evolution of the Monastic Ideal*, London: H. C. Kelly, 1913.
- Zagano, Phyllis, *Woman to Woman: An Anthology of Women's Spiritualities*, Collegeville, Min.: Liturgical Press, 1993.

- *Articles*

- Anson, Peter, 'Papal Enclosure for Nuns', *Cisterian Studies* 3 (1968) 109-123.
- Atkinson, Clarissa, ' "Precious Balsam in a Fragile Glass": The Ideology of Virginity in the Later Middle Ages', *Journal of Family History* 8 (1983) 131-43.
- Aveling, J.C.H. 'Catholic Households in Yorkshire, 1580-1603', *Northern History* 16 (1980) 85-101.
- Beales, A.C.F. 'A Biographical Catalogue of Catholic Schoolmaster in England', *Recusant History* 7.6 (1964) 268-90.
- Benedict, Philip, 'The Catholic Response to Protestantism. Church Activity and Popular Piety in Rouen, 1560-1600', in James Obelkevich (ed.), *Religion and the People, 800-1700,* Chapel Hill, NC.: University of North Carolina Press, 1979, pp. 168-90.
- Bennett, Judith, 'Misogyny, popular culture and women's work', *History Workshop Journal* 31 (1991) 166-88.
- Bernos, Marcel, 'La Catéchèse des filles par les femmes aux XVII° et XVIII° siècles', in Jean Delumeau (ed.), *La Religion de ma mère: La Femme et la transmission de la foi*, Paris: Cerf, 1992, pp. 226-86.
- Blackwood, B.G. 'Plebeian Catholics in the 1640s and 1650s', *Recusant History* 18.1 (1986) 42-58.
- Bossy, John, 'The Counter-Reformation and the people of Catholic Europe', *Past and Present* 47 (1970) 51-70.
- ---------------- 'The Character of Elizabethan Catholicism', in Aston Trevor (ed.), *Crisis in Europe 1560-1660*, London: Routledge and Kegan Paul, 1965, pp. 223-47.
- ---------------- 'The English Catholic Community 1603-1625', in Smith, A.G.R. (ed.), *The Reign of James VI and I*, London: Macmillan, 1973, pp. 91-105.
- Brockliss, Laurence, 'Richelieu, Education, and the State', in Bergin, Joseph and Laurence Brockliss (eds.), *Richelieu and His Age*, Oxford: Clarendon, 1992, pp. 237-72.
- Burke, Peter, 'How to Be a Counter-Reformation Saint', in Greyerz, Kaspar von (ed.), *Religion and Society in Early Modern Europe,* London: George Allen and Unwin, 1984, pp.45-55.
- Byrne, Lavinia, 'Mary Ward's Vision of the Apostolic Religious Life', *The Way Supplement* 53 (1985) 73-84.
- Choquette, Leslie, ' "Ces Amazones du grand Dieu": Women and Mission in Seventeenth-Century Canada', *French Historical Studies* 17: 3 (1992) 627-55.
- Crawford, Patricia, 'Women's Published Writings 1600-1700', in Prior, Mary (ed.), *Women in English Society 1500-1800*, London: Methuen, 1985, pp.211-31.

- Cross, Claire, 'The Religious Life of Women in Sixteenth-Century Yorkshire', in Sheils, W.J. and Diane Woods (eds.), *Women in the Church, Studies in Church History* 27, Oxford, Basil Blackwell, 1990, pp.307-24.
- Cross, Claire, ' "He-Goats before the Flocks": A Note on the Part Played by Women in the Founding of Some Civil War Churches', in Cuming G.J. and Derek Baker (eds.), *Popular Belief and Practice, Studies in Church History* 8, Cambridge: Cambridge University Press, 1972, pp.195-202.
- Cullum, Patrica, ' "And hir Name was Charite": Women and Charity in Medieval Yorkshire', in Goldberg P.J.P. (ed.), *Woman is a Worthy Wight: Women in Medieval English Society 1200-1500,* Stroud: Allan Sutton, 1997, pp.182-211.
- Davis, Natalie Zemon, 'From "Popular Religion" to Religious Cultures', in Ozment, Steven (ed.), *Reformation Europe: A Guide to Research,* St Louis, Mis.: Centre for Reformation Research, 1982, pp.321-42.
- Denis Evinson, 'The Catholic Revival in Hammersmith', *London Recusant* 8.2 (1978) 19-46.
- Dickens, A.G., 'The First Stages of Romanist Recusancy, 1560-1590', *Yorkshire Archaeological Journal,* 35 (1943) 157-82.
- ---------------- 'The Extent and Character of Recusancy in Yorkshire in 1604', *Yorkshire Archaeological Journal* 37 (1948) 24-48.
- Dubois, Elfreida, 'The Education of Women in Seventeenth-Century France', *French Studies* 32.1 (1978) 1-19.
- Duffy, Eamon, ' "Holy Maydens, Holy Wyfes": The Cult of Women Saints in Fifteenth- and Sixteenth-century England', in Sheils, W.J. and Diana Woods (eds.) *Women in the Church, Studies in Church History* 27, Oxford: Basil Blackwell, 1990, pp.175-96.
- Dulong, Claude, 'Education des filles, enseignement des femmes', *Pénélope* 2 (1980) 1-16.
- Edwards, Felicity, 'Spirituality, Consciousness and Gender Identification: A Neo-Feminist Perspective', in King, Ursula (ed.), *Religion and Gender*, Oxford and Cambridge, Mass.: Blackwell, 1995, pp.177-94.
- Escoupérié-Merle, R. B., 'Marthe de Flottes, directrice des Filles de la Providence de Toulouse ou l'enseignement féminin sous l'Ancien Régime', *Auta,* 632 (1998) 8-13 and 633 (1998) 57-63.
- Evennett, H.O., ' Counter Reformation Spirituality', in David Luebke (ed.), *The Counter-Reformation: The Essential Readings,* Oxford: Blackwell, 1999, pp. 47-64.
- Friedman, Alice, 'The Influence of Humanism on the Education of Girls and Boys in Tudor England', *History of Education Quarterly* 25 (1985) 57-70.
- Gorman, Margaret, 'The Influence of Ignatian Spirituality on Women's Teaching Orders in the United States', in Chapple Christopher (ed.), *The Jesuit Tradition in Education and Mission. A 450-Year Perspective,* Scranton, Penn.: University of Scranton Press, 1993, pp.182-204.
- Grisar, Joseph, 'Mary Ward, 1585-1645', *The Month* 12.22 (1954) 69-81.
- -----------'Maria Ward auf dem Weg zu einem neuen Frauentum, *Stimmen der Zeit,* 152. 7 (1953) 20-34.
- -----------'Die beiden ältesten Leben Maria Wards, der Gründerin der Englischen Fräulein', *Historisches Jahrbuch,* 70 (1951) 154-189.
- Gueudré, Marie Chantal, 'La Femme et la vie spirituelle', *Dix-Septième Siècle* 62 (1964) 47-77.
- Haigh, Christopher, 'The Fall of a Church or the Rise of a Sect? Post-Reformation Catholicism in England', *Historical Journal* 21.1 (1978) 180-86.

- ------------------ 'From Monopoly to Minority: Catholicism in Early Modern England', *Transactions of the Royal Historical Society,* Fifth Series, 31 (1981) 129-48.
- ------------------ 'The Continuity of Catholicism in the English Reformation', *Past and Present,* 93 (1981) 37-69.
- Hanlon, J.D., 'They be but Women', in Carter, C.H. (ed.), From the Renaissance to the Counter-Reformation: Essays in honour of Garrett Mattingly, London, Cape, 1966, pp.367-93.
- Hilton, J. A., 'Recusancy in Elizabethan Durham', *Recusant History* 14.1 (1977) 1-9.
- Hobsbawn, E.J., 'The Crisis of the Seventeenth-Century', in Aston Trevor (ed.), *Crisis in Europe 1560-1660: Essays from Past and Present,* London: Routledge and Kegan Paul, 1975, pp. 5-59.
- Kirkus, Sister M. Gregory, 'The Presence of the Mary Ward Institute in Yorkshire, 1642-1648', *Recusant History* 25.3 (2000) 434-48.
- Klassen, Sherri, 'Greying in the Cloister: The Ursulines Life Course in Eighteenth-Century France', *Journal of Women's History* 12.4 (2001) 87-112.
- Lake, Peter, 'Feminine Piety and Personal Potency: The "Emancipation" of Mrs. Jane Radcliffe', *The Seventeenth Century* 2.2 (1987) 143-65.
- Laurence, Anne, 'A Priesthood of She-Believers: Women and Congregations in Mid-Seventeenth-Century England', in Sheils, W.J. and Diana Woods (eds.), *Women in the Church, Studies in Church History* 27, Oxford: Basil Blackwell, 1990, pp. 345-63.
- Leatherbarrow, J.S., 'Lancashire Elizabethan Recusants', *Chetham Society* 110 (1947).
- Le Bourgeois, Marie-Amélie, 'Une Fondatrice d'avant-garde: Anne de Xainctonge (1567-1621) et la compagnie des sainte-Ursule à Dôle', *Revue d'Histoire de l'Église de France* 80.204 (1994) 23-41.
- Liebowitz, Ruth, 'Virgins in the Service of Christ: The Dispute over an Active Apostolate for Women during the Counter-Reformation', in Ruether Rosemary Radford (ed.), *Women of Spirit,* New York: Simon and Schuster, 1979, pp.131-52.
- Lierheimer, Linda, 'Redefining Convent Space: Ideals of Female Community among Seventeenth-Century Ursuline Nuns', *Proceedings of the Annual Meeting of Western Society for French History* 24 (1997) 211-20.
- Lindley, K.J., 'The Lay Catholics of England in the Reign of Charles I', *Journal of Ecclesiastical History* 22.3 (1971) 199-221.
- Lux-Sterritt, Laurence, 'Between the Cloister and the World: the Successful Compromise of the Ursulines of Toulouse, 1604-1616', *French History* 16.3 (2002) 247-68.
- ------------'An Analysis of the Controversy Caused by Mary Ward's Institute in the 1620s', *Recusant History* 25.4 (2001) 636-647.
- Marmion, John, 'Some Notes on the 'Painted Life' of Mary Ward', *Recusant History* 18.3 (1987) 318-322.
- McCarthy, Caritas, 'Ignatian Charism in Women's Congregations', *The Way,* supplement 20 (1973) 10-18.
- McGrath, Patrick and Joy Rowe, 'Anstruther Analysed: The Elizabethan Seminary Priests', *Recusant History* 18.1 (1986) 1-13.
- ----------------- 'The Elizabethan Priests: the Harbourers and Helpers', *Recusant History* 19.3 (1989) 209-34.
- McGrath, Patrick, 'Elizabethan Catholicism. A Reconsideration', *Journal of Ecclesiastical History* 35 (1984) 414-28.
- McMullen, Norma, 'The Education of English Gentlewomen 1540-1640', *History of Education* 6.2 (1977) 87-101.
- Mulligan, Lotte and Judith Richards, 'A "Radical" Problem: The Poor and the English Reformers in the Mid-Seventeenth Century', *Journal of British Studies* 29 (1990) 118-46.

- Norman, Marion, 'A Woman for all Seasons: Mary Ward (5185-1645), Renaissance Pioneer of Women's Education', *Paedagogica Historica* 23.1 (1983) 125-144.
- O'Connor, June, 'The Epistemological Significance of Feminist Research in Religion', in King, Ursula (ed.), *Religion and Gender*, Oxford and Cambridge, Mass.: Blackwell, 1995, pp.45-64.
- O'Malley, John, 'Catholic Reform', in Ozment, Steven (ed.), *Reformation Europe: A Guide to Research*, St Louis, Mis.: Centre for Reformation Research, 1982, pp. 297-320.
- Papy, Jan, 'Juan Luis Vives (1492-1540) on the Education of Girls: An Investigation into his Medieval and Spanish Sources', *Paedagogica Historica* 31.3 (1995) 739-75.
- Pollock, Linda, ' "Teach her to Live under Obedience": The Making of Women in the Upper Ranks of Early Modern England', *Continuity and Change* 4.2 (1989) 231-58.
- Poutet, Yves, 'L'Enseignement des pauvres dans la France du XVII° siècle', *Dix-Septième Siècle*, 91 (1971) 87-110.
- Powis, J. K., 'The Nature of Gallicanism in Late Sixteenth Century France', *Historical Journal* 26 (1983) 515-30.
- Ranft, Patricia, 'A Key to Counter-Reformation Women's Activism: The Confessor-Spiritual Director', *Journal of Feminist Studies in Religion* 10.2 (1994) 7-26.
- Rapley, Elizabeth, 'Fénelon Revisited: A Review of Girls' Education in Seventeenth-Century France', *Social History* 20.40 (1987) 299-318.
- ------------'Women and the Religious Vocation in Seventeenth-Century France', *French Historical Studies* 18.3 (1994) 613-31.
- ----------- 'Her Body the Enemy: Self-Mortification in Seventeenth-Century Convents', Proceedings of the Annual Meeting of the Western Society for French History 21 (1994) 25-35.
- Robert, Michael, ' "Words they are Women, Deeds they are Men": Images of Work and Gender in Early Modern England' in Charles, Lindsey and Lorna Duffin (eds.), *Women and Work in Pre-Industrial England*, London: Croom Helm, 1985, pp.122-180.
- Ronzeau, Pierre, 'La Femme au pouvoir ou le monde à l'envers', *Dix-Septième Siècle* 108 (1975) 9-33.
- Rowlands, Marie, 'Recusant Women 1560-1640', in Prior, Mary (ed.), *Women in English Society 1500-1800,* London: Methuen, 1985, pp.149-180.
- Ruether, Rosemary, 'Prophets and Humanists: Types of Religious Feminism in Stuart England', *Journal of Religion* 70.1 (1990) 1- 17.
- Stone, Lawrence, 'Literacy and Education in England 1640-1900', *Past and Present* 42 (1969) 69-139.
- Warnicke, R. M., 'Lady Mildmay's Journal: A Study in Autobiography and Meditation in Reformation England', *Sixteenth Century Journal*, 20 (1989) 55-68.
- Weaver, F. Ellen, 'Women and Religion in Early Modern France: A Bibliographical Essay on the State of the Question', *Catholic Historical Review* 67 (1981) 50-59.
- Webb, Diana, 'Woman and Home: the Domestic Setting of Late Medieval Spirituality', in W.J. Sheils and Diana Wood (eds.), *Women in the Church, Studies in Church History* 27, Oxford: Basil Blackwell, 1990, pp.159-73.
- Weber, Alison, 'Little Women: Counter-Reformation Misogyny', in David Luebke (ed.), *The Counter-Reformation: The Essential Readings*, Oxford: Blackwell, 1999, pp. 143-62.
- Wetter, Immolata, 'Mary Ward's Apostolic Vocation', *The Way*, supplement 17 (1972) 69-91.
- Willen, Diane, 'Women and Religion in early modern England', in Marshall Sherrin (ed.), *Women in Reformation and Counter-Reformation Europe*, Bloomington, Ind.: Indiana University Press, 1989, pp. 140-166.

- -------------- 'Women in the Public Sphere in Early Modern England: The Case of the Urban Working Poor', *Sixteenth Century Journal* 19.4 (1988) 559-75.
- York, Anne, 'Women and Silence: Expanding the Boundaries of Seventeenth-Century Women's Religious Congregations', *Proceedings of the Annual Meeting of the Western Society for French History* 24 (1997) 441-50.

- Theses

- Annaert, Philippe, 'Vie religieuse féminine et éducation entre Somme et Rhin. Les Ursulines aux XVII° et XVIII° siècles', 6 vols, unpublished thèse de doctorat, université de Louvain-la-Neuve, 1990.
- Bowden, Caroline, 'Girls' Education in the Late Sixteenth and Early Seventeenth Century in England and Wales', unpublished PhD thesis, University of London, 1996.
- Crimando, Thomas, 'France and the Council of Trent, 1560-1589', unpublished PhD dissertation, University of Rochester, NY, 1984.
- Desilets, Roseanne Michalek, 'The Nuns of Tudor England: Feminine Responses to the Dissolution of the Monasteries', unpublished PhD dissertation, University of California, 1995.
- Elwood, Ann Barclay, 'French Nuns and Fallen Women: Social Control and Autonomy in Ancien Régime Convents', PhD dissertation, University of California, San Diego, Cal., 1989.
- Hastings, W. F., 'English Catholic Education, 1580-1800', unpublished PhD thesis, University of London, 1923.
- Le Bourgeois, M. A., 'Les Ursulines d'Anne de Xainctonge (1601). Contribution à l'histoire des communautés religieuses féminines sans clôture', Thèse de Doctorat Sciences Théologiques, Institut Catholique de Paris, 1995.
- Lierheimer, Linda, 'Female Eloquence and Maternal Ministry: The Apostolate of Ursuline Nuns in Seventeenth-Century France', unpublished PhD dissertation, Princeton University, 1994.
- Morris, E. M. D., 'The Education of Girls in England from 1600 to 1800', unpublished PhD thesis, University of London, 1926.
- Seguin, Colleen Marie, ' "Addicted Unto Piety": Catholic Women in England, 1590-1690', unpublished PhD dissertation, Duke University, 1997.
- Strasser, Ulrike, '"Aut Maritus, Aut Murus?" Women's Lives in Counter-Reformation Munich (1579-1651)', unpublished PhD dissertation, University of Minnesota, 1997.
- Taylor, Judith Coombes, 'From proselytizing to social reform: Three generations of female teaching congregations, 1600-1720', unpublished PhD dissertation, Arizona State University, 1980.
- Zarri, Gabiella, 'Living Saints: A Typology of Female Sanctity in the Early Sixteenth Century', in Daniel Bornstein and Roberto Rusconi (eds.), *Women and Religion in Medieval and Renaissance Italy*. Chicago and London, The University of Chicago Press, 1996.

Index